Christopher Steed is a research fellow at Southampton University. He spent twelve years in Whitehall, where he worked on trade policy towards South Africa during the Thatcher years and deindustrialisation. He has twenty years experience as a parish priest and currently works for the Diocese of Winchester. A qualified psychotherapist and counsellor, he holds doctorates in sociology and education from the University of Exeter, and in theology and history from Trinity College, USA. He has worked in education and in senior management roles in not-for-profit organisations. He is the author of *A Question of Worth* (I.B.Tauris, 2016).

'We want to bring a message from the people in the poorest countries in the world to the forum of the most powerful business and political leaders. The message is that rising inequality is dangerous. It's bad for growth and it's bad for governance. We see a concentration of wealth capturing power and leaving ordinary people voiceless and their interests uncared for.'

– Oxfam International[1]

'Hath not a Jew eyes? Hath not a Jew hands, organs, dimensions, senses, affections, passions? Fed with the same food, hurt with the same weapons, subject to the same diseases, healed by the same means, warmed and cooled by the same winter and summer as a Christian is? If you prick us, do we not bleed? If you tickle us, do we not laugh? If you poison us, do we not die? And if you wrong us, shall we not revenge?'

– *The Merchant of Venice*, Act 3 Scene 1, Shakespeare

'Does it really matter that we have more than others? If they worked as hard as me then they too could have what I have.'

– Anon[2]

'History says, don't hope
On this side of the grave.
But then, once in a lifetime
The longed-for tidal wave
Of justice can rise up,
And hope and history rhyme.'

– *The Cure at Troy*, Seamus Heaney[3]

A Question of Inequality

The Politics of Equal Worth

Christopher Steed

I.B.TAURIS
LONDON • NEW YORK • OXFORD • NEW DELHI • SYDNEY

I.B. TAURIS
Bloomsbury Publishing Plc
50 Bedford Square, London, WC1B 3DP, UK
1385 Broadway, New York, NY 10018, USA

BLOOMSBURY, I.B. TAURIS and the I.B. Tauris logo
are trademarks of Bloomsbury Publishing Plc

First published in Great Britain 2018
This paperback edition published 2020

A catalogue record for this book is available from the British Library.

A catalog record for this book is available from the Library of Congress.

ISBN: HB: 978-1-7883-1153-3
PB: 978-0-7556-0181-3
ePDF: 978-1-7867-3399-3
eBook: 978-1-7867-2399-4

Typeset by Riverside Publishing Solutions, Salisbury, Wiltshire

To find out more about our authors and books visit
www.bloomsbury.com and sign up for our newsletters.

Contents

Introduction: Setting the Scene

Paraded across the divides of modern times, inequality is both wide and widening.

In parallel, the very concept of 'equality' is becoming wider. Egalitarianism is a social and political agenda that has varying fortunes on the contemporary scene. Does the embrace of a market society necessarily involve repudiation of 'cradle to grave', or state interventions to level things up? How should societies respond to pervasive concentrations of power that surges through the very language we use about ethnicity, gender, age and intact bodies? Is the trend towards equal identities leading anywhere – should we not just abolish all social categories as oppressive? And what do we do about the obscene disparities of health as well as wealth, among those who live in the same city (let alone the same country)?

What is inequality? When you drill down into it, the term 'equality' is somewhat meaningless. People live such radically different lives. Maybe it is another way of talking about disparities that will inevitably exist in the aggregate, rather than at an individual level, and rather than being a call to arms against social injustice. Does it matter if people in different social locations live different lives and labour under far greater disadvantages? Is 'equality' the ultimate value anyway? This book argues that 'equal worth', open to debate though it is in philosophical circles, nevertheless functions as a social dynamic, and seeks to show how. However problematic a concept, inequality gets under the skin; it provokes a reaction much to do with our own sense of value and worth.

The experience of living with racism is well documented in an unlikely context; that of growing up black in white Australia. Maxine Benebe Clark documents life in Sydney in the 1980s and 1990s where racism was commonplace. Anything unfamiliar was hidden from view and scorned. All the culture was about white people doing white things. A Cabbage Patch Kids doll given her by her mother evoked being overcome with disappointment. The doll had brown skin and would not carry the same social value in the playground.[1] That epitomises the central message of this book. It is about what happens when the externally conferred social value meets with an internal sense of value and the pattern of role-switching that ensues in such transactions.

Discrimination – whether in criminal justice, health care, education or the slog of everyday life – dents people's understanding of themselves and their identities and this is such a huge factor and force today. An overwhelming sense of powerlessness often flows from stereotypes. Being given to understand that you are no good in the classroom and have few prospects in the workplace erodes self-value.

That will be the journey of exploration in this book. Inequality matters precisely because it gets under the skin. Discussion about social anxiety and status syndrome become core issues, not just because of what people experience relative to everyone else but because they dig into the role that our own sense of value and worth plays in human action. How do people build a good life filled with meaning and feel they are worthwhile when, for some, the odds are stacked so heavily against them? How does a young Dalit man do that if his job is to scrape human excrement and clean toilets with his bare hands?

For many, money is the goal of a good life but the flashy confident have opportunities denied others. Or some will not progress very far and be disadvantaged due to the constraints of parental background. People will never be at the same starting point and while the message of aspiration is vital to make a break from imposed limitations – the ideal of 'be who you are' rings hollow. The world over, lives are constrained. Inequality is detrimental and often lethal because, instead of limits coming from inside, someone else gets to define the limits within which life must be lived. As we will explore, refusal to be bound by the definitions of others is the essence of the Protest – 'I am me!'

This is the lure, the demand, but also the challenge of equal identities. Perhaps now it is stagnant living standards for the broad middle of society and accumulation of unusable wealth by the rich that has pushed fairness up the agenda.[2] There is certainly something fundamentally wrong with the way wealth is distributed. The strength of the reception to Thomas Piketty's magnum opus, *Capital in the Twenty-First Century*,[3] demonstrated the interest in this.

The world is changing more quickly than anyone can keep up with. From one breathless headline to the next, we are seeing faster and more disruptive change of global consequence than ever before. Unevenly spread global wealth is a pressing issue. Many social rifts are closing; fresh ones are opening up. On the whole, inequality is rising and wealth more concentrated than ever. The simplest way of measuring income inequality, Gini coefficients, have risen everywhere. The top one per cent has increased their share of the pie dramatically. Oxfam reported that the top one per cent has more than 50 per cent of total global wealth. Just eight men own the same wealth as half the world. One of the six co-chairs at the 2017 World Economic Forum said the increased concentration of wealth seen since the deep recession of 2008–9 was dangerous and needed to be reversed.[4] If there's one theme that dominated discussions in Davos that year, it was inequality. By 2009, as the financial crash was kicking in, researchers were already drawing attention to the link between inequality and a range of social ills. Addressing the World Economic Forum in 2013, the head of the International Monetary Fund (IMF), Christine Lagarde, quoted an American President to warn of the dangers of rising inequality. 'Franklin D. Roosevelt once said, "The test of our progress is not if we add more to the abundance of those who have much; it's whether we provide enough for those who have too little."'[5]

Few had listened, she said four years later, despite many IMF researchers reaching the same conclusion. 'I don't know why people didn't listen, but certainly I got a strong backlash, in particular from economists saying that it was not really any of their business to worry about these things.' Inequality was feeding the rise of nationalism and populism: 'You can be absolutely sure that nations will revert to their natural tendency of hiding behind their borders, of moving towards protectionism, of listening to vested interests, and they'll forget about transcending those national priorities.'[6]

Were those economists right to say that unequal distribution of income does not matter too much in itself? It could perhaps be that the lived experience of most people is focused more on poverty and that the struggle to make ends meet is their daily concern. Where they are positioned on the income distribution curve could be a profound outrage to those looking on rather than those trying to feed their families. But is this right? Is inequality bad for individuals and societies?

Walter Scheidel argued in his history of inequality, *The Great Leveller*, that it is the natural state for society, or as the Nobel Prize-winner in Economics Edmund Phelps had said, it is a mistake to rail against inequality at the top. Economic cycles will come and go: nothing can be done to prevent inequality.[7]

It is not just about chronic disparity of income between rich and poor. Elites do not just possess greater wealth. They have more power. The disadvantaged are excluded through a variety of means. Elsewhere, I try to show that the economic and social system works for those who can pay up and keep up, who look good and who stay young. There are massive divides in educational attainment whereby regimes of testing and assessment are used to sort out different levels of ability.[8] In October 2017, the British prime minister, Theresa May, announced initial findings from a Racial Disparity Audit. 'My most fundamental political belief is that how far you go in life should be based on your talent and how hard you work – and nothing else,' she declared. The audit looked at how people of different backgrounds are treated across various areas of the state, including health, education, employment and the criminal justice system. Huge differences showed up in outcomes for ethnicities in different parts of the country, as well as significant disparities between different ethnic minority groups. Employment rates were far higher for white people – 75.7 per cent – than for black and minority ethnic (BAME) groups – 63.9 per cent – across the country as a whole. White pupils from state schools had the lowest university entry rate. More than nine in ten head teachers were white British.[9]

Inequality is as old as human societies. Differences persist everywhere. As Jesus said, the poor are always with you. Reaction against it is nothing new. The oppressed have always chafed against oppressors. Slave and peasant revolts were rare. The medieval world did not think of social class in the way we do. Their emphasis was on layers and ordained orders commanding loyalty and fealty. It was in the seventeenth and eighteenth centuries that a tradition of radical politics began to emerge that brought a daring idea into the world. The new idea began to resonate both with strong strands of Christian tradition and also the Enlightenment. People could change things. The social order did not have to be this way. Transformation was possible. Socialist politics in the nineteenth century made this daring idea take hold and become a vibrant force. Communism was fundamentally an equality project: Lenin's own father had been influential in trying to ensure equal opportunities for ethnic minorities in the area school district. Driven by hatred, Vladimir Lenin then emerged preaching class war and violent overthrow of society. His motivation was to create an alternative world. Twentieth-century chaos was aflame with those who had such fire in their minds.

Unfortunately, there was a snake in paradise. It is power that creates inequalities. Communism had little conception of power, beyond the general proposition that bourgeois oppressors held the cards. The idea that proletariat revolutionaries could seize the reins of state power and become a viciously oppressive force was not foreseen. Its advocates did not foresee that although capitalism was mired in interests, the state also took on strong interests that did not serve the people in whose name it purported to act. Communism turned out to be only a pseudo equality project. The dream turned into nightmare. What did the emancipation of women count for if so many would languish in the Gulag? To the end of their days, unreconstructed adherents of the far-left could see no flaws in communist regimes beyond a few mistakes made. Class war or violence clothed in anti-imperialism was justified; it was not on the same moral footing as the incarnations of fascism. This blind spot has warped how generations of activists have seen the world. Yet anyone alive to the evil that men do should not have been surprised by Stalin or a Mao. The failure of suspicion about power was terrifyingly naive. Marx argued that capitalism was on the wrong side of history – often an ominous phrase – and that society should be organised in a different way; that a communist society should be set up in which equality is universal. How human beings should live in the world would be radically new. But communist autocracy led to terrifying abuses of human rights and great loss of life. All too quickly, high-minded Bolshevik ideals were betrayed by propensity to violence. All that mattered was achieving an equal society. The masses of people were raw material of social engineering. As Stalin said, 'one death is a tragedy; one million a statistic'.[10] The individual did not count in Soviet Russia.

The convulsions of class war have moved on; the idea perished after 1989 when the Berlin wall came down and the communist nightmare was over. What started out as a project to establish equality among the masses rapidly led to Russia becoming the most unequal of the richer economies (in the Russia of 2017, the Revolution was hardly celebrated). Cuba and North Korea were isolated enclaves and even the One Party State that is modern China became transformed into a market economy despite the Tiananmen Square protest being crushed that year. Western politics had changed out of all recognition. Thatcher, a grocer's daughter, did not have long to run as the UK prime minister but Theresa May, who was often compared to Thatcher, could take power in the summer of 2016 professing to govern on behalf of those at the bottom at the pile, against all discrimination. Thus revived a tradition of the 'one nation' Tory. Theresa May's main protagonist, Jeremy Corbyn, made clear that the UK Labour Party was a movement of social justice 'for the many, not the few', holding a vision of hope where the poor have sufficient to live on and workers are fairly paid.

Forms of inequality had moved on to other locations. Gender inequality, disability, sexual identity, race and ethnicity, ageing – all came under the spotlight in the last decades of the twentieth century as profound questions were asked about the way society worked. These have not gone away: far from it. In *Toxic Inequality*, Professor Tom Shapiro reveals how ingrained, systemic racism is responsible for the widening gap between the wealth of white and African American households in the United States.[11] In Australia, an investigation by the country's sex discrimination commissioner, Kate Jenkins, found that incorrect assumptions are being made that gender equality has been achieved despite disturbing and comprehensive evidence to the contrary. There was 'surprising and concerning' prevalence of opposition to advancing gender equality.

> They're not actively working against equality but there is a sense in the broader community that gender equality has been achieved, which means there is no real motivation for people to do things differently or to promote women or highlight their stories.[12]

It is all very well basing advances in gender equality assuming Anglo-Saxon, heterosexual, able-bodied people, many who feel they are breaking down some of those barriers. Yet women with disabilities are 40 per cent more likely than women without disabilities to be the victims of domestic violence; and Aboriginal women are 32 times more likely to be admitted to hospital as a result of family violence-related assault than non-indigenous women.

New divides were opening up to take the place of the previous divisions in society. Internet media brought an intensified social comparison. Technology is making the world more unequal as a large gap yawns between elites favoured by an automated future and those who will serve in low-paid jobs and wait at tables.

Globalisation – by turns bogeyman and cause of celebration – was blamed or lauded for many situations where jobs were being sucked east. But the real culprit was not the Chinese economy hoovering them up: it was automation. Capital follows cost savings. If jobs in America's rust belt can be done more cheaply by an army of robots, what stops this happening? As Stephen Hawking warned, technology's role in growing levels of income inequality means that this is 'the most dangerous time for our planet'.[13] Inequalities will rise – and fall but technology makes the world more unequal.

If humans cannot do jobs, artificial intelligence can. The diffusion of technology takes time to filter through. What is the future of low-paid, low-productivity work?

I write these words on a day when leaders of the 20 most powerful and rich countries on the planet had concluded their meeting at the G20 in Hamburg. In the shadows of global elites, the anti-capitalist movement erupted into action. At least 40,000 people had gathered and police in riot gear lined the streets. The anti-globalisation ATTAC movement, organising the march, said that about 100,000 people attended. ATTAC coordinator Thomas Eberhardt-Koester said the movement wanted to 'bring our criticism of the G20 and our alternatives for fair global policies onto the streets'. More than 200 police officers were injured in three days of rioting. After a night of rioting in which radicals looted shops, hurled objects and set alight street barricades, the city centre was in lock down with luxury shops along main streets barricaded, protected by security guards.[14] The same day – 8 July 2017 – saw the world's largest Pride festival on the streets of London. More than 26,000 people took part in the parade, watched by a crowd of one million. This came after 100 other similar events in the preceding fortnight. Things had moved on in so many countries. The social landscape was unrecognisable compared to 50 years before, when the Sexual Offences Act 1967 decriminalised homosexuality in England and Wales.[15] All this coincided with a report published by Her Majesty's Inspectorate of Constabulary (HMIC) and Her Majesty's Crown Prosecution Service Inspectorate (HMCPSI). The report pointed out that in a recent study of 358 homicides of women in the United Kingdom, 71 per cent were identified as involving a past or current relationship. Stalking behaviours were present in 94 per cent of cases.[16]

Inequality did not make people angry in the Middle Ages. You accepted you were a peasant and someone else was a king. But in a twenty-first-century capitalist society, it is a major problem. You compare yourself with others. You believe *you* can have it too. This could be because of social envy. But there is a darker side. Economic inequality means people say 'I don't have a stake in this society'.

Inequality has come to be an industry; studies on how to break up concentrations of wealth and power have been at the top of the bestseller charts. Marx's iconic flagship volume *Das Kapital* had an heir for our times. Thomas Piketty's *Capital* went to the top of the New York Times bestseller lists – much hailed and much criticised. Unequal societies were argued to be dangerous for cohesion. A raft of social ills were linked to it. Methodologically, this does not prove the point. Correlation is not the same as causation. There is a curious bifurcation at work. Keen interest among politicians and social scientist in the lack of equality that weighs on society is matched by a general lack of interest among most people in their findings, whose concerns are, primarily, on paying the common round of bills.

Why then is inequality such a problem? Could societies not resign themselves to a lack of equality being inevitable? An unequal social system is here to stay. There will always be winners and losers. After all, the granting of privilege by some to some is deeply ingrained. One person's advantage is another person's disadvantage. In the writings of that paradigmatic Enlightenment figure Jean Jacques Rousseau, equality is an ambiguous concept. 'Man is born free but is everywhere in chains'. Civilisation creates and perpetuates inequality – but we are all equal in misery and equally in chains.

I will argue that inequality does matter. It matters because of the way that equal worth is not merely a philosophical construct but a social dynamic. To set the stall out, inequality may not worry people if by that we mean their perception of where they sit on the income distribution curve. It might not be uneven rewards in abstract terms so much as their reality of having to make ends meet and pay that electricity bill hanging over them or find the money to get out of overcrowded housing. Very likely, being pinched or ground down by sheer lack of resources, in other words poverty, might be what is far more of a pressing issue. As an interviewee said on radio news during the UK election of 2017 when asked about what affects them most in everyday life, 'it is the struggle of living. I have got a job. Yet everything is expensive.' 'It is the cost of living', said another, 'having to buy food.'[17] Though referred to a great deal by political parties, inequality came up only sporadically among voters, who seemed to have intuitive respect for existential complexities politicians often lacked.

Yet lack of equality matters when it affects people personally. As another interviewee said during the UK election, recounting her experiences, 'social inequality is a huge problem. I face it every day. I will never be able to catch up with people I went to university with. Just because I went to Oxford University does not guarantee the same job opportunities. I will never keep up'.[18]

For so many, even in relatively affluent Britain, sub-standard housing and often hunger map on to other social divides such as the widening gap between north and south or situations when zero hours contracts become exploitative. It is when discrimination and other forms of inequality connect with the daily reality of lived experience that lack of fairness in society becomes an issue. It could well be that the average person is far less interested in economic inequality than the politician. Is it primarily social scientists that link the issue of inequality to the issue of poverty?

Nevertheless, inequality is integral to discriminatory or exploitative treatment. It is fundamental to groups in society being handled differently. It matters because of the lack of respect with which it is inexorably associated. We will never be equal; the starting point, the advantages or variation in social circumstances are too profound to militate against full equality of opportunity. Few can grasp opportunity with an equal hand. Systemic inequalities whereby we are not in practice equal human beings should be challenged for at least five reasons:

1. **Religious and philosophical argument.** Social injustice is a moral outrage. To have an inbuilt division between the haves and have-nots has to be wrong if it means some have the dice loaded against them by reason of their circumstances. This is socially corrosive.
2. **The economic argument** – that wealth is sucked up from the bottom to the top. People need to have a stake in the system or they will feel disenfranchised. It is incongruous to observe an economic system in a democracy which channels the spoils to the richest.
3. **The practical argument** – that inequality has a very real impact on people's lives from day to day. The practical effects of inequality could take the form of unequal access by those with disability, preference shown to 'people like us' (PLU) or the glass ceiling.
4. **The argument from intensified social comparison** in an age of anxiety, is harmful to those who cannot keep up. Social status has always been a feature of competitive societies where participants do not simply accept the status quo. It is internet social media that has extended comparative status to such issues of looks and body image where people do not only go third class but are trashed.
5. **The psychodynamic argument: inequality impacts the person.** Consciousness of relative position engenders a counter-reaction that will manifest in various ways. It is this awareness of inferior status relative to others that makes inequality socially corrosive.

Persistently high rates of income or wealth inequality are bad for social cohesion, political inclusion and crime. The evidence for this is overwhelming. Or is it? **The argument is that growing economic inequality exacerbates social problems** such as youth unemployment, gender-based violence and many others. Inequality denies people both their dignity and their voice. It feeds social frustration and the lack of cohesion. Islamic fundamentalism is exacerbated by its appeal to those who feel on the margins. It feeds on broken homes, abusive relationships and petty criminality.[19]

Affective inequality matters. People feel disadvantaged for various reasons. A news piece about social mobility and grammar schools told the story of a young woman who left school with ten good GCSEs. Then her dad died and her nan and her auntie. It was all too much. She got work in a fish factory.[20]

These are the arguments we will rehearse in this essay. Accounts of inequality surely fall short if there is no theory of relativity. As with Einstein's 1905 landmark work in theoretical physics, a theory of social relativity is contingent upon local frames of reference. Relative position needs to be proximate to be felt. Global inequality is a massive issue of our times as the gap between many areas of the world and rich world countries is so stark. It is, though, when people are brought into close relation with each other – such as in a family or between neighbours and neighbourhoods – that relative effects kick in.

We will consider this against the landscapes of our times where inequality is a pressing issue:

- Social worlds moving apart (Chapter 1)
- New class divides such as being due to age and automation (Chapter 2)
- Inequality on a global scale (Chapter 3)
- Gender (Chapter 4)
- War on the skin – racial profiling (Chapter 5)
- Intact bodies and wounded history (Chapter 6)

Behind the entrenched inequalities that are reproduced in these arenas of our times lie fundamental issues about how human beings are valued. Whether it is those who are excluded from social norms, either just-about-managing ('jams') or not able to keep their heads above water financially; whether is those who experience lack or outright deprivation; whether the focus is on everyday sexism and gender stereotyping, racial profiling or whatever, there is a set of beliefs and attitudes.

A century ago, Gandhi responded to the 1919 Amritsar massacre in his newspaper *Young India* that the Hunter Report 'furnishes overwhelming testimony of British officialdom's conception of Indian rights as of little importance and Indian life as very cheap'. It would no longer be subject to colonial power. Such is hidden psychology of politics and of unequal status.[21] The caged bird was now free.

The Infamous Second Verse

A personal word. In the Parish, the most commonly requested hymn at markers of births, marriages and deaths remains the nineteenth-century favourite 'All Things Bright and Beautiful'. Most can still remember it but not the infamous second verse that came up at the time of writing: 'The rich man in his castle, the poor man at the gate. God made them high and lowly and ordered their estate'.

To modern tastes this is a relic of a reprehensible antiquity, reflective of ideas about the social order long since consigned to history (consigned one might add, by the triumphant success of the equality agenda as well as Christian socialism, strong when the hymn was written). It is now obvious in a way that it was not before consciousness-raising became so powerful that this was power in thin disguise.

De-personalisation's disavowal and re-assertion of the worth of social participants who had felt relegated lay behind Brexit, Trump and the populist surge of 2016. It reflects the societal shift we are witnessing towards 'voice and choice.' This contemporary mood is a universe away from the kind of spirituality expressed in the writings of the seventeenth-century mystic and cleric Jeremy Taylor, for example, where people are exhorted to feel under-valued, unnoticed and esteemed of little worth.[22] My own perspective is shaped by a rather different theology plus its practical application in setting up an environment where people do count and they do matter. I have worked on the old council estates where it was pretty clear, pretty quickly that there was a healthy reaction against those who sought to 'do' for people; what was important instead was to value the contributions put forward so people knew they are listened to.

I believe strongly in a society of equals, where it is vitally important to treat people the same, where it is important to mount radical assault to the barriers in a deeply unfair society that prevent them reaching their potential and where society should make it its business to look out for those that have weaker voices. I believe strongly that we must find ways at local level of recreating community that really does allow for participation and reward on equal terms. Recreating communities of equals where social relationships are non-oppressive is vital for human flourishing.

Yet there is a faux reaction often in evidence that mires the progressive left in moral confusion. Banning speakers from a university campus where their words are likely to be disturbing to some is not an expression of the equality principle. Putting trigger words on actions and statements that will evoke predictable cries of protest is not an expression of the equality principle. Questioning misogynistic practices among Muslim communities only to risk accusations of Islamophobia or racism is not an expression of the equality principle. These things should continue to be challenged.

Equality is not the ultimate principle. In overall terms, the value of persons is paramount. That underlies equality in that human beings could be said to have equal value (though that is disputed among moral philosophers). As a Christian theologian, the claim I would make is that the value and worth human beings have is undergirded by God. The Creator – who, as the American Declaration of Independence stated, created us equal and endowed us with certain unalienable rights – alone holds ultimacy. An impersonal, atheistically perceived universe can never be the source of validation for personal human beings of incredibly high value. That is not, and can never be, a licence for human oppression. Quite the contrary, it challenges it at every turn.

The problem with inequality is that we are never at the same starting point. There are plenty who will never progress far because their upbringing and the lack of opportunities constrain them. Inevitably, we are a product of the experiences that shape us – and those experiences are completely unequal. In affirming equal value it is important to allow and encourage everyone to rise to their own level and be who they are. This will vary within societies but also over time.

Part One

Landscapes of Inequality

1

A Tale of Two Cities

'The Labour Party is the party of equality and seeks to build a society and world free from all forms of racism, anti-Semitism and Islamophobia. Labour has a strong record on progressing women's rights and freedoms that we can be proud of.' – Labour Party Manifesto, UK General Election 2017

'We pass through this world but once. Few tragedies can be more extensive than the stunting of life, few injustices deeper than the denial of opportunity to strive or even to hope, by a limit imposed from without but falsely identified as lying within.' – *The Mismeasure of Man*, Stephen Jay Gould[1]

'All the time they kept screaming. The screams moved with the fire.' Far, far too quickly a tower block in West London containing 120 homes and 200 people became a raging inferno. 'It went up,' remarked a survivor, 'like a matchstick.'[2]

It was the best of times, it was the worst of times. Social rifts in London and Paris had evolved beyond recognition from the eighteenth-century urban underworld charted by Dickens when, in France, a revolution dedicated to *egalité* was about to sweep the old order of things away. In the twenty-first century, the banlieues of Paris are present in all their social distress; framed by modernist architecture, they are places where alienation and violence are rife.

It was from the alienated banlieues that terror erupted in 2005.[3] Distressed London is represented by social housing estates and tower-blocks that pierce the sky, built to house the poor and which are crammed with human beings. It was in an area like this that the towering inferno was lifted from a Hollywood disaster movie to become horrific reality one June night in 2017.

Outside cladding that was put on Grenfell House in North Kensington for insulation had become a combustible fire blanket. It seemed as if a dysfunctional relationship between housing standards between the rich and the poor lay at the heart of the horror. With more money, greater protection could have been bought. Do rich lives count for more? Was an inferior quality material being used and is it worth spending more on more important lives? Rapidly, the Grenfell fire became a story about class, ethnicity and poverty. One of the capital's richest councils that had huge reserves of public money had failed to look after its poorest residents. Or so it seemed. Yet on the website, the Royal Borough of Kensington and Chelsea had proclaimed that 'Grenfell Tower in North Kensington, has been undergoing major refurbishment [...]. The large-scale works included the installation of insulated exterior cladding, new double glazed windows and a new communal heating system'.[4]

In North Kensington, contrasting social worlds lived side by side. 'I do feel that poor people have been gated off from this community,' said a local resident.[5] '[Visually] there's no comparison, you've got a Rolls Royce to your right and the slum to the left. It's not a good contrast. There's half a road separating the wealth and the poverty.' A short distance away from the disaster, rich mansions lay empty while BMWs, Jaguars and Audis were parked along tree-lined streets. Some of the wealthiest streets in the country nestle near cramped housing. In the shadows of classy delicatessens for the wealthy lay supermarkets offering inexpensive food for the poor, the migrants and the 'just-about-managings' that have become a slogan in the circles of government.

Those with lower incomes face a housing crisis; they are being evicted by private landlords as a consequence, mainly, of welfare cuts and capping of benefits.[6] In the United Kingdom, 120,000 children are forced to sleep in emergency accommodation, mixing with drug addicts and those with mental health problems. Particularly in London, those on housing benefit face huge problems in obtaining jobs or other accommodation.

Inequality is usually measured by comparing incomes across households within a country. But there is also a different kind of inequality: the affordability of homes across cities. The flight of lower-income people from our cities does not bode well. In many of the world's urban centres, homes are becoming prohibitively expensive for people with moderate incomes. As the 2017 Demographia International Housing Affordability Survey showed, around the world it is highly variable, ranging from Hong Kong (a price to income ratio of 18 : 1) to Chicago (3.8 : 1). In London it is 8.5 : 1.[7]

'This would never have happened in a mansion,' remarked one angry protester about the Grenfell disaster. There was a sense among many others that elites just don't listen; the familiar refrain of our times. The fire revealed the divides of social London. The political morality tale not only highlighted the gap in mortality rates between North and South Kensington, it also revealed the litany against impersonal faces and impersonal forces. Theresa May, prime minister, visited the disaster but received strong criticism for not going among the traumatised survivors.[8]

Conditions are cramped. 'I have lived in a one-bedroom flat with my daughter for ten years,' said one survivor. 'What alternative was there? The Battersea Power Station development is not for the likes of me – riff raff or scroungers or whatever they call us.'[9] This was not housing the less well-off people. Generally, a commitment to affordable homes helps to get planning applications through. Developers often then alter the number of affordable homes they offer. The needs of communities are ignored. In places like these and the old tower block country the author is used to, social worlds are moving apart. In rich societies, the poor have shorter lives and suffer more from every social problem. Malign circuits, characteristic of societies at every level, are greatly exacerbated where you have low educational attainment, poor housing and poor health.

On the same day as the Grenfell fire, the leader of the Liberal Democrat Party in the United Kingdom, Tim Farron, resigned his position. Against the backcloth of his views on gay sex during the 2017 General Election campaign, it would, he said, have been impossible for him to be a Liberal Democrat leader and 'remain faithful to Christ'.[10] In his eyes, this was a moral issue. In the eyes of his detractors, it was an *equality* issue to do with the acceptability of gay relationships as contrasted with heterosexual relationships. Are questions of equality the defining moral issues of our time?

It certainly seems that to go against an equality issue is the ultimate sin.

The UK general election was fought initially on the vexed issue of garnering sufficient support for the right negotiating stance to withdraw the United Kingdom from membership of the European Union (EU).

'Everyone is equal before the law'. So says Article 20 of the European Charter of Fundamental Rights. The Charter subsumed all the rights found in the case law of the Court of Justice of the EU as well as the rights and freedoms enshrined in the European Convention on Human Rights – two contentious institutions to those clamouring to withdraw.

It is today's single most important political principle. Diversity is now to be valued not assimilated. The equality principle is included in all European constitutions. It has been recognised by the Court of Justice as a basic principle of European Community law.[11] Article 21 follows – the principle of 'Non-discrimination'. Any discrimination based on any ground such as sex, race, colour, ethnic or social origin, genetic features, language, religion or belief, political or any other opinion, membership of a national minority, property, birth, disability, age or sexual orientation or nationality is prohibited. In turn, Article 22 proclaims that the EU shall respect cultural, religious and linguistic diversity. The principle of equality extends further into Article 23 – 'Equality between women and men must be ensured in all areas, including employment, work and pay.'

Though poorly understood by Western liberalism, fragmentation into different identities based on nationalism has become the hallelujah (or political menace) of our times. What liberals did grasp was a different sort of identity politics. The classic oppositional movements of the second half of the twentieth century – civil rights, women's liberation, ethnic, de-colonisation, disability, sexual orientation and ageing – represented enormous social changes that were advancing at broadly the same time. The triumph of the principle (though not the practice), has been all but complete among richer countries. Many critics argue that the ideology of equality and diversity has hardened into a dogma which excludes minority views of those who see it as a juggernaut.

As Tepperman notes in *The Fix*, an identity of being on the left has been a way of feeling morally superior; an identity of being on the right of politics of feeling intellectually superior.[12] Nevertheless, an enduring feature of the movements which blossomed in the 1960s – for women's, gay and black liberation – was not their support for but their hostility to the emerging market state. Equality used to be a matter of class and positioning in society. Now it is about culture and identity. If you discriminate against the poor or sections of society, it becomes an equality issue. The voices of alleged victims are entitled to their day in court as much as abusers. To deny that would also be an equality issue. Equality is the sacred cow of our times, the god of our age. Fall foul of equality and this dominant theme and force in our social and political life will rise up and crush you.

The UK general election that was the immediate backcloth that highlighted two different versions of inequality. The two main protagonists were a Vicar's daughter (who believed you should treat everyone with equal courtesy no matter who they were) and a Labour Party leader whose constant refrain was that the political manifesto should be one of governing 'for the many, not the few'. The election campaign stressed again and again that the many and glaring inequalities in society had to be addressed. Theresa May had stood on the steps of Downing Street 11 months earlier and proclaimed the 'burning injustice' of poorer people who died on average nine years sooner than richer brethren. Labour had always stood for equality. Equality was its founding and guiding principle. 'Labour brought in the Equal Pay Act, the Sex Discrimination Act, the Equality Act, the Minimum Wage and introduced Sure Start. Every progressive piece of equality legislation has been delivered by Labour'.[13]

By the time of the 2017 UK election political orthodoxy represented by the postwar consensus had changed. Concentrations of power had become something to attack; the idea of one element of power having too much sway something to oppose. Translated, this resulted in oscillation between the periodic invigoration of the state or the dominant mantra of the times being free market economics. Equality was a key driver behind the political orthodoxy shifting.

The postwar consensus in many Western societies had been that of wedding social democracy, Keynsian interventionist economics and the power of the state to effect change. Re-distributive taxation was both necessary and fair in order to pay for education, health and welfare for all. The taboo about high unemployment being unacceptable only began to be broken after 1979. It was Margaret Thatcher who broke with the postwar consensus. On taking the leadership of the Conservative Party in 1975, she re-invented herself as daughter of a Grantham grocer.[14] This was brandishing of mobility and aspiration on a meritocratic national scale. Economic liberalism became the ideology, firstly of a radical few and then the happy hunting ground of a property-owning, share-owning democracy. The instrument of loosening the power of the state and breaking unintended consequences of the welfare state was an approach in which everything became a free market.[15]

The basis of that market and society capitalism – quickly daubed with the term 'neo' liberalism – was that it is only individuals who act. In his defence of classic liberalism, Margaret Thatcher's favourite author, Friedrich Hayek, stressed that to speak of groups acting is fallacious. Individuals can either be harmed or benefitted. The only way governments act is to affect individuals. People act based on their desires, in turn shaped by beliefs. Paternalism – the notion that governments can help you act better than you can act yourself – must be discarded as socialist baggage. If people are autonomous and free, they are the sole determinant of what is good for them. There is no such thing as society! And so Friedrich Hayek's vision of the world was translated into a late twentieth-century version of laissez-faire capitalism; a vision in which the pursuit of equality was not important.[16] Across both sides of the pond, the word was out that state efforts to reduce the gap between rich and poor end up impoverishing us all.[17]

Yet do we have to choose between the socialist view of equality and expanding the cake? Are more equal societies inevitably societies with proportionately smaller national incomes than less equal societies? In its Third Way, New Labour accepted that social democracy and public services needed to go hand in hand with a pro-business, market approach. Tony Blair and other New Labour ministers came to share the consensus in the Treasury that promoting equality meant sacrificing economic growth. The thrust of government policy was to stimulate the economy, and never mind if the gap between rich and poor widened – so long as the poor became richer too and all boats floated.

The consensus held sway until there was another generational shift. It came in the wake of the financial crash of 2008. That and the era of austerity that followed left the United States 16 per cent poorer than it would have been if previous growth trends had been sustained and Europe 17 per cent poorer. The crash widened inequalities. According to the US Federal Reserve, the incomes of America's poorest 20 per cent fell 8 per cent between 2010 and 2013. In fact, the incomes of all Americans fell in this period, except for the richest 10 per cent – whose income in these low growth years actually rose 10 per cent.[18]

There was never a sustained left-wing push-back against global capitalism on intellectual grounds. Yet all this began to erode the left-right project. The market should not be the arbiter. It should at least be re-moralised or infused with volunteering that conscripted the willing participation of active citizens.

The financial crash had a long tail. It was strongly felt by many that a concentration of power in the financial sector should not be tolerated. Thinkers on the political Right began talking about inequality or the difficulties young people had in getting on the housing ladder. With social democracy dying on its feet across Europe, an era of post-liberalism seemed to beckon. The strange politics of 2016 – exemplified in the Brexit vote to leave the EU and the ascendancy of Trump – showed that many felt powerless in the face of markets where there are no influences to restrain and referee. Through social media, spontaneous movements of 'networked individuals' were transformed into organisations and political movements with a programme to fight austerity. It became abundantly clear most working people in the United Kingdom did not feel a part of the European project. Remote bureaucracy, knowledge economy leading to jobs performed by computers, technocratic managerial solutions to the problems of society – all these things combined to create a strong sense of distance, disempowerment and disconnection. It was a cry of pain. Mainstream politics had lost its way.[19]

A new faith in egalitarianism began to surface. Even in the International Monetary Fund, the new orthodoxy is that inequality is not a concomitant of faster growth, of a bigger cake, but can erode it. So it was that, in the wake of the EU referendum vote in the United Kingdom, the new prime minister could talk on the steps of Downing Street about governing for ordinary working people who are trying to do the right thing but only 'just about managing'. Government should be about the need for fair pay, confronting vested interests. Theresa May remarked that those who held power nationally had more in common with global elites elsewhere than those who lived down the road. Social bonds that held the country together needed attention.

> That means fighting against the burning injustice that, if you're born poor, you will die on average nine years earlier than others.
>
> If you're black, you're treated more harshly by the criminal justice system than if you're white.
>
> If you're a white, working-class boy, you're less likely than anybody else in Britain to go to university.
>
> If you're at a state school, you're less likely to reach the top professions than if you're educated privately.

> If you're a woman, you will earn less than a man. If you suffer from mental health problems, there's not enough help to hand.
>
> If you're young, you'll find it harder than ever before to own your own home.
>
> But the mission to make Britain a country that works for everyone means more than fighting these injustices [...]. When it comes to opportunity, we won't entrench the advantages of the fortunate few. We will do everything we can to help anybody whatever your background, to go as far as your talents take you.[20]

This rallying call to equality and social justice combined with the subsequent Conservative Party Manifesto in the 2017 General Election, though it resulted in a debacle, nevertheless did signify the return of the state.

Society in Layers

Poverty bites people at the core. I think of Barry. Barry (name disguised) was a young man who may not even be alive now. In the London Borough of Enfield, life expectancy in the most deprived area, where he lived, is nearly six years less for men compared with life expectancy in the better off areas.[21] Barry has never grasped the 'five-a-day-message'. Barry took drugs. His younger brother is on the watch-list by social services. Mum had a succession of partners, some of whom abused him, as did his own grandfather. Most drank too much. In that family culture, it is quite usual for the men to beat up their womenfolk when they are three sheets to the wind. The relationships never last. It was against the odds for someone in that setting to feel good about themselves.[22]

Case Study: Tales of the Precariat[23]

I've had what you might call a diverse life. I'm an advanced plumbing and electrical engineer by profession, but I lived on the streets for a number of years when I left home at 16. Mine's a common story. I accumulated debt due to government caps, bedroom tax, that sort of thing. I was living on £1 a day and I was malnourished. I was so hungry I'd walk into a supermarket, pick up a pasty and eat it there and then. I think the security guards knew and were just kind hearted towards me. I knew it was ridiculous that I couldn't afford to buy a pasty.

> People were hassling me, pounding on the door. I think it must be an awful job, doing that. All my bills had threats on them. I nearly lost my home through it. I had no life. I tried to hide it from my children, even when I had a bad bout of depression, but they knew something was wrong.
>
> I was about to hand over everything I had to the council: my tenancy and all my goods, but on the way over there I saw this sign about CAP [Christians Against Poverty], and something prompted me to contact them. The man I spoke to said 'Stop! I'll see you tomorrow.' He came to my house and went through the paperwork and told me that CAP could help me!
>
> They loaded up my cupboards for the first time in ages so I had food in the house. And when the letter came saying I was out of debt, it was like all the worries and stress were gone, and I had a brand new fresh sheet to start again.

Life at the bottom of the pile is tough. As many as 80 per cent of the more than 1.2 million foodbank users in the United Kingdom are forced to skip meals many times a year. They cannot afford basic provisions. Of the 400 households served by a sample of food banks surveyed for a Trussell Trust Report, almost half reported 'unsteady income'; 78 per cent of those households reported having to go without food – sometimes for more than a few days.[24] More than one in ten of those in debt do not have a bed to sleep in at night. The average annual income of those who came to the charity Christians Against Poverty was less than £12,000 less than the average UK income. 'Clients face a relentless financial tightrope which for many renders it near impossible to balance debt repayments and living costs, let alone a savings buffer. Renting beds is becoming increasingly common in "austerity Britain"'.[25]

Welfare assistance schemes had been cut back; the provision shrunk. Enormous pressure due to rising demand and funding cuts had taken their toll. Low income was found to be the main cause of household food insecurity. One in three adults in the past year was worried about not having enough money left over each month to save for the future or cope with financial emergencies. Food often had to be foregone; meals skipped.[26] Failure to act would create widespread destitution, and put even greater pressure on already over-stretched housing, health and social care services.

This is one face of contemporary poverty. What it does *not* show is a sense of inequality looming large within the consciousness of those who have unsteady income, who often have to go without heating or toiletries. Rather than where they place themselves, perhaps a sense of inequality comes more when external observers look at their lives and place them on the income distribution curve.

Inequality though is characteristic of income disparity. The complaint of different outcomes for different people is familiar litany in health care debates. In the author's immediate experience, in UK cities such as Southampton and Portsmouth, wide disparities show up within a few miles of each other or even in the streets next door.

Asking us to consider the causes of avoidable ill-health, Michael Marmot looks beyond such factors as smoking, poor diet, pollution, stress and risky behaviour to a social environment that pulls people down or conversely protects them from ill-health. It is not just the immediate social environment but the nature of the whole society that shapes outcomes. Despite appearances, healthy living cannot be reduced to personal choices. In an environment of poverty and social disadvantage, how a whole society is organised shapes outcomes. The surprise though is that the social gradient affects health higher up the scale; the disparity in health outcomes is not just observed at the bottom of the pile.[27]

Economic inequality magnifies the effect of social status. It digs into a sense of absolute value people have; it constitutes a core challenge. In *Happiness*, the economist Bruno Frey argued that we may not value absolute income but we set a high store on earning more than those around us.[28] Arguably, we value a higher relative income because we then value ourselves more by comparison. The thought that we are earning more than others promotes happiness.[29] To get on and go up is less satisfying if everyone else is also rising. Status-consciousness is about relative position, arguably because the relative betrays the absolute. We ourselves are called into question; our being is wrapped up with what we are earning and the 'positional goods' we are buying. Money often functions as fancy gold, a false indicator of well-being. Its lack feeds a sense of relative deprivation. When a personal sense of value is tied up with financial or asset value, the resultant confusion will lead to the soul under threat when the external value is eroded. It does not make for a sustainable future.

Once there is enough to assure the basics of life for all, wealth is not harmful because it reduces the amount left for another, but because it raises the wealthy person to a higher rank. As social status rises, so do health prospects and life expectancy. The causal pathway Marmot identified was the psychic benefits of 'being in control' of one's life. Autonomy in this sense is related to socio-economic position. Making society more participatory and inclusive should increase public health.[30]

The tale of two cities and health inequalities are not just between postcodes. Record levels of violence and abuse against vulnerable patients at mental health trusts were reported in 2016 amid accusations of 'endemic' use of force in the UK National Health Service. More than 5,000 serious incidents involving both children and adults were investigated, including hundreds of suicides, dozens of killings, more than 2,000 cases of self-harm and even deaths of children.[31]

The next day, an alarming epidemiological study by the University of Manchester was published showing that people from the north are far more likely to die from so-called 'diseases of despair' – drugs, drink and suicide. Poverty and lack of opportunity were factors behind growing geographical health gaps, most dramatic in early adulthood, researchers said. The chance of dying early was 20 per cent higher in the north than in the south – those aged 35–44 in the north were 49 per cent more likely to die – a disparity that had grown from just three per cent in the 1960s. Those aged 25–34 were 29 per cent more likely to die early – up from 2 per cent 50 years before. The findings suggested that 2,698 people aged 25–44 who had died in the north in 2015 would have survived had they lived in the south. Behind it lay a crisis of social identity, especially among men.[32] A stark difference in premature deaths highlighted a systemic inequality, in the words of the Bishop of Liverpool, that had proved indifferent to interventions from government.[33]

Despite the sharp divide of social worlds within the capital, London had a favoured status by comparison. In recent years, £900 per head more had been spent to improve people's lives. Notwithstanding a tale of two cities, this was a tale of two Englands. Metropolitan areas had been privileged by globalisation. A big gap had opened up. The south had re-invented itself as a knowledge economy: the north had swapped coal mines for call-centres. The de-industrialisation of the 1980's changed countries like the UK profoundly. On a personal note, during my time in the Department of Industry between 1979 and 1986, we saw jobs in manufacturing shrink from 7 million to near 5 million. the the economic winter wasteland, wealth migrated south. Opportunity no longer knocked for a generation where skills, traditions and communities were ripped apart.

2

Winners, Losers and New Class Divides

'Guided by the belief that every life has equal value, the Bill & Melinda Gates Foundation works to reduce inequities and improve lives around the world.'[1]

'I used to work in a shoe factory. I was like a slave. I sought the revolution.' – a Venezuelan worker articulating the devaluation that lay at the heart of his anger[2]

'Despite the huge progress of the last four decades in reducing poverty, economic inequality is becoming a critical problem within countries, whether rich or poor. Inequality means abundance for the few and injustice for the many; this is a denial of the rights of millions of people. In more unequal societies, rich and poor alike have shorter lives, and live with a greater threat of violence and insecurity as inequality creates conditions in which crime and corruption thrive.' – Oxfam[3]

For generations, social life and the field of politics were agitated by class. They still are. New forms of restless inequality are being thrown up by production on the contemporary scene that is starting to rely heavily on automation. It forces us to re-think what we mean by work.

Classic Class

When it came, a century ago as I write these words, the social explosion in Russia was a release of pent-up forces.

'The social constrains,' argued Emile Durkheim, the founding father of sociology in the nineteenth century.[4] This was nowhere more true of class. A traditional society constrained the kind of lives people lived and defined their place in the world.

The dice is loaded against many children even before they start school. Their prospects are predictable from the lives of their parents. Echoing Salman Rushdie in *Midnight's Children*,[5] of two tiny people who might be born at any time, one is already poor and the other born rich. Both will be handcuffed to their history. The problem is to explain such differences without some idea of class.

In traditional society, social location was determined primarily by land and therefore inheritance. Slave-owners and then feudal aristocracy felt themselves to be different kinds of people, a species apart with blue blood coursing through their veins that they passed on together with their land. The poor were unheard and unseen. Serfs in medieval England only began to have greater value placed on them when their wages rose. With the development of capitalism, the rise of merchants and professional groups, it was the economy that acted as the means by which value was assigned. How much you were worth was inextricably linked with what you did and how much you were paid. As the twentieth century wore on, forces that held the class system in check were no longer in place.

That lay in the future for Durkheim, who watched as his country entered into a political alliance with Tsarist Russia in 1893 and lived to see the overthrow of the Romanov dynasty and the events of 1917. Social attitudes of the Russian aristocracy undoubtedly contributed to unrest that turned violent as social frustration boiled over. 'The old government knew better how to deal with this peasant scum you call the people', one squire wrote to Prince Lvov, prime minister of the Provisional Government of 1917. Yet Prince Lvov saw this as the revenge of the serfs. 'If only Russia had been blessed with a real landed aristocracy like that in England, which had the human decency to treat the peasants as people rather than dogs. Then perhaps things might have been different.'[6]

Durkheim developed a theory of social class based on the idea of the division of labour in society. The normal state of affairs he saw as being social solidarity – conflict arising from industrialisation was but temporary anomie.[7] Yet what constitutes class has been more influenced by Marx with his conflictual account of social divisions. Karl Marx, the German émigré and journalist who had arrived in Paris 15 years before Emile Durkheim was born, was the inspiration behind the politicised form of class war that social upheaval took in Russia.[8] In 1844, the young Karl Marx met Friedrich Engels who had just published his *Condition of the Working Class in England*. It was a stirring essay on the de-humanising effects of industrialism. Friedrich Engels famously described housing in Manchester, the premier manufacturing city of the world of his day, as resembling 'cattle-sheds for human beings'.[9] Marx wrestled with the problem of how to promote a communist revolution in a country that was predominantly agrarian. The urban working class was small in Russia. Nevertheless, it is clear from contemporary Russian accounts that factory workers struggled with social influences that wanted to hold them only slightly higher up the ladder than the peasants. Some factory owners, unconstrained by legislation, could order arbitrary and humiliating punishments or prescribe how workers should dress at all times. This was resented as an affront on their personal dignity. 'We are not even recognised as people but are considered as things that can be thrown out at any moment [...] outside Russia, even horses get to rest. But our workers' worth is worse than a horse.'[10]

Durkheim died a few days after the Bolsheviks seized power. Soon after, Lenin declared war on privilege. Every village and town, he said, 'should be left to develop its own means of "cleansing" Russian land of all vermin, of scoundrel fleas, bedbug rich and so on'.[11]

It is largely due to Marx that we think of class as being shaped by the power of money and by exploitation, whether you are boss or a worker. 'The German Ideology' argued that the alienation inherent in the human situation is not a problem to do with how people think about the world. It is not mental in origin at all but caused by economic and social conditions. Change economic relationships and the inherently exploitative nature of the capitalist money system, he argued, and new social conditions will forge a new humanity. 'Our conception of history depends on our ability to expound the real process of production, starting out from the simple material production of life'.[12] The material elements of a complete revolution against the social order he defined as productive forces combined with revolutionary mass.

I want to argue that behind the reproduction of class and forms of social difference that cramp and constrain is not just a set of economic relations but a society that ascribes different scales of worth. Before the Russian Revolution, one young Russian peasant coming from the country to live in St Petersburg was very conscious of prejudice from the urban working class he sought to assimilate into. These skilled workers, the labour aristocrats of their society, took a pride in their appearance that seemed to convey 'their consciousness of their own worth'.[13] It was this sense of dignity that the young peasant, Kanatchikov, sought to achieve. Learning the skills of elite workers gave him greater confidence in his own powers and thus a greater sense of his own worth. Marx, the inspiration behind the social upheaval that followed in Russia, misses this aspect of devaluation in his clarion call to change our relationship to the means of production. 'Let the ruling classes tremble at a Communistic revolution. The proletarians have nothing to lose but their chains. They have a world to win.'[14]

Here is a boy from 1950s Huddersfield, heartland of the British industrial working class once characterised by overcrowded streets, long hours in the mills and personal cycles of poverty amid many positive ways communities were knit together – kinship and family webs, friendships, club, union and chapel. He is conscious of the possibility of mobility from a working class home through university into the junior ranks of management but conscious too that there, the line ended:

> There were two kinds of graduates that they took. There was me and my kind. But there were others that joined at the same time – right regiment, background, right car, knew how to handle a pair of guns and a fishing rod. They got on like houses on fire. Up and up they went, just like that. They'll be on the board of managers now. But I felt I was being left behind in a corner, just neglected. No matter what I did. No matter how good the ideas. Nothing happened. After two and a half years, they offered me a job that I could have done when I was sixteen. That I could have done quite well at sixteen. Nothing more. So I wasn't going to start at the bottom again. Not after two and a half years. It was like playing snakes and ladders, only my kind being the kind that comes down the snakes. I gave my notice in.[15]

It is the language of not fitting in, of never feeling one quite belongs. Languaged differently but expressing the reality of social value, here is a village lad in Somerset in Edwardian England in the days when the term 'respectable' was used to denote the families who were poor and did not mix and went neither to church or chapel: 'I remember during our last days at school, Oliver talking wistfully to me knowing I was going to start a career on the railway. "Of course", he said, "your family is respectable and mine isn't".'[16]

Many examples could be adduced to illustrate how de-humanising attitudes reproduce class inequality. One thinks of Lord Salisbury, a prime minister at the beginning of the twentieth century, who regarded the lower classes as 'scum' and was clearly not happy about further extension of the franchise. Depressive, devaluing factors have pushed the very worth and felt value of people down. Social forces affect their being, not just social and relative position. They are not merely external. What is needed to translate this process into a whole class of people is systems thinking. Oppressive forces act at the level of beyond the individual and are transmitted through sets of systems. The main field of activity that assigns value and worth is the economy. Where the power lies in society lies with those who dictate the terms of value.

'Where I come from, it was all put-downs. "You'll never amount to anything, it's no good teaching you lot!"' remembers someone growing up in the East End. 'You may have wanted to get out of here but when Mums and grandmas scrubbed steps or cleaned toilets and Dads went into the factory, what was the point. Low expectation, low-self worth comes from being told – "that's all you're worth". The emotional poverty was crushing. When I tried to brighten up the community centre, people resisted at first. They had got used to the rubbish surroundings because it was saying to them, "this is what we are – rubbish!"'[17]

Class shows up in devaluing acts and attitudes, many of which reflect hidden, largely unconscious bias. It might be strong-minded professionals who think they know better and who would rarely communicate that working class or poor people are to be listened to; their contribution valued.

The process of devaluation is set to continue. According to a report on social mobility in the United Kingdom, seven out of ten jobs created in the future will be professional jobs.[18] Arguably, talk of social mobility detracts from larger inequality. Poorly skilled men and women trapped in poorly paid jobs experience the conditioning effects of devaluation resulting in the poverty of aspiration that is the real enemy of personal progress. Social justice has been side-lined. It removes working class young people out of the communities that need them. Aspiration is not realisable. The assumption that there are jobs available is a deficit model of the working class – if only we can get more educated! There are simply not enough jobs at the top, in managerial, white collar roles. Most jobs do not require high levels of education. The United Kingdom is an economy of retailers and care workers while the middle class run faster to keep up. People should be able to live lives of dignity whether they rise or not. There is no real model of movement between classes, just a vague idea of everyone doing better than their parents. Or does this fly in the face of observation that social stratification is lessened?

Due to the influences of Marx and Weber, analysis of exploitation and inequality has focused on economic, power and status systems. In *Distinction*, a more recent theoretical analysis, the French writer Pierre Bourdieu emphasised the concept of different forms of capital – economic, cultural, social and symbolic – which together empower people in their struggle for position. As a result, individuals occupy a space with those who also experienced the same conditioning.[19] When it comes to the choice of occupation, people often end up doing the most natural next step. This used to mean going down the mines because your father did. What Bourdieu is suggesting is that it is not just economic relationships that shape your life chances. Cultural capital also mediates the fundamental conception of life you inherit, giving people the ability to function on the abstract register, to be reflexive, more imaginative and cultivate options. This is probably another way of saying that people who have money confer their advantages on to their children. In all societies and classes, offspring benefit from parents who transmit experiences and expectations. Unless class and cultural capital is addressed through education, the status quo will go on reproducing itself.

Poverty as an economic category can never be mapped straight on to class, a cultural and social category. Not all working class are poor or vica versa. The rich are not necessarily elite and the elite are not necessarily rich. The problem is that all efforts to study these vexed matters are so loaded that research into social classes is bound up with political campaigns to create a more equal society. Nothing wrong with the latter but as Heisenberg's uncertainty principle reminds us, the stance of the observer – by implication the method of choice – affects observation.

A tool is now to hand which still incorporates occupation and wealth but also includes this new emphasis on cultural capital. More than 161,000 people took part in the Great British Class Survey, the largest study of class in the United Kingdom. Traditional categories of working, middle and upper class are outdated, fitting only 39 per cent of people. Class has traditionally been defined by occupation, wealth and education. But the research found a new model, depicting the elite at the top to a 'precariat' – the poor, precarious proletariat – at the bottom. The BBC Lab UK study measured economic capital – income, savings, house value – and social capital – the number and status of people someone knows; cultural capital, defined as the extent of interests and activities.[20] Drawing on this conceptualisation, a major survey in 2013 suggested that people in the United Kingdom now fit into seven social layers.[21]

- **Elite** – the most privileged group in the United Kingdom, distinct from the other six classes through its wealth. This group has the highest levels of all three capitals.
- **Established middle class** – the second wealthiest, scoring highly on all three capitals. The largest and most gregarious group, scoring second highest for cultural capital.
- **Technical middle class** – a small, distinctive new class group which is prosperous but scores low for social and cultural capital. Distinguished by its social isolation and cultural apathy.
- **New affluent workers** – a young class group which is socially and culturally active, with middling levels of economic capital.
- **Traditional working class** – scores low on all forms of capital, but is not completely deprived. Its members have reasonably high house values – this group having the oldest average age at 66.
- **Emergent service workers** – a young, urban group, relatively poor but high social and cultural capital.
- **Precariat, or precarious proletariat** – the poorest, most deprived class, scoring low for social and cultural capital. This was the 16 per cent of people whose lives are insecure and often dysfunctional. They live precarious lives in that income is uncertain; often walking a financial tightrope.

The cultural dimension had been left out of class analysis. But the survey led to a spike in theatre tickets purchases as markers to new class identity!' While the elite group had been identified before, this is the first time it had been placed within a wider analysis of the class structure, as it was normally put together with professionals and managers. At the opposite extreme, said researchers, the 'Precariat', the poorest and most deprived grouping. These two groups at the extremes of the class system had been missed in conventional approaches to class analysis, which have focused on the middle and working classes. It was all about how much capital had been accumulated, though capital should be re-defined to include cultural and social capital as well as economic. As an online survey, however, it was heavily skewed towards middle-class computer users. Where do the elderly fit in – secure in their relatively low income pension?

Research by the University of Kent used data from the European Social Survey to examine the part played by education, social network membership, individual attitudes and ability and resources in explaining why the children of the middle class end up dominating professional and managerial jobs.[22] It concluded that, while education is the dominant factor in reproducing privilege, social network contacts play an important subsidiary role, accounting for 15 per cent of the advantage middle class children have in getting professional jobs in landing high status jobs (education accounting for about 50 per cent). This highlights how devaluation operates. Devaluation reproduces the inequalities of the world, especially the systemic disparity between rich and poor that has been the mainspring of social ranking. The point is that class plugs into what people are worth in economic and social terms and through that, into an absolute sense of themselves. It constantly generates issues of value.

Yet the way that cultures of devaluation operate is complex. It is not just a top-down social force. People position themselves in a way that feeds a sense of their value. Here is a white man in Newark saying how, in his new job, he meets a better class of people than when he worked in warehouses and factories. 'The grade of the people you met just wasn't appealing to me – they didn't have a direction in life, and they lived from week to week.'[23] People draw boundaries between themselves and those below. It is key to the construction of subjectivity. Relative position will occupy us later.

A common theme of contemporary commentary is that the notion of a fixed class is increasingly irrelevant as an analytical lens. Class 'is an increasingly redundant issue!'[24] 'The notion of class society is useful only as an image of the past.'[25] Traditionally, ownership of material culture used to define worth and value. Today, it can seem as if cultural production generally, super-charged by the middle class take-over of what to see and hear, vis-à-vis working class reaction in favour of popular culture, has come to replace class.

Class has a variety of meanings. The term needs to be de-constructed. It can be used to describe groups in the pecking order of society, social standing or prestige and markers of material advantage or occupation. But class also has political overtones; implying social forces that can change things. Such variety of meaning led to a lack of clarity in debates about whether it was still relevant.[26] Sociologists began to develop accounts of social class that looked at data about patterns of work,[27] historical accounts of how class is formed[28] and how class is constructed culturally in consumer society. Class identity is shaped and reproduced through value; high value people compared with low value folk. What it means to be respectable is always present. Some working-class families used not to support the idea that children can improve themselves. Was this in reaction to being told that they're no good? Or was it because the families feared social mobility would result in alienation?[29]

Class has been a major organising concept as in industrial society, production, distribution and regulated work are vital. In the West, there was the landless labourer, the worker who was free to sell anywhere what he or she had. Their labour became a commodity. For Marx, the problem was the experience of work that defined the relationship to the means of production. Society did not arise from the individual; it was the other way round. Weber disagreed. It was the way you found work and the rewards from it that was important.[30] People's life chances will vary according to their access to a wide range of sources of economic power. For some, it will be property, for others their capital will add to more than the value of the property. But status was also important to Weber. Different individuals or groups are viewed or valued differently and have greater privileges.[31]

Many factors are thus important in the pecking order – education, housing and occupational status. Weber argued that non-economic forces such as status were important, alongside the economic, in determining life chances. People judge each other as being inferior or superior according to the values they have in common. When people act in conformity with those values, they build up a good reputation and a high status in their community. More typically, a person's status follows from what Weber called 'the style of life'. People have low status according to how their way of life is perceived. Dirty work may be seen as demeaning, 'women's work' may be valued less than masculine. Effective claim to social esteem or honour is based on positive and negative privileges. 'Classes, status groups and parties are phenomena of distribution of power within a community.'[32]

The sharp end of class is that inequalities impede opportunity. Addressing unequal outcomes through redistribution has long been the remedy on the left of politics. Another form of equality of opportunity is less common – making sure the playing field is more level for everyone, not just those born lucky with inherited wealth and potential (a tricky word if there ever was one).

Age

Wealth inequality cuts two ways. One is the gap between class, rich and poor families. The other is between the generations.[33] In contemporary Britain, opportunities are determined more by wealth than by education or even income.[34] Property wealth in particular is skewed. That matters because the assets tied up in a bricks and mortar often represent the savings people need to fall back on during the unexpected or when work is precarious. The lack of accordable housing means that while some have assets as well as a home; many have neither. Growth in income inequality over the past 30 years has slowed yet wealth inequality is much higher than income inequality and is rising.

Younger people are better able to cope with technological overload than older people, who are often bewildered at the high speed of change. Nevertheless, those who are under 30 face new forms of inequality. In the United Kingdom they have witnessed an increasingly 'pay-as-you go' social welfare, contributing to their higher education through taking out loans. They struggle to get on the housing ladder.

There are inter-generational divides that may be getting worse after the financial crash of 2008. Many are trapped in low-paid work. They have done all the right things responsible citizens are supposed to do – looking for work and contributing to society. Yet all that many have to show for it is shoddy housing and wages that have hardly risen in real terms. There are not many jobs featuring young people who get ahead in these circumstances, making work pay and who elicit the dignity of working people.

By contrast, older people attract a range of welfare payments ranging from winter fuel to free passes on buses. They have seen their homes rise in value. Pay-as-you-go public pension schemes mean that the young are paying for the pensions of the older members of society.

Falling birth rates and growing lifespan means that in the rich world, societies are ageing faster than in the developing world. Among Organisation for Economic Co-operation and Development (OECD) countries, the share of over 65s is set to increase from 16 per cent in 2015 to 25 per cent in 2025. Ninety per cent of the population live to celebrate their 65th birthday in good health. To cash in on this dividend warrants over 65s and the recently retired being turned to creative, economically active pursuits. That will help ensure they remain net contributors to rather than net recipients of welfare. Economic growth thus generated would help young and old alike.[35]

In many EU countries, during seven years of economic crisis the intergenerational income and wealth divide widened.[36] In Greece, Golden Dawn attracted many without jobs, feeding off an unemployment rate among young people approaching 50 per cent. The divide between young and old in the EU increased. Youth unemployment and youth poverty rates grew; government spending shifted away from education, families and children towards pensioners.[37] Unemployment in the 15–24 age group increased by 7.8 percentage points between 2007–13.[38] The more precise measure of forced inactivity of young people is the 'not in employment, education or training' (NEET) rate (which varied significantly between EU countries). During the crisis, the material deprivation rate increased substantially more for the young compared to the old.[39] By all these measures, young people were significantly poorer: poverty among pensioners was reduced.[40]

The intergenerational divide tends to grow in times of recession.[41] What was needed was both action to restore fairness in government spending so the young are not disadvantaged, and also pension reforms that share the burden fairly between generations.[42]

As the New Economics Foundation observed, age was the determining factor in the unexpected results of the UK election of 2017. The palpable injustice of the generational wealth divide was one factor that tipped young people into voting for change. Housing was a critical issue in this debate as was any proposal to tax wealth. Both coming together may have cost the Conservative Party dear.

> Little is said of the systems that suck wealth from younger to older generations, or from debtors to lenders, or north and south of the UK's staggering regional divides. Newspapers extol the virtues of equal opportunity, while simultaneously arguing against 'death taxes' and 'garden taxes' as they violate our freedom to pass our wealth to our children, with no recognition of any contradiction.[43]

The UK Office for National Statistics showed that the gap between the richest and poorest fifths of society fell markedly in 2016. Against that, the generational divide is growing. Growth in pension payments masks the struggle of many other households to keep afloat.[44] The UK Resolution Foundation demonstrated that at age 30, a typical UK-based adult born between 1981 and 1985 had just half as much total net wealth as someone born five years earlier at the same age. This trend of younger groups faring worse than the cohort before them was largely a question of luck and being able to own a house at the right time in economic cycles. The fact is that record levels of wealth is still held in few hands. The extent to which wealth is taxed has barely changed since the 1960s.[45]

The high speed world into which young people are entering as they come into the job market is of a different order to that which their grandparents inhabited. Nowhere is this more obvious than in the world of high finance. Wall Street denizens earn more money than most people. And that means they become accustomed to the perks, such as eating at restaurants that might strain the budget of those less well situated. It is the bastion of class consciousness.

But the firms are white collar sweatshops with glamorous trappings. Anecdotally, you do not know how hard you can work, short of slavery, unless you have been an investment banking analyst or associate. It is not merely the hours, but the extreme and unrelenting time pressure. Priorities are revised every day, numerous times during the day, as markets move. You have many bosses, each with independent demands and deadlines, and none cares what the others want done when. You are not allowed to say no to unreasonable demands. The sense of urgency is so great that waiting for an elevator is typically agonising. If you manage to get your bills paid and your laundry done, you are managing your personal life well. Exhaustion is normal. On a quick run home en route to the airport after an all-nighter, a co-worker tried to shower fully clothed. Investment bankers have signed a Faustian contract: You have no right to personal boundaries.[46]

The problem with re-distributive policies designed to produce an egalitarian society is that you cannot redistribute wealth until it has been created. Even countries with a strong culture of the riches of wealth creation such as the United Kingdom are very poor at sharing it out. The biggest single element in the record levels in the United Kingdom of £11.1 trillion of wealth holdings are private pensions (£4.5 trillion), followed by property (£3.9 trillion) and financial wealth (£1.6 trillion). The top 1 per cent of the population now owns 14 per cent of all UK wealth, while the bottom, 15 per cent have zero wealth or are in debt.[47] This is not just a social disparity in one country. Across OECD countries, amid much pensioner poverty, the wealth of the baby-boomers is increasing relative to other groups in society.[48]

This is not to deny another reality and form of inequality that is all too prevalent. Ageism is rooted in a lack of equal treatment. Along with homophobia, it is one of the biggest cultural challenges in the West. Its ambiguity is that as society grows younger in attitudes, lifestyle and clothing, older people yearn to capture a piece of their childhood. The ideal is to be young. Ageing has formidable power to set up internalised reactions, framed in terms of loss of value. There are fewer opportunities for older workers. It is about social value. 'At the end of your career, you feel under-utilised and under-valued as well as under-motivated!'[49] What may very well be intended as on a relative scale in comparison with other, younger workers, is experienced as a threat to one's absolute sense of self.

In areas of the world such as sub-Saharan Africa and the Indian sub-continent, the proportion of young people is rising. In Pakistan, nearly 55 per cent of its peoples are under the age of 25. In India, two-thirds of the population are under the age of 35.[50] Yet in China and Japan, people are living longer and having fewer children. Baby-boomers in the West are levelling off into retirement. Fertility rates are falling below those needed to replace each generation. In Germany, concerns about an ageing workforce were underlined by a European Commission Report warning that the population could shrink and those of working age fall from 54 million to 36 million by 2060 – a serious fall of 19 per cent.[51]

The pinch point is that life expectancy is rising at the same time as fertility rates are falling. There are numerous implications. Economies the world over are undergoing a transition from youthful to ageing societies. Growth is being driven by increasing numbers of older people and by the expansion of the global middle class. As these two groups grow, the higher levels of healthcare they demand will cause seismic shifts in the amount of money being spent in the health sector, driving employment. Increasing longevity makes pensions, health care and other social services costlier.[52]

By 2020 the over-50s will constitute over 40 per cent of the British population. By 2040, 30 per cent will be aged 60 or over. The question for policy makers is 'which sections of the older population will live healthy, active lives and which will be dependent on formal and informal sources of support?' What are the patterns of inequality in health? How does the relationship between health and economic position vary with age? The extent to which material well-being differs across ages, across income and type of wealth is an important issue to understand – one that at the time of writing, is the subject of a large-scale longitudinal study by a UCL Health and Social Surveys Research Group.[53]

Inequality due to age is becoming much better understood. Global public consultations held between September 2012 and January 2013 fed into the formulation of the future development goals. Older people experience inequality in economic, political, environmental or social domains. Inequalities are reinforced by discrimination older people face as they are perceived to be independent and no longer capable. Often this results in being denied equal access to health services, property rights, decent work and livelihood opportunities. Similarly, older people living with disabilities experience 'double discrimination relating to their age and disability status'.[54] Ageism generally is intensified when it is gender-based discrimination. It is now a legal offence in the United Kingdom and many countries to discriminate against people in the workplace because of their age. At the same time, everyone is being encouraged to work for longer as the retirement age is raised. It is often hard for people over 50 to get another job.

> Our elderly are arriving at their twilight years and finding themselves cast off as nuisances, best kept out of sight and out of mind. In our frantic world of commerce, once you are old you are invisible – even advertisers forget that you exist.[55]

Fat Cats

'The growth of CEO and executive compensation overall was a major factor driving the doubling of the income shares of the top 1.0 per cent and top 0.1 per cent of households from 1979 to 2007.'[56]

Another landscape of inequality is the divide in earnings between those at the top of the corporate ladder and those many rungs below. The twenty-first century could shape up to be the most unequal period in history. Massive inequality marks a growing separation between the wealthy and everyone else. Increasingly, fault-lines force apart the way the economy is dividing. For the most part, the rewards are channelled to those at the top who pay themselves 120 times more than the average full-time worker. (Compare this with 47 times at the beginning of the millennium.) In 2014, the income of company directors had risen by over 20 per cent in the previous year; wages overall had fallen.[57]

J. P. Morgan, the classic American financier, reportedly said that in the interests of fairness, the ratio of pay of the Chief Operating Officer to the median worker should be about 20 to 1. The multiple of top executive pay to the median was 25 to 1 throughout the twentieth century, then from the mid-1980s, it rocketed to 150 to 1 (a six-fold rise). In the 1980s, the ratio of top executives to average salary levels in the organisation was 30 : 1. By 2012, it was 110 : 1. In the United States, the ratio was *c.*500 : 1.[58]

The benefits of globalised capitalism have been profound. Free markets have raised hundreds of millions out of poverty. Yet the cost has been a widening gap between a global super-rich and the rest. Arguably, this gap threatens our democratic institutions. The United Kingdom's richest 100 people have the same combined wealth as 30 per cent of UK households. Top directors now earn 175 times the average worker's salary – up from 45 times since 1998. A growing divide yawns between those with good salaries and those who are on the edge of society with dead-end jobs. The left behind are left out. The Institute of Public Policy Research report predicted that poor households will see their earnings rise by just two per cent over the next 14 years, while the average FTSE 100 chief executive's pay is predicted to skyrocket to £9.5 million.[59] The IPPR forecasts Britain's corporate fat cats will earn 350 times median income, up 144 times from 2016.

The growing inequality is not a good basis for a coherent society. Surely, a massive gulf between those at the bottom ad those at the top harms everyone? Or does it?

Automation

To the Luddites, groups of masked men who smashed up textiles machinery in Yorkshire, Lancashire and the East Midlands between February 1811 and June 1812, the benefits of automation seemed to lie entirely with employers. This was only a few years after Thomas Paine had proposed a universal basic income at a rate of £15 per person year.

Unlike the first industrial revolution where machines were based on amplifying force for the purpose of reducing human heavy lifting, contemporary machines are different in that they are increasingly learning for themselves. They have learned how to learn, a quality that has until now been exclusive to humans. With machines now performing this role, often better than us, how valuable will the human – or 'non-routine' – aspects of work be in the future? Machines are becoming much better than us at making important non-routine decisions involving our health, finance, navigation or entertainment, for example; what value will humans add? According to McKinsey, robots and computers can not only perform a range of routine physical work activities better and more cheaply than humans. They are also increasingly capable of accomplishing activities that include cognitive capabilities once considered too difficult to automate successfully, such as making tacit judgments, sensing emotion or even driving.[60] In 1972 the philosopher Hubert Dreyfus asserted that computers would never be able to perform simple tasks such as driving! Now, autonomous driving vehicles are commonplace.

The problem with income inequality appears to be accentuated by political geography where elite suburbs are thriving and former manufacturing areas struggling to offer skilled trades, not just university degrees. Having too few jobs is compounded too by lack of opportunity for meaning, self-improvement – let alone dignity. It is now made worse, at least at this stage, by the rise of the robots. The digitisation of the world economy – converting everything into '1's and '0's so it can be stored in machine intelligence – is the astounding breakthrough, changing all landscapes of present and future. In the run up to the American election of 2016, globalisation was blamed for taking American jobs. Those jobs are not coming back. It was robotics that are stealing blue collar jobs rather than Asian workers – witness petrochemical plants in the United States that don't need working-class workers. One person with a PhD in chemistry and dozens of robots will do the job more cheaply. The world seems to be approaching a tech-driven employment crisis. This fed Donald Trump's surprise victory in the US presidential election. As outgoing US Secretary of State John Kerry observed, 'trade is not the most culpable entity for the loss of jobs. Eighty-five per cent of job loss in America is because of technology. I can't wait to see how the incoming administration deals with AI.'[61]

Many counter-voices are raised against the alarmists. After all, China now has the greatest population of robots and heavily encourages their use.

Maybe they have come just in time to save the de-population and ageing time-bomb! For now, automation of factories has already decimated jobs in traditional manufacturing but employment remains high in the more developed world. Developing nations have not yet de-industrialised to nearly the same extent. In the foreseeable future, garment factories will rely on soft-touch human hands.

Nevertheless, the rise of artificial intelligence is likely to extend this job destruction deep into the middle classes, with only the most caring, creative or supervisory roles remaining. 'Deep learning' technologies are now demonstrating that they can do much more than just the type of work we have thought of as routine. So can we now replace fears that automation will erase jobs with hopes that advanced AI will actually improve rather than displace human work? How do we build a future that doesn't leave humans behind? How do we need to respond – as individuals, communities, companies, institutions – to harness technological progress for the benefit of the many?[62]

Observing a young American democracy, Alexis De Tocqueville thought that with the division of labour in the industrialisation that was growing steadily in the 1830s, the horizons of the workers were constrained. All they needed to know was one thing – how to operate the machine. The mind of the masters and factory owners, however, expanded with division of labour. The master needed to know many things in order for the enterprise to flourish. Bound up with power, such compression of knowledge or its contrast was leading inexorably to new social polarisation.[63]

Beyond doubt, artificial intelligence and automation are about to transform the nature of work. Every production line in every country is starting to feel the impact of robotics. Additive (3-D) manufacturing is linked with the shortening of global supply chains as local needs can be tailor-made to extend product ranges everywhere. Where automation in the past affected low-skill jobs, smarter machines and artificial intelligence automation could affect a much broader range of jobs in the future. This will surely shape high-paid, high-skilled positions. Although machines are getting better and better at doing jobs people have done, technology is taking out middle-income jobs.

Paul Mason argues that technology is not some deus ex machina intervening in the system periodically. Overlaying the more frequent and periodic booms and slumps that capitalism undergoes are longer cycles – or waves – marked by the invention and dissemination of certain key technologies: steam-powered machines and canals; railways and telegraphy; plastics electricity, the telephone, production management techniques; automation, aeroplanes, semi-conductors, and nuclear power; and now, the internet and information technology.

> Working-class resistance can be technologically progressive; it forces the new paradigm to emerge on a higher plane of productivity and consumption. It forces 'new men and women' of the next era to promise and find ways of delivering a form of capitalism that is more productive and can raise real wages.[64]

There will be a considerable time-lag. Every technological revolution has destroyed jobs well before new jobs emerge. Optimists argue that many jobs will be created. Yet as Mark Carney, Governor of the Bank of England, suggested, 'the fundamental challenge is that, alongside its great benefits, every technological revolution mercilessly destroys jobs and livelihoods – and therefore identities – well before the new ones emerge'.[65]

There are big questions here for what it means to be human. How does future society cope with widening rungs on the social ladder? Who owns the robots? A universal basic income could be needed to provide a means of livelihood. It is the unskilled who will lose out. Owners of capital and proprietors of invocation will remain winners. Labourers with only modest skills would be vulnerable. This stands in marked contrast with previous waves of industrialisation. There may not be a job bonanza this time.

3

Global Divides

'Sidaram Manji was shot, not because of what he had done but because of what he was, a Dalit, formerly known as untouchable, living in a mud hut on the edge of Mauri in Bihar, north-east India. He worked as a bonded labourer in the field of his killers, Bhuminar landowners whose large brick houses occupy the centre of the village. He drank from a different well, used a different temple and never strayed over the invisible line segregating Dalits from Bhumihars. His crime was to fish in a pond deemed out of bounds by the landowning caste that controls the village.'[1]

The process by which markets, people, goods and culture become more integrated has a name. It is a name that for many has become the pantomime villain of our times. For others it is an essential means to defeat poverty and bring multiplier benefits of international free trade to millions.

Globalisation is not new. Pre-industrial worlds had variants of it. The second half of the nineteenth century saw improved transport links via steam ships and the railways, and improved communications, via the telegraph network, bringing huge wealth worldwide – despite being wrapped in imperial preference and colonial exploitation, while wholesale migrations populated new continents.

In many Western advanced countries income inequality is significantly higher than it was until about 1980. It had been both stable and relatively low for three decades since World War II; a halcyon era of inclusive economic growth. A period of state intervention in the economy in reaction to the Great Depression and unemployment of the 1930s had reinforced that in the West at least.

By the age of five, seven out of every 1,000 American babies have died. By the same age, 300 out of every 1,000 babies in Sierra Leone have died. As Andrew Oswald observes, there is:

> nothing much one can say when one hears those statistics, is there? If a visiting Martian professor said to me that the human race should be ashamed of itself, I cannot think what I would say as a good counter-argument before she stepped back into the flying saucer.[2]

Millions of people around the world suffer and die from treatable conditions because medicines are priced too expensively. That led to the campaign group Global Justice Now launching a new campaign in the autumn of 2017 for access to medicines. Sibongile Tshabalala and many other South Africans fought against drug companies charging rip-off prices for HIV medicine. They set up the Treatment Action Campaign (TAC) and eventually won the right for South Africa to import cheaper versions of the drug. The TAC demanded the right to health for all South Africans. Formerly the World Development Movement, Global Justice Now campaigns for a world where resources are controlled by the many, not the few. They are in solidarity with social movements to fight causes of poverty and injustice.[3]

The coefficient that measures inequality varies between zero and one; it is named after its originator Corrado Gini. At a Gini of zero, everyone has the same. When the measurement is 1, one person has it all. Between the mid-1980s and 2011/12, the Gini coefficient increased in 16 out of the 21 OECD countries. As the OECD notes, average incomes at the top of the distribution have seen particular gains. However, there have also been significant changes at the other end of the scale. In many countries, incomes of the bottom 10 per cent of earners grew much more slowly putting relative (and in some countries, absolute) income poverty on the radar of policy concerns.[4] The question of who Gini is for, whether for the population as a whole or some sections of it, is never really answered.

Inequality in labour earnings rose quickly though the 1980s in both the United Kingdom and the United States, though was slower in the rest of Western Europe. More widely, globalisation has taken off the runway since the 1980s. It is not just air transport. A new era of container shipping, financial flows and the emerging infrastructure of the internet has created an interlocking global system of trade, transport and instant communication.[5] Results were spectacular. A billion people were lifted out of poverty.

Around the globe, leaders of governments and other stakeholder institutions entered 2017 facing a set of difficult and increasingly urgent questions. Fiscal space is very tight, interest rates near zero and demographic trends are disadvantageous for many countries.[6] Fears are the world economy faces a protracted period of low growth. The world economy is at a crossroads. Global growth is slow by post-World War II standards. Concerns are growing about social participation. Can inequality be satisfactorily redressed within the prevailing liberal international economic order? Can those who argue that modern capitalist economies face inherent limitations in not distributing rewards equally be proved wrong? Should transfer payments be expanded to ensure fair shares for all?[7]

Globalisation has many faces. European football is one of them. The Dubai-based airline Emirates sponsors household name teams in England, Spain and France. According to Kuper and Szymansk, the Spanish national football team's success went markedly upwards in tandem with the country's integration into economic markets. Growing interest in the United States is linked to the two groups keenest on the beautiful game – immigrants and coastal elites – being the most globalised Americans.[8] More than 20 per cent of UK Premier League teams are managed by American owners. Over half the clubs in England's top two divisions are owned by foreign investors. Chinese companies have invested heavily in clubs across Europe, as well as investing in football in their own country, encouraged by the personal enthusiasm of President Xi. Football usually generates winners and losers.

Globalisation too is rarely a draw. China has gained hugely from globalisation, with hundreds of millions being lifted from poverty, accounting for 19 per cent of the growth in global prosperity over the last ten years. But even globalisation is occasionally attacked. On 6 December 2016, *Global Times*, a jingoistic newspaper published in Beijing, ran an opinion piece blaming globalisation for China's income inequality, housing bubbles and the ravaging of its environment. China's own policy failures can be criticised. But its government has sensed the danger of rising public anger created by the divide between rich and poor. Working-class Chinese and the new middle class alike, worried about rising inequality, the impact of mass migration from the countryside into cities and job losses. Many felt that inequality and social mobility were growing. In turn, the middle class fretted about the growing new plutocracy who owed their fortunes to corruption, nepotism and networking, not hard work.[9]

Arguably, this is an inevitable result of the dynamic economic system unleashed by capitalism. Modern Communist China is the story of a nation which was dedicated to equality. Creating a society where everybody was exactly equal meant doctors earned the same as drivers. Then came China's economic miracle. China changed from a highly equal society to a deeply unequal one (though the signs are the Gini coefficient is starting to reverse once again due to rising rural incomes).[10]

The Credit Suisse Research Institute's Global Wealth Report is the most comprehensive source of information on global household wealth. It provides complete estimates of wealth, covering all regions and the entire wealth spectrum. The 2016 Report suggested that the lower half of the world's population collectively owned 1 per cent of global wealth while the richest ten per cent of adults owned 89 per cent of all wealth.[11] The number of super-rich has doubled in recent times. At the extreme end, using data from Credit Suisse and Forbes, Oxfam observed that eight billionaires who had the same wealth as the bottom half of the planet could fit into a buggy on golf courses for the elite.[12] The question is – does such massive social unfairness matter? Is capitalism inevitably an engine for social unfairness?

Inclusive growth is now high on the global economic policy agenda. The OECD has researched how far redistribution through taxes and transfer of benefits helps to moderate income inequality. The result is what Peter Lindert calls the Robin Hood Paradox.[13] The highest levels of redistribution occur where there is less inequality. Redistribution towards the poor tends to happen least in those times and polities where it would seem most justified by the usual goals of social welfare. For instance, among OECD countries, the highest levels of redistribution occur in the Scandinavian countries and the lowest in Mexico and Chile.[14] As Lindert notes, government redistribution cannot explain all epochal reversals in equalisation of income. Market forces and economic growth would produce a similar pattern even without government policies due to demographic change and unbalanced technological advance.

Winners and Losers

Winners of the globalisation league table are strongly in evidence. According to the World Bank, trade has helped halve the number of people living in extreme poverty since 1990.[15] Integrating the world economy gives an incentive for countries to specialise and demand worldwide access to sources of cheap raw materials. Sourcing the cheapest materials from around the world increases profits. Greater trade leads to sharing knowledge and technology resulting in more employment.

On the debit side, multinational companies switch investments between countries in search of a free pass by regulatory regimes. They can push wages lower than the free market equilibrium. Unfair free trade causes loss of jobs in domestic markets. Structural changes arising from globalisation often leads to the slow erosion of an economy's manufacturing base. *Deindustrialisation causes* structural unemployment. In this way, the gap between rich and poor widens. Globalisation cannot but generate winners and losers and increase inequality both within countries and internationally as richer nations benefit more than poorer ones. In the global village, inequality has to be configured globally. The gap between rich and poor has to be extrapolated to richer and poorer countries.

Case Study 1

I write these words in Nepal where gaps between poor and less poor mark out social divides there as anywhere. Health, educational attainment and housing that are markers of social divides in richer countries are richly in evidence. Our guide up in the high passes towards Everest, Myla, is not a mountain man. His family are not subject to the endemic poverty that grips the foothills and mountain regions. Myla is a farmer. The Khumbu valley is a more prosperous region. Yet such disparity is played out amid relative poverty that political parties feed on. Recent years have seen not only an homogenous entity called 'a Maoist insurgency' but no less than 15 Maoist or Leninist parties vying for supremacy on the left. Each is saying that there is nothing for the people. Each highlights how education, health and welfare is sorely lacking. The rich carry on getting richer.[16]

The differences *within* a country about the way people are valued by income are paralleled by major differences of wealth *between* countries. In a global society, we have to think bigger when it comes to inequality of poverty and wealth. One of the most degrading life-conditions, in all societies, is poverty. Poverty de-humanises people, creating social inferiors and a contrast between those who have and 'the have-nots'. In the struggle for survival and the way that they are more easily exploited, the poor have less status. Their life chances are far worse in education and health. The poor are routinely shunned and shamed, treated as idle or of low worth. Africa especially highlights the way that we live in an extremely unfair world. The issues that concern young people in our society – 'Will I find a job? Will I find the love of my life? Will I be safe and secure?' – are on a very different scale.

There are many causes of global poverty: economics and trade, politics, the history of a country, its geography, war and conflict. All these factors hold back development. But poverty is also shaped by issues such as class and social expectations. Multi-nationals often exploit poorer countries by paying very low wages and abusing the rights of workers.[17]

The number of people hungry around the world is now rising again. An estimated 815 million people go to bed hungry – an increase of 38 per cent from the previous year. Levels of undernourishment have slowed. The vast majority live in countries affected by conflict. Inequality is driven by conflict.[18]

Different standards apply. One manufacturer inserting the maximum 1 per cent mercury into sun tan products in the West gets away with 3 per cent mercury levels in Kenya, where a lighter skin is prized. Because that has harmful effects on the face, the same company sells a treatment! In practice, as the tragic story of the aftermath of the Union Carbide factory disaster in India makes clear, one life does not seem to have the same value as another around the world. Class and wealth divide people into social layers but also have the effect of devaluing those who do not have any status.

Case Study 2

The following notes were made by a link diocese in Rwanda about their experience of poverty.[19]

- People are aware that 'persistent poverty' is evident in their community. The tangible indicator of poverty is malnutrition, poor housing, poor clothing, lack of health insurance, poor hygiene and sanitation.

- People lack knowledge about the available resources to use in order to fight that persistent poverty.
- The solution to the problem of persistent poverty in their community is through farming, that is crop production and small animal breeding.
- We have already small saving and credit groups to begin the journey of community transformation.
- Pigs and hens are the possible animals to breed that can help at the same time in agricultural production both in Kibuye and Musebeya Parishes. In Kibuye Parish, women have began that project.
- Vegetables, corns and cassava trees are the crops which can help change people's lives quickly.
- Building capacity of local people through training helps create awareness of opportunities available, training them on how to begin small generating income enterprises, training them on how to breed and take care of small animals especially pigs and hens.
- Gathering funds to support the existing initiatives and begin others in order to boost the socio-economic transformation. People working together in groups can be given loans to buy animals or to begin small scale industries. After generating income, they bring back money to be given to others.

Gaining Economic Power

Global poverty and inequality implicates us all. Drinking tea in the fifth largest economy in the world is made possible in large measure because of 200,000 people employed on the tea plantations of Sri Lanka. Many Tamils had been brought over from India by the British to work on the terrain of the central highlands in order to water the growing demand at home. Their descendants often live in isolated communities. The hardest work is done by women. 'Tea pickers are considered the lowest of the low, despite being the backbone of the Sri Lankan economy.'

> They live in poor accommodation on the estates and work in all weathers, on steep plantations slopes, in bare feet, at risk of being bitten by insects and snakes. Needless to say, it is very hard work. They are paid a minimum wage by the kilo picked.[20]

Compounded by the lack of resources, plantation workers are regarded as foreigners and second class. They have few rights, have to fight hard to obtain identity cards and have few medical facilities. If someone is unwell and takes time off to visit a clinic, their wages will be reduced. People often go without treatment. Their homes are tiny and might house as many as eight people, with no electricity for light or for cooking. Children of the plantation often fall behind in their education.[21]

Or take a lesser known crop, a special variety of deep-rooted peas. These are much better able to cope with the devastating reality of weather patterns that makes other crops, such as maize, fail when the rains fail meaning that farmers are unable to make a profit. Unscrupulous middlemen take advantage by buying directly from farms using illegal buying scales. The result is that prices are driven down and farmers are unable to send their children to school or feed their families properly. 'It is very pathetic, as a father, to feel helpless like that, to feel like you cannot provide food for your children and that there is nothing you can do to make them better.'[22]

Such cameos illustrate the anguished gap between the way poverty and inequality is intertwined; between those who have resources and those who have few, those who struggle to feed their families and those who feed on those who struggle to feed their families.

The Clay Cup

Perhaps nowhere on earth is inequality more deeply entrenched than in the caste system. Most conspicuously in India, caste reflects a deeply layered society endemic across southern Asia.

The Dalits are the people living at the very bottom of the hierarchy of India's caste system. Since one in six Indians is a Dalit, there are nearly as many Dalits in India as there are people in the United States. Sometimes known as the 'untouchables', Dalits are regarded as subhuman outcastes. They are history's longest standing oppressed people group and constitute the largest numbers of people categorised as victims of modern day slavery. Hindu scriptures call them the 'unborn', which translates as: it would be better if they had never been born. Because of India's social, economic, cultural and spiritual hierarchies, Dalits suffer unthinkable discrimination, humiliation and lack of basic human rights, such as education, healthcare and freedom of conscience. Only 10 per cent of rural Dalit women can read and write. Dalits generally must work in the most 'unclean', dangerous, and inhumane occupations. They suffer overwhelming rates of violent discrimination and sexual abuse. Many are condemned to a life of debt bondage and bonded labour.

The word 'Dalit' literally means crushed, broken or oppressed by the social hierarchy above. Their history can be symbolised by a clay cup. In 70 per cent of India's rural villages, members of other castes will not eat or drink with a Dalit. When a Dalit person asks for a drink, he or she is given a clay cup – which is to be crushed on the ground after use. Why? So no other person risks being polluted by it.

Due to their low position in Indian society, Dalit people are used and spent without consequence. They are raped, held captive in brothels and temple ceremonies, and forced to work as bonded labourers, without education, without economic opportunities, without healthcare, without hope for their future. For 3,000 years, the Dalit people of India have been considered 'untouchable', less than human; worthy only to be slaves, to be broken and crushed.

Inequality matters in practice here. Dalit families lack the educational opportunities that enable them to create a better future. They are denied access to proper health care and services. Dalit families are without a means to gain marketable skills or income.

The Dalit Freedom Information Network is seeking to change all that, as a new generation of Dalits is standing up for the rights of their people to go to school, to be healthy, to be free, to never be called an untouchable again. Through a foundation programme of education, economic empowerment and healthcare, children gain necessary skills in a safe, encouraging learning environment away from the hands of traffickers. Dalit women learn valuable trade skills so they can stand independently long-term. Its founder, Bishop Joseph D'souza came from an upper-caste origin, living in what he now calls 'Christian ghettos' surrounded by low caste and Dalit people.[23] Speaking in October 2006 before a US Congressional hearing, D'souza said that:

> India's tragedy is that society continues the practice of the caste system, with rule of law not being applied when Dalits are being discriminated against, even though the practice of untouchability stands abolished by the Constitution.[24]

In India, caste lays down those whom society values most.

> The caste system constitutes a hierarchy of social-status ranks [...]. Social inequality is a keynote of the caste system. There is an interrelationship of superior-inferior attitudes all the way from the dark roots to the topmost blooms of the system.[25]

A strong argument can be mounted that the colonial encounter resulted in the British class system being mapped on to Indian society in a simplistic way with the result that caste became projected and then fixed.[26] As one descends the hierarchy, traits of superiority decrease and those of inferiority increase; the lower the caste, the fewer the number of castes from which it can expect deference.[27] Caste locks someone up in their own *jati*, a micro-caste, so they are cut off from other castes. Inferiority is as much a social fact as superiority and accepted with equanimity. 'It is a virtue to leave lower-caste people to their fate, for to question the justice of inferiority is to question the caste system itself.'[28]

In Sanskrit, the word 'Dalit' means oppressed. There are 200 million human beings who are deemed so impure that they are placed outside normal society. These customs have not ended. In a recent narrative, Sujatha Gidla recalls Dalits scrambling to their feet whenever a Hindu appears. They were regarded as defiled; good enough only to carry out labour in the fields and remove human waste. They cannot touch Hindus, come near a village well or enter a Temple. Every day, they must act out their lowly status and pay unstinting subservience.

Dalit Case Studies

Ritu Dharamender Siwan

Ritu comes from an impoverished Dalit family. She is a brilliant student and has stood first in her class right through from kindergarten to Grade Ten, even though, in the light of generations of marginalisation and poor opportunities for education and gaining some marketable skills, her parents and ancestors were relegated to one of the lowest economic rungs of the society.

Ritu's father is a low-paid manual labourer who does whatever odd jobs he can find in this town. Her mother is a homemaker. Ritu has a younger brother and a sister. Ritu had another brother immediately next to her but due to a severe ailment coupled with her parent's economic poverty, they could not take him for the best possible treatment. He succumbed to it after a few months.

Kala's Story

When Muniappa, a manual scavenger and his wife Savitri, a street sweeper, had their second girl child, they felt that their world had fallen apart. Having a girl child in India is like landing yourself in a financial crisis! As Dalits, all they were destined to do for generations together were menial jobs. Even though they suffered from a host of health problems and had witnessed many sewer cleaners dying of suffocation in the toxic environment of manholes, they had no choice but to continue doing this very job. Theirs was a desperate existence. Having a second girl child was like the final nail in the coffin – until the villagers noticed that the baby girl was good looking and suggested that she be dedicated as a Jogini.

The illiterate and superstitious parents consoled themselves that they were doing a service to their god and took pride in the fact that their little girl was to become a 'goddess'. Their daughter was barely five when they began preparations for her dedication. As part of the preparations, they often visited the house of an older Jogini (senior shrine prostitute) who lived in a shack near the temple. Kala had to spend a few nights alone with this Jogini once every few months to imbibe her spirit.

Young Kala dreaded those days and was particularly terror-stricken when the older Jogini went into a trance. But though she cried and pleaded with her mother not to take her to this Jogini's home, her mother hardened her heart and claimed that this practice was necessary for her to become a Jogini too. Eventually, Kala would be married to the local deity, obliged to wear red and white beads around her neck to advertise to the people around that she too was a Jogini. The deeply distraught older sister, who tried to intervene on behalf of Kala, would be proudly told by her mother, that her little sister was soon going to become a goddess. For their mother, this seemed to be the only sense of validation in an otherwise hopeless existence.

When Kala turned six, plans for her dedication service began. This came to the notice of one of our social workers who was located in the same village. Swinging swiftly into action, she mobilised support from other activists and approached the parents and relatives of Kala and explained the illegality of the Jogini system and the cruel consequences of such a dedication. The parents, who were under tremendous pressure by the local villagers to dedicate the child to become a Jogini, requested that their children be immediately taken away to a safe place.

The caste system generates psycho-social distance and even a sense of being polluted by lower orders of society. In Bihar province, upper caste people ask an aid agency to move Dalits away from the wells. If untouchables used the hand pump, it would contaminate the entire place. 'When will people understand we are also human beings?' complains one such Dalit. 'Let me be born again as an animal rather than a Dalit. We face more humiliation than they do.'[29] Yet as Nehru observed, 'If merit is the only criterion and opportunity is thrown open to everybody, then caste loses all its present-day distinguishing features and in fact, ends.'[30]

A final word. After industrialisation, inequalities *between* countries became more important. Despite global divides, as those gaps narrow due to dramatic economic change, greater differences in income between rich and poor may once again be within countries.[31]

4

Half the World: Identity Wars

'The Bank's response to a male who is abrasive, rude and confrontational is to accept these features as a positive and do nothing about them. In a female, they are seen as wholly negative.' – a female City executive who began an £11 million law suit after claiming that she became suicidal after being harassed and humiliated by her male boss[1]

'Woman is like a flower, with honey just for one man; man must be like the honeybee and gather all he can.' – *The King and I*, Rodgers and Hammerstein[2]

'Would men but generously snap our chains.' – *A Vindication of the Rights of Woman*, Mary Wollstonecraft[3]

The experience of being human has always been agitated by there being two types of human. Only two? What is basic; what is inherent?

Gradually, prejudices are tumbling. The fluidity of gender is now taken for granted in the same way that fixed, stable categories were until recently. Whatever private suspicions people may bear about inferiority of another's gender, class or ethnicity, it is increasingly taboo to say so in western societies.

As I write these words, the BBC has revealed a huge gap between the pay of its top male and female stars. Two-thirds of its presenters earning more than £150,000 were male, one-third female.[4] To its critics, this was a disturbing example of gender inequality. How could men and women be paid at different rates? Even the wealthy professional women were paid less than their male counterparts!

Some BBC executives and commentators threw oil on the fire by pointing out that the position of men and women in the workplace will never be the same since it is women who go off to have children. A renowned former female presenter remarked that there will never be equal pay for men and women 'until men have babies'. 'Women always end up doing most of the work with children, which rightly take up most of their attention'.[5] Or as a current female presenter commented, 'I don't want women to be undervalued or for bosses to assume that they can get away with treating us as discount items.'[6]

For others, that sense of moral outrage missed the point. It had nothing to say about gender discrimination in wider society. The story was about 96 rich people surely, not those on lower salaries. So what lens should such an issue be viewed through?

Following that report, a 3,000-word document by an unnamed Google engineer that circulated inside the company in August 2016 claimed that 'Google's left bias has created a politically correct monoculture' which prevented honest discussion of the issue. The engineer argued that women are naturally drawn to empathy rather than systematising and therefore resulted in fewer female programmers.[7] The comments caused predictable outrage though others argued that it is illiberal that all such opinions cannot be aired without the advocates being pilloried. Was there a kind of thought police in which it is betrayal for a woman to choose to have a role designated as stereotypical? Would building an open, inclusive environment mean fostering a culture in which those with alternative views, including different political views, feel safe sharing their opinions?

Equality and Diversity programmes have done considerable work to raise awareness of these matters. In the United Kingdom, the Equal Pay Act of 1970 stipulated that when it was a case of 'like for like' and men and women doing the same job, they had to be paid at the same rate. That of course came at a historical moment as feminism was burgeoning into consciousness, raising and exposing patriarchy.

There is much that is both persistent and puzzling about the gender pay gap, whether it is generational or due to occupational segregation. Who gets which jobs, and why, is more important than earnings ratios per se.

Women in their early 20s are now racing ahead, outperforming men. Yet the average British woman's salary is 29 per cent lower than the average man's. It is like women stop working for pay in September. But women make just one per cent less than men who work at the same company, at the same level and with the same responsibilities. Across Europe, the gap is similarly small. Is this about gender or class?

Every age has its own battles. Every age has to decide what feminism means. For white middle class women, much of the battle is won, the glass ceiling penetrated. The lived experience of many others reveals everyday sexism to be an occupational hazard. Structural issues such as lack of childcare are important. Yet unconscious bias and stereotypes are hugely controlling. We teach boys that engineers and scientists are valued more and pay them accordingly. We demonstrate that nurses and teachers are default female careers.

A trawl through websites about contemporary feminism is illuminating and confusing in equal measure. Some of it is 'victim feminism', treating women as in need of protection from words and ideas; hapless, hopeless creatures requiring safe spaces in order to flourish. Others celebrate female power and 'the return of the girl'. Still others deride what they see as largely cosmetic change, both metaphorically and literally.

A wrecking-ball to the whole tendency within contemporary feminism to accommodate itself to a system which is still so often a man's world, comes with a book such as Jessa Crispin's *Why I am not a feminist.*[8] Women should not simply be *allowed* to participate in the world as it is shaped by patriarchy but should shape their own experience rather than fit into prescribed shapes.

It is certainly the case that Western ideas about speech are shot through with myths and biases. The idea in popular culture that women talk more than men has been shown to be completely without foundation. It's just that men hear women being more talkative![9]

There has been an industry in recent years demolishing a previous industry, disproving the notion that the female brain is somehow different (stereotypically, men have had more spatial awareness but less emotional recognition and so on). Is there a blue brain or pink brain? Are behavioural differences something we are born with right and therefore inherent? Or is this learned behaviour with patterns forming almost from the beginning as tiny people play with a doll or a digger?

As a generalisation, the advance of feminism has usually been with reference to a raft of social factors that hold women back. Counter arguments have been with reference to inherent biological or 'essential' characteristics proving that women are 'not up to it'. When those arguments are shown to be deeply flawed, proving only that women are limited by cultural constraints as scientists, engineers or whatever, the counter-attack moves on to another target. Menstruation or rearing children were held up as reasons to hold women back because of hardwired difference. It was discovered that there was a gene for everything.[10] Before women were permitted to drive in Saudi Arabia, it was solemnly declared by clerics that the female brain was not up to the task!

Tradition has it that boys are good at counting and girls are good at reading. Mattel once produced a talking Barbie doll whose stock of phrases included 'math class is tough!' A 2008 study by the European Institute in Florence showed that cultural explanations account for much of the difference in Maths scores.[11] The gap in Maths scores between boys and girls virtually disappears in countries where there is a high level of sexual equality. Measures were used such as the World Economic Forum's gender-gap index which tracks economic and political opportunities, education and well-being for women or an index of social attitudes towards women. The result demonstrated that the gap in Maths scores was greatest in countries with the least equality (Turkey); virtually nothing in Scandinavia where sexes are on par. It seems the social position of women affects cognitive testing.

Where do stereotypes come from – nature or cultural forces such as exposure to adverts? After all, girls are given dolls, perhaps as a rehearsal for their social roles. Shaped by hormones in the womb, the levels of testosterone result in a boy's brain being more masculinised, or how far each part of the brain talks to the other parts. If there is a distinction between pink brain and blue brain, it manifests itself in the frequency of connections between hemispheres of the head. Neural pathways in the male brain follow a different pattern. The brain is far more plastic and flexible than supposed.

Decrying a radical distinction between pink and blue brain, Lise Eliot will have none of it. Eliot argues that infant brains are so malleable that small differences at birth become amplified over time as parents, teachers and the culture at large unwittingly reinforce gender stereotypes. Most differences kick in during the teenage years, which could be either social pressure or physiology. Gender identity reflects how much boys and girls are treated differently, affecting the choices they make and the way they learn sex differences. Drawing on years of exhaustive research and her own work in the field of neuro-plasticity, Eliot urges society to close the troubling gaps between boys and girls and help all children reach their fullest potential.[12] Or the argument of Cordelia Fine could be cited among many others in the growing literature about this. Sex discrimination is not a distant memory. Dispelling pseudo-scientific claims about the differences between the sexes, Fine shows how old myths, dressed up in the scientific finery, help perpetuate stereotypes.[13] Science is clothed as being 'the real science', in contrast to books exposing 'myths of science' or evolutionary biology.

An intriguing experiment on primary school children observed the way that boys and girls are treated differently. This includes how they are spoken to (language has power). At just aged seven, girls consistently under-estimated how clever they are – they had low academic self-confidence. Boys found it harder to express their emotions; 50 per cent of the boys described themselves as 'the best'. Girls used words to do with looks to describe themselves. There were biased views on what boys and girls were expected to do. Already, they had set ideas of what they wanted to do when grown up.[14] Attributing mathematical ability to gender differences cannot explain why that particular disparity is greatest in Turkey but insignificant in Scandinavia.

What are we to make of all this? The structure of the brain is the same for boys and girls. It is, however, plastic. An experience-hungry baby is born into a tidal wave of cultural differentiation. The influence of culture on identity is clearly profound. The biologist Robert Sapolsky describes how 'no brain is an island'. Culture and learning shape everything we do.[15] Due no doubt to being shaped by different levels of hormones, innate differences are there but they are small. It remains virtually impossible to separate the formative influences of physiology from the effects of cultural forces or parenting styles and how children are brought up slightly differently. And so the debate unfolds.

The pendulum has swung back. The current state of play counters the belief that men and women are inherently different. Fundamentally, male brains are the same. Pink and blue are cultural constructions. Angela Saini in her book, *Inferior*, shows that the greatest barrier is 'the one in our minds'.[16] This was of course what 'consciousness-raising' feminism proclaimed back in the 1970s.

In Simone de Beavoir's book of 1953, *The Second Sex*, the French philosopher observed that one is not born but becomes a woman. It is a long saga of inequality costumed as the accepted order of things. Experiences of being devalued have been powerful in the way female subjects are formed by comparison with the definition of masculinity through the ages. A major struggle in our world has been the fight for the value of humans – all of them, not just half the world. Seeing women as less than the legal and social equals of men has contributed to a way of viewing women only as sexual objects or mothers. Until recently, the standard for being human was male. With some exceptions, female human subjects were silent and invisible. Gender imperatives and those of ethnicity and many other forms of inequality structure the way that value is embedded and then reproduced. This is profoundly about power relationships. Issues of development, human rights, asylum seekers, literacy and employment were debated without recognising it was women and their children who were most affected. For the most part, women constitute the oldest segment of ageing populations.

The binary distinction has been policed with dishonour. Across the world, wealth and power assumed gender roles which created inequality and relationships of slave as a foil to the tyrant. As a sub-text to the whole Enlightenment project in the West, there has been the questioning of gender roles and rethinking notions of sexual identity.[17] In 1792, revolution was in the air; the social order up for grabs. Mary Wollstonecraft published *A Vindication of the Rights of Women*. It was a revolutionary text, appealing to men's self-interest to encourage more fulfilled wives and daughters:

> I entreat them to assist to emancipate their companion, to make her a help meet for them! Would men but generously snap our chains, and be content with rational fellowship instead of slavish obedience, they would find us more observant daughters, more affectionate sisters, more faithful wives, more reasonable mothers – in a word, better citizens.[18]

The idea that a woman was expected to be 'the toy of a man' was now under scrutiny. It was a fascinating reflection on the way that the master–slave relationship has always been linked. By oppressing one party, both are oppressed; liberating the one party, both emancipated. Could it really be the case that women could not only be sweet beings for men to feel better about themselves but equal partners? Henry James describes this well in his novel *Portrait of a Lady*. Isabelle objects to being graciously passive; waiting for a man to bestow a destiny upon her.[19]

There was a long road of political and social history to travel. Inequality haunted society, made all the more insidious by virtue of it being accepted as intrinsic to the social order. Mary Wollstonecraft attacked writers who argued that a woman does not need a rational education. It was the mind they said that was the most important and highly valued way of being in the world. Girls were trained to be emotional: boys to be rational. To the victors went the spoils; a collation of talent and virtues associated with masculinity. In an echo of Plato writing about ancient Athens, moral character required that reason direct the passions. Femininity was second class.

The notion of equality of the sexes is much less used today. A hundred years ago, one might have defined feminism as a movement towards the equality of the sexes – 'by now this is hardly apt [...]. A commitment to sexual equality does not by itself tell us what shape that equality should take.'[20] No longer were women the same as men but women's lives were seen to be different and it was this observation that needed explaining.[21] Men were regarded as complete people with potential and basic rights. A women's position was defined by the functions she served in relation to men. Traditional matriarchal roles involved self-sacrificing and long-suffering qualities in contrast to the household breadwinner. Men in conservative societies disputed that, arguing that equal value does not mean we are the same and that different spheres of work or home are 'natural'. Such attitudes disguised a de-personalisation that was both widespread and persistent.

Human devaluation is deeply embedded within the construction of gender differences. It remains, though its force has considerably diminished.

> I do think companies need to make women who are pregnant feel valued. We should be treated with respect, not made to feel guilty. Employers should listen and understand that just because they are pregnant or they've had a baby, their minds haven't gone out completely to pasture. That's how I was treated, like I couldn't do my job anymore.[22]

Challenges are Himalayan. The rise of the alt-right in Europe and elsewhere raises the profile of a political movement that is deeply misogynistic. What is valued most highly is the heterosexual strong man who is the saviour. This is contrasted with the homosexualised, feminised gentle man.[23]

In the West generally, women have been breaking down traditional attitudes. The Equal Pay Act of 1970 in the United Kingdom gave all women the right to the same pay as someone else doing the same job. The Sex Discrimination Act of 1975 made it unlawful for anyone to be discriminated against in the workplace because of gender. Equal opportunities were enforced by law. The struggle for equality brought about radical social change. Was it only a generation since women were treated as second class citizens in the workplace, liable to casual sexism and expected to fill the most menial of jobs?

The gender pay gap narrowed, though children usually spelt career death for professional women. Today it is a choice that attracts far less stigma. Yet women still struggle with being grossly under-represented in pay,[24] achieving the top positions and the implications of pregnancy. The Sex and Power survey of the Equal Opportunities Commission showed that the glass ceiling still prevented women from access to the top 33,000 jobs in the boardroom, politics and the courts.[25] In Germany, women (along with immigrants) are under-represented in the labour force. It is not because of education. Women comprise a majority of those who pass high school and university. Child care is scarce.[26]

Much has been achieved. New identities proliferate: new possibilities abound. The days seem distant when a professional women could feel she had to justify herself either if she stayed at home or went out to work. The growing commercialisation of sex raised the shout that women would be seen more and more as objects for male gratification. Humans are mind, body and spirit. And they are valuable. If the body is treated with disrespect, the whole person is up for grabs. This is the cry against the 'objectification' wherein some body shapes, conditions and sizes are more valued. 'A hierarchy of body worth is established and in this context of worth, bodies of old, disabled, black, lesbian women are valued less.'[27] Will there be full equality until the *Beauty Myth* is swept away? Naomi Wolf argues that images of beauty continue to be used against women. A compulsive search for beauty enslaves women, she argues. Not only does the myth of female beauty make women obsessive, it drives pornography, violence against women and girls as well as global hunger.[28]

Half the World

Yet battles to shatter the glass ceiling in the West were very much further along the development spectrum than problems faced by women in poorer nations, working long hours in the fields. As Hillary Clinton pointed out at the United Nations Women's Conference at Beijing in 1995:

> The great challenge of this conference is to give a voice to women everywhere whose words go unnoticed and whose voice goes unheard. Women comprise

> more than half the world's population, 70 per cent of the world's poor and two-thirds of those who are not taught to read and write. We are the primary care takers for most of the world's children and the elderly yet much of the work we do is not valued. It is no longer acceptable to discuss women's rights as separate from human rights.[29]

Strictly constraining gender stereotypes remain highly potent in western societies. Yet that is on a spectrum of difference from the developing world where women are often chattels. 'Half the world' is not just a way of capturing the extent to which half of global wealth is held by just eight men who could travel in a golf buggy on a course for the super-rich. It also designates the half of humanity that hold up the sky.

Outrage is always a good thing. It tells you that people and situations are worth fighting for. In their angry polemic, *Half the Sky*, Nick Kristoff and Sheryl WuDunn set out to expose the abrasive injustice perpetuated on women in developing countries. They argue that the situation is so dire that it requires a massive moral outrage on the scale of the protest against slavery or the holocaust. There are ten times as many women trafficked across international borders as at the peak of the slave trade in the 1780s. Buying up a child prostitute in Cambodia, they came face to face with the gruesome reality of those who would auction her virginity. Even the police were on hand to ensure that, if she escaped, she would be returned to her owners![30]

From honour killings and genital mutilation to rape as a weapon of war and sexual slavery, the thread in the experience of many women in those situations is the attitude of many developing nations towards women. Women are not allowed to be active members of society. They are disregarded as human beings.

One of the Millennium Development Goals adopted by the United Nations is to promote gender equality and empower women.[31] The strategy is to eliminate gender disparity in primary and secondary education by 2015. Across the world, from childhood, women are taught that they are inferior to men, often to blame for violence inflicted upon them. As wives or partners, they must hold the family together, at any cost. Devaluation of women has been endemic in social regimes that draw boundaries that exclude half the world as less prized and defined by lack.

Prejudice against girls starts early. The life-cycle of violence starts with sex-selective abortion and infanticide in countries where girls are valued less than boys or considered an economic burden. Boys are regarded as a blessing;

future breadwinners who will look after parents in old age. But many parents still see girls as a financial burden. In India, 10 million female foetuses may have been aborted in the last 20 years.[32] In China, 30 million girls are missing because government birth control policy used to restrict families to one child. This is 'gendercide' in full throttle.

From infancy, girls may receive less food, less medical care and less education than their brothers. From being girls to adults, women continue to be at risk. The World Health Organization (WHO) estimated that one woman out of every five will be a victim of rape or attempted rape in her lifetime. Each year, thousands of women and girls are trafficked into forced prostitution. Many studies in different countries say that between 20 and 50 per cent of women have experienced domestic violence.

Female genital mutilation (FGM) is practiced widely as a social custom in sub-Saharan to try to ensure pure female subjects. Each year, more than 2 million girls in 30 countries are subject to female mutilation. It is sexism not Islam that has shaped their experience; FGM is not representative of Islamic societies.

In India, the dowry system can lead to tragic results. More than 6,000 brides are murdered year after year by their husbands; angry that they received no money along with their brides.

In Pakistan, the Human Rights Commission reported 670 rapes in the first ten months of 2004. Most rapists and killers go free because of poor policing and the victim's fear of speaking out. Gang rape and honour killings of women remain common in a country where feudal and tribal systems still too often hold sway. Mukhtaran Mai was the victim of a particularly appalling rape in 2002 and refused to accept what had happened to her. She was determined to speak out and became a champion of oppressed women; an inspiration to human rights activists everywhere.[33]

The differences are everywhere. In Iran, the penal code dictates that the penalty of stoning requires that men be buried up to their waste whereas women are buried up to their necks. In theory, escape can be made, but self-evidently it is not possible to wriggle free if only the heads of women show.[34]

Devaluation generates violence. In countries like the Democratic Republic of Congo, where rape has been a weapon of war, sexual violence has not been seen as a serious offence. The ancient preference for sons in traditional societies has brought what has been described as 'gendercide' through abortion and infanticide. The preference for sons and devaluation of girls in countries like India and China generated a brutal question. Where are the 120 million missing girls?[35] Due to that ancient preference for sons and the regular abortion of female foetuses, a culture of downgrading women in India is implicated in a dowry system that results in wives being battered or economic disempowerment. A nation of half a billion women earn less than a third of the male average.[36]

On the face of it, the position of women in societies that encourage polygamy may seem to give security to those who would be left to fend for themselves. The reality is that polygamy devalues women. Someone's dreams are crushed when a new wife joins the household. The only person who revels in it is the husband who gets to enjoy variety. A woman will become nothing more than a dish at the buffet.[37]

In Islamic cultures, the social position of women is fraught. Some women can find the Chador liberating because it is their cultural symbol, their national dress and prefer it to wearing western clothes.[38] The issue is not the Chador and certainly not Islam. The reality is more complex than that. It is important not to deny women their own narrative and not to hear voices like Umm Mustafa, a women living in Cairo's City of the Dead:

> During my twenty eight years that I was married, I rarely left my husband's house. He provided me everything I needed. I was completely safe and secure inside the house. I never had to face the hubbub of the streets. I'm proud I lived this way.[39]

However as Fatima Mernissi, a Moroccan sociologist acknowledges, 'there is a fundamental contradiction between Islam as officially interpreted and equality between the sexes.'[40] In a culture where men dominate women, equality between men and women is latent, not patent. 'Deprived of economic and hereditary rights, everywhere behind men in education, women are formed into an inferior class.'[41] Religious text seems to reinforce this. 'Men are the Protectors and Maintainers of women.'[42] Men and women occupy a different universe – the public outdoor world of work and decision making and the inner world of the home where husbands are guests of their wives. 'From the Islamic point of view, the question of the equality of men and women is meaningless. It is like discussing the equality of a rose and jasmine. Each has its own perfume, colour, shape and beauty.'[43]

Yet Islamic society prizes men. 'Wealth and sons are allurements of the life of this world'.[44] Divorce hangs over the life of a Muslim woman who can only produce baby girls. Often, a girl feels that:

> from the moment she is born and even before she learns to pronounce words, the way people look at her, the expression in their eyes, their glances somehow indicate she was born 'incomplete' or 'with something missing'.[45]

The issue of women and the Burkha can seem to deny agency to women in saying they cannot make this stance themselves. Yet we should not accept that claim uncritically or lose sight of the fact that it is usually men who are making this decision for them. It is men who are gatekeepers of women's access to the outdoor world. It is men who are guardians of the chastity of their wives (and their own lineage) by enforcing the wearing of the veil. Women are not free to choose. Rules are imposed and enforced by men. Male-dominated culture turns woman into objects, not subjects of the laws of society. Their testimony in law is often half that of a man.

According to a study released by the Egyptian Centre for Women's Rights (ECWR) in 2008, 62 per cent of Egyptian men admit to sexually harassing women, and 83 per cent of Egyptian women reported being harassed. Half say it happens every day. It was the first study of its kind.[46] It exposed the explanation that seclusion of women and male reactions is purely cultural rather than reflecting a male dominated society. If women in such a society report an incident, they face loss of respect and honour. This is a strange state of affairs. Women endure loss of respect in the court action yet will face loss of respect if they report. It is a double whammy.

The reality is far more nuanced than this summary attempts. The treatment of women is indeed 'Islam's biggest weakness'.[47] Yet being denied their rights in the name of Islam invites comparison with, for example, those of the United States where one in six women are victims of sexual assault annually – according to the US Rape, Abuse and Incest National Network.

Violation of women and girls is a key part of the global problem of violence. Men have claimed divine warrant for their violence. Violence against women is everywhere, in the womb with selected abortion, in acts inflicted on women's bodies, in enforced marriage such that traps girls as young as eight, in honour killings with women who break all the rules, in sexual assault on the streets and in armed conflict; in the hundred women killed every year by men in domestic violence. Rape is power, inflicted ruthlessly where it will hurt the most. Challenges to the ideology of masculinity disallow revolutionary change. Where socially conscious people become more aware of how power play takes centre stage, the ways power impedes love being freely given is much more of an issue.

There is still a large gap between women in the West whose concerns are with proper child care and equal opportunity in the workplace and women in developing countries who struggle for basic education, better health and protection from violence and exploitation.

Yet whatever the context, it is the value system that is at fault surely. People given lower significance are especially prone to violence.

The Configuration of Genitals (and Other Wars)

We close with another face of inequality, that due to sexual identity. It is worth emphasising that freedom for people to love whom they will is widely regarded as another triumph for equality. Sexual identity and gender identity are now down to the freedom and consent of the individual. As I write these words, the 50th anniversary of the Act in the United Kingdom to de-criminalise homosexuality is being marked. The distress of people being treated differently is integrally bound up with their being regarded as different in some way. Looking back, it is clear that the Act did not end discrimination. Harassment continued at all levels, including that from the police. Controversy remained on such issues as how far homosexuality should not be referred to in the school curriculum (Section 28) and differential age of consent for sexual expression (16 between heterosexual, 21 and then 18 between homosexual couples). Same sex marriages have been lauded as a crucial test of modern liberal democracy.

The feminist unravelling of gender began to take place in the 1960s. Under assault were what seemed to be human givens, that men are essentially strong, dominant providers, that women are essentially fragile, submissive nurturers and that heterosexuality is the only possible route in expressing human relationships. Then came the 'queer theory' of the 1990s; a complete anatomical dissection of gender, homosexuality, bisexuality, trans-sexuality and all stations in between.

Homophobia is still rife in Western societies. Derogatory statements or negative images of homosexuality in the media highlight and sustain prejudice. In sport, business or the military, portrayals of gay or lesbian people reinforce homophobia. In Africa, attitudes towards same sex relationships are replete with overwhelmingly negative comment and legal sanction. Homophobia devalues people; it writes them off. Lying behind centuries old opposition to homosexuality have been social attitudes that relegated gay, lesbian and transgender subjects into objects, objects that were less than normal.[48] Movements to change things such as lesbian feminism, gay liberation, bisexuals and trans-sexual activism (LGBT) were initially about social equality and acceptability. Faced with years of ostracism, these communities often saw themselves as a fixed class; a minority group struggling for recognition.

> For lesbian and gay movements, cultural goals include (but are not limited to) challenging dominant constructions of masculinity, femininity, homophobia and primacy of the gendered heterosexual family. Political goals include changing laws and policies to gain new rights, benefits and protections from harm.[49]

By contrast, queer movements have struck a note of defiance.[50] Categories of gay and lesbian are repudiated as being restrictive; they 'reinforce rather than challenge a cultural system that will always mark the non-heterosexual as inferior'.[51] Equal value and worth are the drivers as ever.

There is a wider cultural trend towards the abolition of gender. Whether human identity can be neatly parcelled out into two distinct sets of being is increasingly questioned; of which more later.

5

War on the Skin

It is a curiosity of history that white people in the time of Queen Elizabeth I used to prize their skin colour so much they would rub whiteness into it. Now a sun tan is a mark of health and vitality. It is, though, a tragic curiosity that so much misery has been played out on the surface of human beings. A casual observer looks at this central phenomenon of history with complete astonishment.

If the configuration of genitals has evoked so much historical agitation, how come that, in addition it has been the colour of skin, and not just the colour of money that has so sharply divided the human consciousness? Who was responsible for this? If the answer is, 'we did it', then who are the 'we' who subjected our fellow men and women to such unimaginable cruelty and abuse? Why would we do it? After all, with class inequality, Marx was clear enough. Almost insurmountable social differences arose from the exercise of wealth and power by those who controlled who went to war and how things were made. Gender differences became so controlling because the norm was male. The dominant position in society was held by the testosterone-fuelled conquerors who took a lot of convincing that they should relinquish some of their power. Oppressive regimes were perhaps more obvious.

But who determined that skin should witness such mortal combat? Who set the pattern that the darker the skin the greater the inferior status sustained by excoriating domination? Racism has been so deadly because it combines the sharp divides of history into lethal challenge. As Niall Ferguson points out, the twentieth century was darkened from the outset with poisonous ideas of race.[1]

This is all the more surprising since 'race' is a largely artificial construct, as is 'religion' with which it is closely intertwined. Does either actually exist as the basis for pernicious cultural inequalities? Education has to be the great answer to inequality everywhere so it is a question worth pondering.

The race and religion dynamic has become freshly important in the post-colonial era as previous inequalities and legacies were exposed, discussed and often dismantled. Modern Western 'race-making' is on a par with similar attempts to frame the meaning of religion. Attempts to distinguish racial identities or religious people from the attributes of others are largely artificial, extrapolated from a process of differentiation that is both western and modern. Defining religion by either piety or practice misidentified root from fruit. Religions cannot be conceived apart from direct traditions in which they are embedded.

Race is a social construct.[2] It is not real in any genetic sense, neither is there a classification that all blacks or all whites have in common. In Brazil, someone who would be categorised as black in the United States would be considered white. In a society where being white (regardless of one's socio-economic class background or other disadvantages) means living a life with white skin privileges – such as being presumed safe, competent and noncriminal – whites who begin to experience discrimination because of having a partner who is of a different skin may begin to no longer feel white. Lived experience and previous self-perception of racial identity become separated.[3] What is fundamental in the battlefield of equality are the social, political and economic meanings of race. Racial meanings attach to how human beings classify others shape things profoundly.[4]

It is all entirely short-sighted. Corporate America is clearly missing out on one of the biggest opportunities of our time for driving innovation and growth: creating business value by advancing racial equity. The potential gains are considerable. US GDP could be 14 per cent or $2 trillion higher, if the wage disparity between white employees and employees of colour was eliminated.[5]

Although completely artificial, the concept of 'race' has huge practical implications. America experiences wide disparities of wealth but also health. Inequality in health care outcomes means that the death rate for black men from cancers is 24 per cent higher than it is for white males. For breast cancer, death rates among black people are 42 per cent higher.[6] The UK government's audit of racial inequality showed more uncomfortable truths about Britain today:

- Black men are almost three times more likely to be arrested than white men.
- Black children are excluded from school three times more than white children.
- Black, Asian and mixed race women are most likely to experience common mental health disorders.
- British white households are more than twice as likely to own their home as some other ethnic groups.
- By age five, Gypsy/Roma children are three times less likely to be doing well in school.
- Poverty's impact on school performance varies starkly, according to ethnicity.
- The unemployment rate is double among ethnic minorities as among white people.
- White people have consistently received shorter prison sentences.

There is a correlation between ethnicity and poverty. A number of prominent BAME (black and minority ethnic) activists – including former deputy London mayor Munira Mirza – hit back at the government's 'crude and tendentious' approach to the issue, saying the policies could 'harm the very communities they aspire to help'. 'All too often statistics are misused in a way that casts minorities as victims of racism and "white privilege",' they wrote.[7]

The last acceptable form of racism is that of Romaphobia – the prejudice and discrimination directed at the various communities who make up Europe's Roma minority. Anti-Roma attitudes pervade European society; stereotypes that cast the Roma as 'thieves, beggars, criminals and parasites'.[8] In the United Kingdom, for instance, Roma travellers are considered old if they are over 50. Life expectancy is ten years less. Nomadic people are forced to settle, harried from from pillar to post. Rates of anxiety and depression are much higher, along with rates of youth offending. The Roma find themselves more segregated and unequal than ever before; such are the consequences of this discrimination at the root of our democracies.

'We don't want much, only to be treated as equals,' protested two Gypsy immigrants from Romania, who had come to live in Italy six years before.

'We had to come; we couldn't afford to feed the children back home.'[9] Devaluation has been virulent in attitudes towards migrant workers. In twentieth-century Britain, the whites felt they were superior to the blacks and the Irish. As later waves of immigration challenging competition for jobs and housing, older migrants were suspicious of Polish workers, asylum seekers or refugees.

> So I have a new name – refugee.
> Strange that a name should take away from me
> My past, my personality and hope.
> Strange refuge this.
> So many seem to share this name – refugee.
> Yet we share so many differences.[10]
>
> Rubimbo Bungwe, a 14-year-old Zimbabwean refugee

One Night in Miami

Before race was a concept, it was an experience of the black man as a different sort of human from the white man.[11] By definition, racism is the belief that some people from another race are intrinsically inferior because of their ethnic or country of origin. Race is of limited usefulness as a means of classifying human beings. Skin colour is only skin deep.[12] It was not always thus. Attitudes evidenced by the Deep South in reconstruction years after the Civil War 'rested frankly upon the premise of the Negro's inferiority'. Supposedly free black people were reduced to serfdom.

> The intention openly averred was to give an inferior people an inferior life, to this end the new system excluded colored man from politics by disenfranchising him, rendered him impotent economically and isolated him by extensive practices of segregation.[13]

Simmering whitelash surfaced as I wrote these words; 12 August 2017 saw a 'pro-white' rally to protest a decision in Charlottesville, Virginia to remove the General Lee statue. About 6,000 people were expected to attend, before it was declared an unlawful assembly. It came after a night where torch-wielding white supremacists marched through Charlottesville, Virginia, shouting 'unite the right' and 'you will not replace us' while calling for a split from the United States, again advocating for what the Confederates tried and failed to do: secede from the Union. Hundreds had descended on the city either to march in or rail against a 'Unite the Right Rally', a major gathering of white supremacists, nationalists and other supporters of the so-called 'alt-right'. The League of the South's long-time president, retired university professor Michael Hill of Killen, Alabama, posted a message in July that began, 'Fight or die white man' and went on to say southern nationalists seek 'nothing less than the complete re-conquest and restoration of our patrimony – the whole, entire South'. Prof. Hill's message, posted on the group's Facebook page a day after one rally, said:

> And that means the South will once again be in name and in actuality White Man's Land. A place where we and our progeny can enjoy Christian liberty and the fruits of our own labour, unhindered by parasitical 'out groups'.[14]

The result, however, was three deaths, including a woman killed after a car was deliberately driven into a group of anti-racists; the car was allegedly driven by James Alex Fields Jr Fields grew up mostly in Northern Kentucky, and had been raised by a single mother who was a paraplegic. Especially disturbing was the failure of the President, Donald Trump, to condemn the white supremacy movement amid the shocking public display of both the Ku Klux Klan, who had helped put him in the White House and beyond question, part of the base he had energised.

In disturbing synchronicity a film was released that depicted, in the cinematographic brutality of realism, race riots 50 years before in the city of Detroit. In 1967, amid the chaos of the Detroit Rebellion, with the city under curfew and as the Michigan National Guard patrolled the streets, three young African American men were murdered at a motel. The film, using this as front stage of its portrayal, shone a light on America's racial past. Speaking about the marginalisation that was still alive and well, the main character John Boyega observed, 'black experience is so unique. Trying to explain it to someone else is like teaching someone Chinese'.[15]

Anti-semitism was mixed into the lethal cocktail. How the Nazi Swastika could be brandished in America in 2017 was appalling to practically all commentators. What did it mean to conflate both white supremacy with anti-semitism? Southern nationalism seems to have been swept up into the larger white-power agenda in recent years, in part reaction, no doubt, to a perception of having lost out. According to the US Census, 55 per cent of the nation's black population lived in the South in 2010, and 105 southern counties had a black population of 50 per cent or higher.[16]

A meeting of four men in Miami provides the crucible for the alignments of blackness in America. A recent play by Kemp Powers is set at the Hampton House motel on 25 February 1964. This is the night that Cassius Clay beat Sonny Liston to become the new world heavyweight champion. He is about to declare publicly his commitment as a Muslim and to announce he is to be known as Muhammad Ali. With him are three other men on the brink of change. Jim Brown is in the process of turning himself from star footballer into a movie star. Sam Cooke, 'Mr Soul', is debating whether to move from smoochy to politically engaged, gospel-driven numbers. And, triggering dispute among them, is Malcolm X: utterly committed, but about to leave the Nation of Islam, trying to rouse them into explicit political commitment, though his own dilemma is entirely unexamined.[17]

Outside, the Civil Rights movement stirs and crashes, and the melody of 'A Change is Gonna Come' hangs in the air. But each of those black American men know that they will emerge into a white world, that they are united in inferior status, despite the radical challenge each will make to it.

The sound of fury, the lash of the whip and the thunder of the guns have lashed the face of America; the same America dedicated to the proposition that all men are created equal and that they are endowed by their Creator with certain unalienable rights. Social landscapes of exclusion stand out in the reproduction of all the social forces that shape and constrain people's lives and assign them a lower value. We may think we have heard all we need to about race, which has been much studied arising from white and black consciousness in conditions of slavery onwards. Yet its legacy still dominates. Slavery has been central to America's economic development.[18] The land of the free was a slave society, built upon extinction of one 'race' and the subjugation of another. In *Between The World And Me*, Ta-Nehisi Coates writes movingly about the plunder of black lives and how 'our very bodies' are transfigured into sugar, tobacco, cotton and gold.[19] It was an economic system built upon profound inequality. Indeed, a case can be made that slavery and global capitalism were at that time, connected but different systems for the commodification of labour. What sought to be a more nuanced account of the history of the American form of slavery capitalism was noted for bringing a Marxist perspective to the study of power, class and relations between planters and slaves in the South while seeking to demonstrate that the economic system was built on a paternalism in which the self-respect slaves could engender might compel slaveholders to recognise their humanity.[20] Its author,

Eugene Genovese, was accused of playing down the truth that slavery, by definition, demonstrates the cruellest kind of racism.

> Beyond doubt, the devaluing experience of race and ethnicity profoundly moulds subjective experience as it constitutes a basis for discrimination. In *The Prison School*, Simmons analyses how mass incarceration and privatisation of both public security and prisons are related to educational inequality. One in three black males born today will spend time in prison in his lifetime.[21]

Nevertheless, 'race' can be a card that is overplayed. As I write these words, a scandal was exposed that involved perpetrators abusing white girls in Newcastle UK. The fact that in Newcastle as elsewhere before it, the perpetrators were from ethnic minorities and largely Pakistani, was hugely difficult for many in statutory bodies to cope with. Always there lurked the spectre of the most troubling accusation of all – of being racist. That prevented the situation being faced up to. It is time, said a former Director of Public Prosecutions, 'to identify the abuse by south Asian gangs as a profoundly racist crime and misogynist crime'.[22] Official comment was desperate to avoid any slur on the Pakistani community in case that would be seen as racist. The surprising opponent of multi-culturalism, Britain's former chairman of the Equality and Human Rights Commission Trevor Philips, called for the authorities to admit that most men in sex grooming gangs are Muslim. Elites have, he said, replaced their old fear of being labelled racist with a new bogey – the 'charge of Islamophobia'.[23]

Social devaluation is nuanced and complex. Some data about IQ scores seem to indicate that black students do less well than other ethnicities.[24] This is explosive, contested territory, implying as it does some racial hierarchy in mental capacities. Leaving aside the question of how far such scores capture the realities of intelligence and encapsulate cultural bias, it is clearly not possible to separate debate about race and IQ from cultural pressures which act on families. There is an ethos about the kind of people highly prized in social environments where to be intelligent is to be white, and act white.

In the inter-subjective field of social encounter, 'white' can seem to be colourless, neutral. Yet it is a building site of enormous labour in constructing power-laden assumptions, usually about superiority. To be white is a powerful position to come from. It is of course a meaningless category. White is as much a colour as non-white. No one is white anyway. The taken for granted ways that being white constitutes an invisible knapsack of resources need unpacking. 'I was taught to see racism only in individual acts of meanness, not in invisible systems conferring dominance on my group', observes Peggy McIntosh, describing assumptions in everyday life enjoyed by white folk.[25]

The social upheaval in Russia in 1917 was not just about the oppression of the peasants and emerging working classes by the system. A major cause of the Revolution was that the Tsarist regime failed to come to terms with nationalism. There was an ethnic hierarchy, parallel to the social one, in which non-Russians existed in layers down to the five million Jews at the bottom of the pile. These were subject to 1,400 different statutes and regulations which all added up to 'a Tsarist's version of the Hindu caste system with the Jews in the role of the untouchables'.[26]

Colonial Subjects

The evolution of population control policies is laden with attitudes towards colonial subjects and the poor that descends into inhumanity. The problem with the natives was that they are born too much and they don't die enough, complained a public health official in French Indochina in 1936. The previous year, India's Council of State was told that control of population was necessary for the masses – 'it is not what they want but what is good for them'.[27]

Traditional inequalities have been generated along the main axes of gender, race or ethnicity and class, though new forms of difference then arose along other axes, such as disability, age and between societies. These are complex, linked realities. 'Gender, race and class cross-cut each other in various complex ways, at times reinforcing, at times weakening impact of existing inequalities.'[28] That at least was the narrative. It assumed there was a Big Three to which newer forms of identity politics based on age, disability and the demand for social acceptance of homosexuality were subordinate. Then came post-colonial studies. It arose as reflection on imperialism's aftermath. Colonisation is another face of the devaluation that, I am suggesting, is a generic principle behind forms of domination. Marx argued that the imperialist expansion of his day represented the incorporation of various regions of the world into the capitalist system.[29] Debates continue about the nature of this process which took in huge swathes of Asia, Africa and Latin America.

It has been argued that the ideology accompanying modern colonialism was Social Darwinism, the survival of the fittest understood not in terms of species but races and nations.[30] Dominate or be dominated!

The post-colonial world was marked by unequal structures of trade and power. 'The notion of dependence emerges today as a key element in the interpretation of the Latin American reality,' wrote Gutierrez, the doyen of Liberation Theologians, a generation ago.[31] The system of *external* domination was being experienced, he contended, as *internal*. Defending the status quo was seen as in the interests of global capitalism and the dynamic elements tied into world markets, leaving the backward elements to fend for themselves. Imbalances between developed and developing countries were, on this reading, caused by relationships of dependence.

In post-colonial representation, even in the way non-white people are constructed, natives have often been defined in terms of a lack of something.[32] Colonial subjects were seen as backward; inferior versions of a Western master-subject – a consciousness and often a self-representation from which they needed to liberate themselves. As the main character, Paul Rusesabagina, says in the film 'Hotel Rwanda' about the lack of any real help for victims of genocide, 'they are saying, "we, the Western powers think you are dung, dirt, worthless"'.[33] The portrayal of the powerless UN colonel shows disgust at the cowardice and, the film suggests, the racism displayed by Western leaders.

That may or may not be justified. Human devaluation was endemic to the reproduction of difference. The reaction to it has so often involved resistance to a notion. Subjects need not go second class! Beset by Anglo-Saxon exceptionalism, there can be little doubt that an African life was not worth as much as that of a European or North American.

6

Intact Bodies, Wounded History

The hand you are dealt with is what people have to handle life. How they play it is crucial in shaping their destiny. To compete on equal terms is, however, impossible. Often people lack communication skills and the means to exercise voice. Others lack the mysterious quality of resilience, of capability. We will return to this via another major lens on inequality: what is usually termed 'disability'.

Human beings are constrained for a variety of reasons – some physical, some emotional. Being one of the lucky few is not just a question of the right social group, class and colour. The odds can be stacked against people for constraints that affect their mental health. In rich countries, a smaller gap between rich and poor means a happier and more successful population. If we halved inequality, mental illness would reduce by a third, suggests the Equality Trust.[1] Natural (or cultivated) advantages become part of a successful life in an economy defined by production and consumption. Increasing success and wealth is inadequate unless it is matched by public validation. Having the right looks, appearance and personality usually associated with youthfulness gives some people a head start. For others, having the right religion or sexual orientation are vital markers in life while for many, being able-bodied will make all the difference as to how far you can progress.

If the notion of equality is complex, so too is that of ability and disability. In the context of equality, we might well contest the definition of 'ability' and what it means to say that we equal ability to grasp opportunities at any given time. What though are we to make of 'disability' in this discussion?

When it is considered in terms of privileges and power, the condition of being equal or unequal is usually cast in the clothing of the gender or class and occupation gap. Significant inequalities exist though in the form of skin colour, 'race', sexual orientation, age and disability. In the United Kingdom, a single Equality Act was passed in 2010 to consolidate eight separate acts and sets of regulations that had been developing since the 1970s. You are disabled if you have a physical or mental impairment that has a 'substantial' and 'long-term' negative effect on ability to do normal daily activities.

At heart is the question of social value. Devaluation has framed what it means to be a human subject for every group of people not standing in the centre of real power and influence. Those that experience disadvantages due to class have their subjectivity formed by society ascribing lesser value to them. The way subjects are formed by devaluation has been central to the construction of gender, to race and ethnicity, age and also to experiences of disability. It is the notion of intactness and its relationship to inequality that we will look at now.

Disability is now a major social category. Definitions are crucial. Who is disabled? The girl or boy in the wheelchair, the child who is blind or the one who has never had a book read to them? Being disabled or no is completely dependent on context. It is not a label certain people have to wear in all situations. A wheelchair user is not disabled in a meeting but a blind man or woman would be disabled climbing a mountain. The deaf, however, would not.

To say that disability is about 'limitations' does not resolve the issue. The person who gets to define who is disadvantaged or limited has a considerable position in a relationship of power. Having a disability is a limitation for that moment in that situation in which someone is not able to compete on level terms with others. Overcoming disability involves removal of limiting constraints.

Disabled people developed the social model of to explain their personal experience of disability and help to develop more inclusive ways of living. The social model of disability says that disability is caused by the way society is organised. The medical model of disability says people are disabled by their impairments or differences. The medical model looks at what is 'wrong' with the person, not what the person needs. It creates low expectations and leads to people losing independence, choice and control in their own lives.[2] It is now no longer acceptable to talk about 'disabled people' as if they were incomplete people.[3]

The search for a social explanation of the exclusion that disabled people were facing began in 1966 through the work of Paul Hunt. For a significant amount of time, Hunt lived in a residential home in Hampshire. He with other residents, through the 1960s were unhappy with the way in which the management of the home were treating residents, and requested the assistance of the Tavistock Institute to help resolve the problems. In the eyes of the residents, the conclusions reached by the Tavistock Institute agreed with the way in which the management of the home operated, which not only fuelled further mistrust between the residents and the management of the home, but also mistrust between disabled people and academics. In a chance meeting with Vic Finkelstein, an academic but also an anti-apartheid inmate of the South African regime, they developed an understanding that disability was not a physical condition but a social condition.[4]

Because of this understanding in 1975 they formed the Union of the Physically Impaired Against Segregation (UPIAS).[5] In 1996, Michael Oliver began a discussion that intended to find a theory that would explain the social nature of disability.[6] The debate that ensued was dominated by a discussion over whether it was society that disabled people and whether an individual's physical impairment should be ignored.[7] Subsequent research has tended to focus on the experiences of disabled people or the elderly, much to the annoyance of disabled people who have argued that they would prefer their problems being resolved rather than discussed.[8] The important aspect of Finkelstein's contribution was the recognition that any given problem faced by disabled people can be viewed from different perspectives dependent upon the relationship and experiences of those viewing the problem. This could apply to any group in society, not just vulnerable people. The solidarity exhibited between disability awareness and anti-apartheid campaigner is instructive. Inequality has an inner thread of human devaluation. To this we return.

Oliver went on to describe four models of disability: the social model, the moral model, the tragedy model and the medical model.[9] The medical model and the tragedy model in particular become not so fruitful ways to adopt a frame of authority. 'We tend to label what or who we do not understand, and by these labels achieve personal comfort denied the bearer of the label.'[10] Language often keeps changing, especially in the field of disability. In 1990, Action Research for Crippled Children became Action Research. The Spastics Society became Scope. The term 'disabled' is now firmly on the political agenda. Yet devaluing attitudes persist. Mothers with a high probability of passing on a genetic cause of disability are often advised to consider being childless. Older mothers can test for Down Syndrome during pregnancy and offered a termination.

Since December 1996 in the United Kingdom, it has been unlawful to treat disabled people less favourably than other people for a reason relating to their disability. As disability moved from being an after-thought to centre stage, corrective legislation defined it in the 1996 Act as 'physical or mental impairment which has a substantial and long-term adverse effect on his or her ability to carry out normal day-to-day activities'. Greater recognition constructs arrangements on basis of non-disabled norms.[11] This has made a big difference. Yet still significant prejudice remains. At a core level, it is about value.

'Whenever someone treats us as if we smell bad, we suffer a profound decrease in self-esteem.'[12] Such devaluation shapes how people are treated. The term 'disabled person' itself is incapacitating; perhaps 'intact' or not maybe a better descriptor, opening out a spectrum of wholeness we share.

Similarly, mental illness is often misunderstood and gives rise to differing scales of how people fit in. Those affected are devalued; routinely shrouded in prejudice and fear. Dementia, the mental plague of our time, can be a de-personalising condition in which its sufferers, usually the elderly, are lost before their time. Dignity can creep away along with rationality. Observers can write them off.

Some approaches endeavour to correct the de-personalisation and restore dignity. Specialised Early Care for Alzheimer's (Specal) has three commandments for treating sufferers as people – don't ask the person with dementia questions, don't contradict them and learn to love repetitiveness. In short, people with dementia may be going back to old experiences in order to make sense of the world.[13]

Organised self-advocacy has been an important manifestation of the emergence of autonomy and self-determination for those with disabilities. One such advocacy group in the United States has been 'People First'. In 1995, advocacy groups established a national advocacy organisation called 'Self Advocates Becoming Empowered.'[14] The United Nations declared that the aim of its World Programme of Action Concerning Disabled Persons was to:

> promote effective measures for prevention of disability, rehabilitation, and the realisation of the goals of 'full participation' of disabled persons, in social life and development and of 'equality' [...] an equal share in improvement of living conditions resulting from social and economic conditions.[15]

'Valuing People' was the title of a UK government White Paper in 2001 about delivery of services and support for adults with learning disabilities.[16] A follow-up UK Parliamentary Report said vulnerable adults were still likely to be exploited and suffer lack of respect.[17] Negative stereotypes were the culprit. The key message was that people with learning disabilities are, above all else, people and citizens with skills, ambitions, aspirations, replete with potential. The learning goes two ways. By entering into a relationship with someone with a learning disability, a transformative effect becomes possible. They become as they really are – not as we fear them to be.

On closer inspection, the definition dissolves. We are all disabled in some way.

Affective Inequality and Wounded History

With Marx and Weber, it is the trilogy of social class, status and power that have become defining terms of inequality. We are arguing here for issues of value, especially the worth of the human, as being a dynamic that operates in social space. This affects the emotional and mental well-being of participants. For lack of a sense of value, dimensions of inequality are opened up that are not normally the focus of attention. The sociology of emotions and mental health challenges the hegemony of the rational actor who is competent to take full advantage of opportunities if offered. In place of oppressive regimes externally, emotions are internal; often arising from wounded history.

Equality has various dimensions – equality of resources, of working and learning opportunities or of power relations. Among the strength of reaction against the forms inequality takes, the demand for respect and recognition is significant.[18] Yet when people are not just beset but actually crippled by a devalued self, they may find it an uphill struggle against those who have greater internal resources. Indeed, it is the accumulation of internal resources that marks out someone who has 'voice,' the ability to respond to life positively as a person of worth. For many, the capacity to exercise the choice that seems so obvious to others is not there. Internal resources need building up first. Almost always, growth in confidence is related to growth in a sense of a valuable self. Teachers try to promote the worth of each student so as to find areas of attainment in which they can shine.

The fact that the same opportunities may be presented to each child does not mean they can grasp them equally. This is where moral outrage about inequality, however valid, can miss the point. Happiness may make people earn more. As a generalisation, the emotional well-being of children and adolescents is key to their future success – a strong reason for the need to create an emotionally healthy home environment. Being cared for is a prime requisite for human development. Devoid of this, lack of a sense of value and belonging will impair the psyche and provoke human deprivation. Relationships of love, care and empathy are unevenly spread. These are wrongly conceived as being private matters.

Mental health or its lack is key to capability. A survey in May 2017 by the UK Mental Health Foundation found that only 13 per cent of those questioned felt they had good mental health. Four in ten said they had suffered from depression, a quarter had experienced a panic attack and the majority of people out of work – 85 per cent – had a mental health problem. As the Mental Health Foundation notes:

- Mixed anxiety and depression is the most common mental disorder, affecting 7.8 per cent of people.[19]
- In England, 4–10 per cent of people will experience depression in their lifetime.[20]
- Common mental health problems such as depression and anxiety are distributed according to a gradient of economic disadvantage across society. The poorer and more disadvantaged are disproportionately affected by such problems and their adverse consequences.[21]
- Mixed anxiety and depression are estimated to cause one-fifth of days lost from work.[22]
- One adult in six had a common mental disorder.[23]

To say this is to focus on the role that emotional life of humans should have in egalitarian theory, about which there has been a considerable ambivalence.[24] The notion of 'affective equality' was introduced by Baker et al. in order to show how inequalities operate in affective domains of life.[25] The background to this was how inter-linkages of different kinds function in the care field. Their point was that social relations are fundamental to the systems through which society functions – the economy, the political, the socio-cultural and that of affective care. Primacy has been given to the economy. The affective, emotional sphere was generally regarded as dependent on other systems – a by-product. Neglect of the role of emotional labour has had an effect on gender studies, such as the lack of research on masculine identities.[26] Unequal division of love, care and empathy have become subjects of research but this is only due to feminist scholarship leading the way.

With some, the capability to respond to opportunity is limited. An analogy suggests itself. As I write these words, the distant South Atlantic island of St Helena has just received its first flight. An airport has been constructed. Until then (October 2017), the ability of the island to grasp economic opportunity was limited. So with human beings: the infrastructure has not been there to respond. A variety of factors affects the degree to which some people are disadvantaged by comparison with others. A difficult early childhood, stress in early life or wounded history cast a long shadow forward.

Part Two

Why We Should Not Just Accept Inequality

7

Moral Outrage: Religious and Philosophical Arguments

'Am I being unfair to you? The first shall be last. And the last shall be first.' – Margie Savage, Women's World Day of Prayer[1]

We have surveyed some of the landscapes of inequality that haunt our times. The question we must now focus on is why inequality matters? Why do we not just accept inequality as an inevitable result of differences within human society?

The impetus towards equalising things out in society moved from equality before God, to equality before the law, to equal votes for all, and then to social and cultural equality of groups in society.

The idea that all people are moral equals has become so accepted in moral and political philosophy that critics of this principle will risk being branded as members of the alt-right in America. 'Basic equality' or the notion of treating persons as equals surely holds commanding heights of culture that no anti-egalitarian challenge need be taken seriously outside the political fringe? Is that actually so?

'Equality simply does not exist', affirms an interlocutor. 'We are and never will be equal.'[2] That is to load 'a question of inequality' with the heavy weight of 'equality of outcome' – something that few theorists outside Marxist circles believe is possible. Most theorists recognise the very different lives people lead and, rather than try to level those lives out and achieve uniformity, attempt to ensure those from diverse backgrounds have the same potential as everyone else to make our way in the world. On the contemporary scene, there is not a hierarchy of value, rather endeavours to ensure equality of value. Diversity is to be valued not assimilated. There is a broadly accepted 'right of recognition'; a basic right to be seen as a human being, a member of a political community.[3]

The first type of argument we will consider is the religious argument, before going on to observe moral and philosophical accounts of why inequality matters. This is not just a conceptual problem. Our aim in Part Two is to ask these questions with a view to a better understanding of how equal worth functions as a social dynamic. What are the social and political implications of this idea? But although seemingly obvious, does the notion of 'equal worth' hold philosophical water in the first place? Does an abused woman owe equal respect to her abuser as she would towards her own child?

Equality Before God

The essence of the religious objection against inequality is that human beings are equal before God. Our being on level ground stems from having the same value before the Lord who created us, irrespective of our social setting.

The notion of 'equality' was not a driver in the ancient near east that was the cradle for the Judaeo-Christian belief systems and Islam. These great monotheistic religions were cradled within societies that were intensely hierarchical. Yet equal status before God was, in the final analysis, the determining factor behind the way that people accessed their faith. This most obviously applied to the wrinkles and even the sharp divisions of class. Whether men and women had equal moral and spiritual validity was another matter entirely, as was the status of those outside the faith, such as Gentiles.

Grotesque inequalities of wealth were a feature of ancient societies, probably even more so than today. In biblical literature, concentrations of power among the rich that adversely affected the poor became the focus for cries for social justice. The lives of the poor ought not to be burdened by exploitation and unfairness. When the rich had it all and those without had nothing, something was profoundly wrong. Moral responsibility was called for; grinding the faces of the poor unacceptable.

> Thus says the Lord. For three transgressions of Israel and for four I will not revoke the punishment; because they sell the righteous for silver and the needy for a pair of shoes – they who trample the head of the poor into the dust of the earth.[4]

'Let justice roll down like waters and righteousness like an ever-flowing stream!' Amos thunders. If the people claimed to believe in one God, there was an ethical imperative that was flowed from it, such as the righteousness and justice the herdsman from Tekoa demanded.

The gospels do not portray the prophet from Nazareth as preaching equality directly. Inhabiting the role of a divinely attested Messiah, Jesus did, however, act in ways that struck his contemporaries as different to the institutional religion of his day. He mixed with everyone – rich and poor, men and women. Luke's gospel is the clearest example of this; indeed it is a theme in his theology that the little people disregarded by everyone else and have little value are given extraordinary value by God.

One parable offers an intriguing window on how equality and justice do not always cohere. In Matthew 20, Jesus speaks of a vineyard owner (literally, a 'house-Lord' – Matthew 20 v 1) who is looking for casual, fruit-picking labour. The house-Lord gives his rewards as he wishes: salvation is a free gift. That seems to be the message overall. Yet the casual labourers he recruits are looking for a fair wage. After some collective bargaining, they agree on the standard rate of one denarius a day.

That was early in the morning. By 9am, he goes again to where the unemployed gather. He is in the market for hire at midday, at 3pm and 5pm. Though late in the afternoon, the work requires more labour – and there are those willing to supply (without haggling). When the time comes for payment shortly after 6pm, the lesson immediately kicks in that the first shall be last and the last paid first. That in itself speaks of those who arrive late (Gentiles, non-believers) being treated the same as those who have long been in the faith and in the traditions (Jewish believers). The point is though that they all receive equal payment. Those that had been bearing the heat and burden of the day since the morning expected to receive greater consideration. By comparison with those that are recruited later, the original labourers have a grumble (the very word in v 11 is onomatopoeiac; a sound imitation). Their dissatisfaction is not that they were placed on the same footing as the late-comers but that the new arrivals had been placed on the same basis as them!

Justice might say they had a point. Why should a ten-hour day be remunerated at the same rate as a one-hour day? Even within the piece-work conditions of the time, it is not fair! Yet none were promised any more remuneration than anyone else. The dilemma of the daily rate was applicable to all. They were, however, placed on the same level of equality.

The Corinthian correspondence is not normally the 'must-go-to-place' for signs of the new order of things that had broken in upon the present. Yet one marker that the new has indeed come and the old has gone is in the first letter. Paul writes of the many who are one body together. 'Because there is one bread, we who are many are one body because we all partake of one bread.'[5]

Paul writes about 'varieties of gifts but the same Spirit; varieties of service but the same Lord; varieties of activities but the same God who activates all of them in everyone'.[6] It is where that discussion takes us that seems especially relevant. Paul will not allow the tricky notion of complementarity to imply inferior status. The Body of Christ imagery points to every part of the body being needed, just as with a human body. Those parts that seem to be of lesser importance are clothed with honour and respect – an interesting perspective in itself in an honour culture that was the background against which Paul wrote. He is keen that there should be an equality in the body, that no part should claim pre-eminence. 'For in the one Spirit we were all baptised into one body – Jews or Greeks, slave or free – and we were all made to drink of one Spirit'.[7] This of course has strong resonance with the first Christian writing. 'There is no longer Jew or Greek, there is no longer slave or free, there is no longer male and female: for all of you are one in Christ Jesus.'[8]

The Jews saw the world as being divided into two categories – the Jews and everyone else. This 'us/you' contrast has been made obsolete. They are no longer divided by the law. Slave and free were the other two most obvious differences. Slavery was not yet regarded as immoral and degrading but it was an extension of the principle that in Christ, the profound barrier of the law has been ended. The last trio is gender. Josephus – 'the woman, says the law, is in all things inferior to the man.'[9] Some have seen an echo of the Jewish male prayer that he was not created either a woman or a slave.

It is perhaps going too far to see in this verse a manifesto of a new kingdom. Jews were still Jews; Christians did not cease to be slaves. Women were still making their way in a man's world. Nevertheless, as Dunn remarks:

> Paul's choice of contrasts covers the full range of the most profound distinctions within human society – racial/cultural, social/economic, sexual/gender. The language implies a radically reshaped social world as viewed from a Christian perspective, equivalent to the 'kingdom-perspective' which informed Jesus' ministry – a powerful integrating force for the different social groups in the earliest diaspora churches.[10]

These distinctions thought to imply relative worth or privileged status before God no longer have that significance. They have been relativised. The Jews were no longer more highly regarded by God. How Paul saw the application of this idea to the role that women or slaves could play in the churches he founded is complex. Nevertheless, here is a clear marker that gender, social status or race is no longer a barrier to the spread of the gospel.

Paul would have agreed with the theologian Martin Schmidt who commented that: 'equality before God does not exclude differences among people but includes them, and the true expression of the religious life is not mechanical uniformity but organic individualism'.[11]

For early Christian theologians, the new faith they were preaching broke down existing barriers based on the old division of the world. This was especially true of the Jewish–Gentile ethnic divide. 'For Christ is our peace, who has made the two one and has destroyed the barrier, the dividing wall of hostility [...] creating in himself one new man out of the two, thus making peace'.[12]

But it went further into a levelling of social divisions. Early Christianity was passionate in its advocacy of an equality in those who had come to faith in which 'there is neither Jew nor Greek, slave nor free, male nor female'.[13] Paul develops the concept of the Christian church as the Body of Christ embodying the new humanity but espousing difference. Diversity within unity is the theme of important statements in the New Testament about the church. 'The body is a unit, though it is made up of many parts: and though all its parts are many, they form one body'.[14] The totality of Christians constituted an international and societal commonwealth but it was an entity fully capable of accommodating, even celebrating diversity. The vision was that of a new humanity in Christ, a new understanding of history, a signpost to where the redemption of the world was leading inexorably.

Enlightened Egalitarianism

The notion of a common humanity was familiar territory to Enlightenment thinkers such as Kant and Rousseau and before them, Stoic philosophers and Christian theologians, concerned to develop the idea of a new, common humanity in which the old barriers of race and ethnicity were broken down. Equality as an ideal became a central trope of politics. The concept of equality of opportunity is strong. What you achieve is down to your own hard work rather than God's will.

In the Roman world, these ideas developed in tandem with those of the Stoics, who philosophised the notion of a common humanity and global citizenry based on recognition. Stoics have some interesting, though partial, lessons for the twenty-first century.[15] Diogenes refused to be defined simply by his local origins and group memberships, rather in terms of more universal aspirations and concerns. 'When anyone asked him where he came from, he said, "I am a citizen of the world".'[16]

The Stoics developed his image of the kosmopolites, or world citizen, arguing in effect that each of us dwells in two worlds, the local and the global. Stoics said the latter community is 'most fundamentally, the source of moral and social obligations.'[17]

Stoic ideas influenced Rousseau as well as the American Republic through the writings of Paine, Kant and Adam Smith. The latter was wrong to object that Stoicism sought to minimise difference. There is no need, the Stoics insisted, to disband local group identities which can be a source of great richness. We are surrounded by a series of concentric circles, beyond them being the largest one, that of humanity as a whole.

But can the notion of a common humanity be conceptualised in terms of equality? It can be argued that a recognition of humanity does fit in with the view that everyone should be treated equally. But human value is not a 'good' to be distributed. If the status of citizenship, for example is extended to all competent adults, it is vital that every member of the political community is given an equal vote. There is no hierarchy of membership in the political community.

Recognition of a common humanity is not the same as laying stress upon equality. The ideal of equality is very much contested territory. Equality can be seen to be a requirement of justice and thus enforced by the state, an ideal that individuals can choose to pursue or a social ideal which is not a requirement of justice. Inequality is objectionable for some because it constitutes a bad state of affairs (the telic view) objectionable to others because it involves injustice (the deontic view). Does it mean political equality, equality before the law or that everyone should be equally well-off? Equality has for some the notion that there is something to be re-distributed.[18]

It is fair to say that until the radical tradition of seventeenth-century England, there was little emphasis upon political equality. As we have observed, Biblical and faith traditions more generally had a strong sense of humans being of equal validity and worthy of both divine favour and protection. This was not, however, translated into any idea of making people equal in their social status. The Peasant's Revolt of 1381 did not espouse a political philosophy of abolishing distinctions between peasants and kings. Nor was there an imperative to level things up in society. That distinction fell to the Levellers. The idea that the ordinary person has potential for meaning as much as a King has been vital to political debates about both democracy and equality since the seventeenth century. 'The poorest he hath a life to live, as the greatest he,' proclaimed Colonel Thomas Rainborrow in the Putney Debates following the English Civil War. Our single most important political principle comes to us from these debates.[19] The Levellers adopted an Agreement of the People, in effect a social contract by which people would establish and set limits to the power of the government.[20] Though no such agreement was ever put into practice, their significance was that here were ordinary people engaging in politics.

While espousing diversity and self-determination, philosophers in the flowering of modernity set in train by the Enlightenment argued for a substratum of equality. They questioned the traditional notion that some were born to rule, others to be ruled and that inequality was justified legitimately by both church and state. As the banner of political equality began to be unfurled, it was argued that all people were equally able to reason and think about morality, thus qualifying for civil rights. In his second treatise, Locke, an early liberal, argued that since all human beings had identical faculties, notably reason and since they were equally dependent on their Creator, they are equal both in dignity and rights.[21] He was, however, against any notion that American Indians warranted respect in contrast to a European way of life.

Both Vico, the Italian political philosopher (1668–1744), and Montesquieu (1689–1755) were more sensitive to cultural diversity though clearly Eurocentric.[22] Montesquieu in particular believed that each society was different and developed distinctly human capacities on its own terms. But although he celebrated diversity and was not shocked by cultural practice or beliefs, he still took European society as the norm and assumed his vision of the good life was preferable. A later figure, Herder, demonstrates the extent to which Enlightenment liberalism espoused universals while simultaneously generating thinking about difference. Every culture is a unique expression of the human spirit according to Herder, not a by-product of a universally shared human nature. Herder still endeavoured to find a space for a common humanity, arguing that humans belong to a single species and share rational, physical, emotional and cultural needs. All cultures are equally valid in trying to meet those needs. Significantly, Herder's thesis links cultural production with language.[23]

The Enlightenment position is best referenced, however, through what Charles Taylor calls the standard bearers of the call to universals – Kant and Rousseau. Immanuel Kant's deontological formulation of the categorical imperative relied on a statement of universalising an action to make it theoretically applicable to everyone. 'There is [...] only one categorical imperative. It is: Act only according to that maxim by which you can at the same time will that it should become a universal law.'[24]

In short, no principle can be considered morally acceptable if it cannot be universalised. If an action is right for one, it is right for all. No action is permitted unless 'in the same situation, all people should act in the same way'.[25] To allow exceptions would have a corrosive effect on society.

Kant's second principle by which the categorical imperative was formulated contained a significant statement of human value. Humans are an end in themselves, never a means to an end. Humans should never be used by others who want to exploit or enslave them. Unlike Benthamite utilitarianism, there can be no use of the one for the sake of the many. Each person demands unique treatment. 'So act that you treat humanity, both in your own person and in the person of every other human being, never merely as a means but always at the same time as an end.'[26]

Kantian universalism is problematic. His stricture against using people as a means to an end restricts hard choices for the common good. Sometimes, duties conflict. What is significant here though is the rationalisation of Kantian ethics, grounded in an account of intrinsic (and equal) human dignity – a property that consists largely in autonomy, in the ability of each person to determine a vision of the good life.[27]

In *A Discourse on Equality*, Jean Jacque Rousseau argued for two forms of inequality – natural differences due to age, health, strength of mind and body and moral or political inequality. He tells a story of the noble savage, man in a state of nature.

> If we compare the prodigious diversities of upbringing and of ways of life which prevail among the different classes in the civil state with the simplicity and uniformity of animal and savage life where everyone eats the same foods, lives in the same style and does exactly the same things, it will be understood how much less the difference between man and man must be in the state of nature than it is in society.[28]

In short, civilisation produces inequality. Differences came when individuals were forced to compare themselves with each other and to take account of the continued dealings they have with each other. According to Rousseau, wealth, rank, power and personal merit are the sources of difference by which one is measured in society, contrasted with the universal, the pure state of nature. Dependence on others to get what we want promotes a deformation of the self as people become the characters they believe others value as attractive or socially useful. Extensive rationalisations are developed to justify the power and position that underpin hierarchies and ideologies.[29] These ideas have been celebrated by those who see Rousseau as having profound insight into the false promises of modernity; how, in other words, can we avoid greed, competition and status?[30]

Equality? We are, declares Rousseau, equally immiserated: 'man is born free but is everywhere in chains'. Society corrupts the individual. In his *Confessions* Rousseau, telling the story of his life, analyses with sharp insight the relationship between an elusive but essential inner self and the variety of social identities he was led to adopt.[31] How Rousseau's account of the personal qualities of each unique individual maps on to his conception of equality is ambiguous.

Rousseau's ideas fed the French Revolution with its call to liberty, equality and fraternity. In 1789, the French Declaration of the Rights of Man proclaimed men to be equal, though 'only in respect of their rights'. The second of the new ideals of the revolutionary era heralded as an object of belief, *egalité*, represented, 'a type of social and economic community based on equality'.[32] It was rooted in Rousseau's notion of equality and in his social contract: a unification of the community on a new basis that would reject inequality and difference.

Equality went on to become 'a child of the great revolutions that inaugurated the modern world'.[33] Before *egalité* became a rallying cry of the French Revolution that Rousseau unwittingly fed, it was the keynote of the American Revolution with its Declaration of Independence and stress on the belief that 'all men are created equal'. Equality had emerged as a political ideal.

The notion of equality at this time is highly contestable. The promise of *egalité* in the French Revolution stood in strong contrast with the reality of the kind of society arising from post-1789 upheavals.[34] The Napoleonic Code conferred equal right to the protection of the law on those who had a stake in society – that is, owners of property. As Theodore Zeldin observed, this made the penniless worker almost an outlaw.[35] Before that though, the rhetoric of the 1776 US Declaration of Independence had struck a chord with nascent European political awareness – 'We hold these truths to be self-evident, that all men are created equal, that they are endowed by their Creator with certain unalienable rights, that among these are life, liberty and the pursuit of happiness'. The goal of the US experiment is expressed in the Latin phrase that appears on the nation's seals and coins – *e pluribus unum* (out of many, one); that is 'to forge a long-lasting stable nation state [...] out of a population of diverse races, ethnicities, incompatible beliefs, values, orientations and agendas'.[36]

During the drafting of the Constitution, southern spokesmen warned that they would not tolerate interference with their slaves, whom they regarded simply as their property. White settlers insisted on equality but it did not occur to them that the assertion might include others who were neither independent nor male nor white. Patrick Henry, the revolutionary orator, could famously declaim 'Give me liberty or give me death' while admitting that slavery was repugnant to humanity and that his black slaves could only accept the first at the price of the second.[37]

America was thus born with a conception of itself as a land of equal and self-reliant citizens. That was its founding myth.[38] However, seems hard to understand how Thomas Jefferson, a slave-owner, could declare 'that all men are created equal' as a philosophical justification for the break with England. Nevertheless, the subsequent growth of liberalism arose from the Enlightenment. The quest for universals and the practice of liberalism inevitably had a levelling influence as rich and powerful were compelled, in Western Europe at least, to yield political rights. In the democracies, it became harder to deny universal suffrage to working men and then to women. Even in the early eighteenth century, before the high noon of the Enlightenment, questions were being asked by female voices: 'if all men are born free, how is that all women are born slaves?'[39]

Looking at America some 60 years later, Alexis de Tocqueville thought he saw that this new type of society had generated a sense of 'equality of condition'.[40] Gone were status hierarchies of the *ancien régime*; in its place was a social order characterised by a sense of an equal condition and a structure of feeling and mentality undergirding the new democratic society that 'we're all in this together'.

Participation in the public sphere was governed by criteria of achievement, property and interests applicable to men only. Liberalism had limits because it reproduced the patriarchal division between public and private life as male and female. The logic of liberal theory demanded what was a long time coming: the emancipation of white and black women as well as racial emancipation in itself.[41] For early feminists as for advocates of racial justice, the goal was emancipation: emancipation from systems of domination. This could be stated a century later in these terms: 'Radical feminism is working for the eradication of domination and elitism in all human relationships'.[42]

Twentieth century British socialists like R. H. Tawney were to object profoundly that the class divisions strengthened by capitalism's concentration of economic power placed people in very different circumstances. Wealth and income were the determinants of individual value. Consequently, it was immensely hard to instantiate theoretical equality of opportunity.[43] In practice, 'perfection of individual human beings' presented impossible barriers. Inequality of circumstances was against it.

Karl Marx had defined in his *Critique of the Gotha Programme* the essence of socialism in terms applying to a political community ('the needs principle') – 'from each according to his ability, to each according to his needs'.[44] Marx had already argued in *Das Kapital* that a worker is compelled to sell his capacity for labour for 'the whole of his active life'. The Eden-like state of innate rights of man is deeply corrupted by capitalist exploitation under which 'theft of alien labour time' becomes normative and the worker subordinate.[45] Marx was very hostile to universal truth yet clearly condemns capitalism for its violation of a normative concept of justice rather than just arising from historically specific class consciousness.[46]

The notion of equality of the sexes is much less used today. Phillips comments that a hundred years ago, one might have defined feminism as a movement towards the equality of the sexes – 'by now this is hardly apt [...]. A commitment to sexual equality does not by itself tell us what shape that equality should take'.[47] Marx had criticised the Gotha Programme drawn up by German socialists in 1875 who demanded that all members of society have equal right to the proceeds of labour. Applying that to feminist debate, how can that be fair if one woman is a black single mother; another a white middle class professional? 'Right' must mean applying a single standard to all.

In an outline of a Feminist Ethics, Linda Bell suggests that the notion of equality is double-edged; it reinforces domination by men. Sexist oppression is not the only form of oppression to be fought, she concedes. But it is a vital one.[48] Hooks suggests that when feminism defines itself as a movement to gain social equality with men, it obscures real problems besetting women's lives.[49]

Enlightenment thinkers did not assume people were alike; rather that differences defined their particularity, not their humanity. All this was to change as modernity progressed. Subsequent social theory readily embraced the emphasis on diversity and multiculturalism. It accorded with the mood of late (or post) modernity that denied vantage points and authority to fixed positions and traditional perspectives.

Munro is right to point out that 'the current tendency is to reject universalism and, in line with a greater respect for the linguistic integrity of specific practices, go the other way, preferring the emic to the etic, local distinctions to global abstractions'.[50]

This is problematic. How do universal values get generated if they are clothed with suspicion? But, following Montesquieu and Herder, modernity generated not only universals, however, it also generated an awareness of difference and, in time, enormous anxiety about civil and legal rights as well as those being exercised in the political sphere. The growing emphasis on difference was in some respects a natural outgrowth of the emphasis on equality. The United Nations could not for long espouse human rights discourse post-World War II without a growing clamour for recognition of black Americans and also women. The heady days of the 1960s and 1970s brought about sweeping social change ranging from civil rights and legislation about discrimination through to a new world of equal opportunities for all.

'Seeing' difference has mixed fortunes in the contemporary world; sometimes being viewed as having positive valence such as welcoming diversity. Often, seeing difference can be viewed negatively as with ethnic conflict in Bosnia. Nevetheless, disadvantaged groups have been subject to discrimination, a lack of justice requiring re-distribution. 'Valuing diversity and committed to equality of opportunity' – a notice at the bottom of job advertisements in the public sector recruiting staff; a slogan for our times. It sums up the motive behind the contemporary focus on difference.

Values transcend particulars of birth and position. Yet justice recognises there are inequalities. In what is now a classic account of justice, John Rawls argued that reconciling liberty and equality requires the notion of fairness. Humans are both rational and reasonable, endeavouring to achieve our aims, if possible co-operatively and legally. To find principles that are satisfactory all round, given our differing needs and hopes, Rawls argues for an original position in which we had 'a veil of ignorance' about what others had or wanted. In such circumstances, we want to protect equal basic liberties such as conscience and freedom of expression but also wherever we were on the pecking order, liberties that were meaningful options for us. Equal rights to pursue freedom of assembly might be less important to the desperately poor slum dweller. But we would also want to affirm the 'difference principle' – those with comparable talents and motivation should face similar life chances.[51] Rawls subsequently modified principles of justice. Each person has equal claim to the same scheme of basic rights. Any inequalities must be available to all under fair conditions of opportunity and especially help the least advantaged.[52]

Maybe political philosophy needed an injection of grand theory! Rawls' account became highly influential.[53] At any rate, in *Anarchy, State and Utopia*, Robert Nozick took Rawls to task. Such a complex model of justice cannot be a model for society. It unfairly benefits the poor at the expense of the rich. Justice is about entitlement – 'I am entitled to my acquisition as long as I stay within the law'.[54] Rawls has also been much criticised on the grounds that his celebrated account of social justice downplayed the moral weight of group and family loyalty or community identity.[55]

In the West, it has been argued that when the system gives some people a flying start and easier access to better jobs, resources, housing and health than others, it is unjust. Gradually barriers were dismantled so everyone has the same chances in life. Inequality in all its forms was seen as a matter of unequal access to advantage. Yet the ideal of equality always needs to be translated into the circumstances that people and groups find themselves in. Theirs is a race in which people start from very different positions on the track. Controversially, by insisting that the essence of justice is fairness, Rawls advocates as great an equality of outcome as is feasible. And so the liberal account of egalitarian justice was given powerful new clothing.

Equal Worth?

In Rawl's account of justice, the interests of each one of us can lay claim to be equally important. The essence of equality is having the same human status and value. It seems to serve as a commitment to the contemporary approach to political philosophy. But is this really the case?

It is neither straightforward nor obvious. George Sher notes the enormous empirical variance among human beings. We simply are not equal in any obvious sense. Yet each one is a separate subjectivity that is structured by common assumptions about time or motivations people have. Though this individual consciousness may be channelled into a wide variety of distinctively human lives, it is the fact of being structured in recognisable ways that supplies a basis for equality. We all have capacities for rational agency that are common ground in our humanity.[56] Richard Arnesson argues that attributing in a similar way the notion of all persons having equal basic dignity and worth is hard to sustain. Interpretations of the basic equality claim face the challenge of clarifying what it means to be a person and the resultant equality idea it generates.[57]

It is by no means obvious that the concept of equal worth is directly relevant to considering what moral rights people have – the abuser or Pol Pot, for instance, in contrast to a selfless charity worker. As we have noted, Kant pre-supposes that humans have an absolute value or worth. Yet a concept of relative worth is available which is less problematic. Weighing moral merits on the scales would result in some positive but many negative assessments of human action that are hardly equal.

It may be objected why the mere ability to decide and act morally or immorally should shape what moral rights people have and whether these are equally valid by dint of capacity. The rapist and the raped should no doubt be treated unequally but the right of justification to explain their actions and response deserves to be taken seriously. In this way, they could be said to have equal dignity.

The reality is that not all philosophers do subscribe to the claim of equal moral status and are therefore egalitarians. Leaving aside obvious differences, it is only as neutralised humans reduced to a core essence that we might be considered identical. The state does not owe equal consideration to criminals and their victims. Humans do not have equal rights and the fact of having species-level 'basic rights' does not translate into political egalitarianism. Uwe Steinhof objects to recourse to a 'norm-generating' fundamental such as the 'original position' that John Rawls advocates. In his view, liberal egalitarianism is unsuccessful and should be abandoned.[57]

The notion of equality in contemporary society is characterised in terms of fairness and being inclusive of difference. Equality of opportunity is espoused far more than a communistic equality of outcome though this in turn leads to a uniformity and suppression of individual identities. The construction of identities is a huge theme in the landscapes of today and to this we now turn.

8

Why Inequality Matters: Economic and Practical Arguments

'We have reached a tipping point. Inequality can no longer be treated as an afterthought.' – OECD Secretary-General[1]

There are two forms of explanation we will consider in this chapter. The first is that inequality matters economically; the second that it matters in very practical ways that affect everyday life.

Economic Arguments

An analysis of income inequality in 28 countries over 30 years had, as its design cover, a grossly unequal distribution of peanuts between two piles.[2] This was a simple but powerful pictorial device to draw attention to a concern with growing traction in political, economic and social commentary.

I happen to write these words on the tenth anniversary of the start of the financial crash of 2007. On that day in August, the French bank BNP Paribas was forced to close two of its hedge funds, admitting they were in effect worthless. The Wall Street bank Bear Stearns had already found, suddenly, that it could not find a buyer for any of its investment funds and that they were worthless. Its customers were unable to withdraw money from two of its investment funds. Now the actions of Paribas fanned the flame and the fire began to spread. One year later, the result of financial pyramids teetering on shaky, slim foundations, came the collapse of Lehman Brothers and the events of a September Sunday when careers were carted off in boxes and banks had to be rescued.

Those events had a long tail. The financial crash made many realise that the economic system was not only unstable and cyclical, it was also deeply unfair. 'Occupy' became a new social movement that highlighted the inequality in western societies. Its key banner was 'we are the 99 per cent', in contrast with the 1 per cent at the top who cream off most of the rewards because they made the system work for them. The strong and seemingly universal sense of unfairness that the system was rigged for elites was no doubt a major factor in the strange politics of 2016. Chickens had come home to roost!

Capitalism is by nature an inequality project. Markets are supposed to be efficient, matching supply with demand. The angry shout that the economic system was failing for so many reflected a perception that it was not distributing rewards all round but concentrated its favours on those who had a considerable amount already. What added fuel to the fire was the feeling that hardly anyone went to prison for allowing the Crash; the bankers who had engaged in predatory lending and clever financial re-packaging were let off the hook but everyone else had to pay for the bankers' misdeeds.

To work efficiently, the system should distribute the proceeds from economic activity to those who put in. In theory, the standard of living of most citizens should be improved, and citizens should not live in fear of losing their homes and jobs.‘ It ought not to be the case that those at the top are further enriched and that to those that have, more will be given while everyone else has to struggle. The consequence of the rich getting richer, 'the middle' being squeezed and pay for the others hardly rising is political instability.

The usual measure of inequality is the Gini coefficient. If income were matched to the proportions in the general population, the top 10 per cent of the people would get 10 per cent of the income and the Gini coefficient would be zero. At the other end of the scale, if all went to the a few richest billionaires, the Gini measure would be one. There are of course no societies on earth that manifest such perfect inequality. Countries with the greatest level of entrenched inequality and contrasts of wealth have a Gini measure of 0.5 or above. According to the World Bank, for 2014, this elite group were mainly Latin American countries such as Brazil, Columbia, Honduras, Panama and Paraguay.[3] More developed countries such as the United States, South Africa and China are not far off that half-way mark.[4]

In 1800, Dorothy Wordsworth wrote that very soon, there will be only two types of people: the very rich and the very poor.[5] Economic inequality has been observed for centuries and studied for decades. The US National Bureau of Economic Research was founded, back in the 1920s, to take a serious look at the issue of economic inequality to address concerns that, under capitalism, the rich were getting richer while the poor getting poorer. It has made a come-back in recent years. Commenting on global inequality, the OECD pointed out that it can no longer be considered an afterthought but has to come clearly into the focus of policy. There are weighty political arguments for taking action but also economic ones. The case against inequality was that it tends to drag down GDP growth, due to the rising distance of the lower 40 per cent from the rest of society. Lower-income people have been prevented from realising their human potential, which is bad for the economy as a whole. New policies are required, such as structural labour market changes with rising job polarisation; tackling persisting gender gaps; the challenge of high wealth concentration, and redistribution.[6]

Janet Gornick and Markuss Jantti brought together an analysis of income inequality in 28 countries over 30 years through the Luxembourg Income Study. The main focus was not on those at the top or bottom (the usual suspects) but the 60 per cent in the middle. An important insight from the study was on the inequity of the gender pay gap and the economic consequences of the working lives of women is factored in and the value of unpaid work in the home. Increased female participation in the workforce has, nevertheless, had the effect overall of equalising income distribution.[7]

Lack of equality in society may have an adverse effect on economic growth though it is not clear what the precise causal connection might be. Equality or its lack seems to be a cultural, sociological term rather than economic. Researchers are mapping one concept on another. Work needs to be done to re-integrate economics and sociology to see income, wealth and occupation more clearly.

The economic problem with inequality is that it does not circulate gains to those who contribute. Indeed, it siphons off wealth to those who already have it. The uber-rich do spectacularly while most were getting worse-off or stagnating. This is not just about income inequality. Disparity in wealth is even more marked. Wealth inequality goes beyond the variations in income inequality that will be apparent in any one year. For the most part, middle income earners have their wealth tied up in housing, the price of which fluctuates notoriously.

Even before financial crash, as the US Congressional Budget Office pointed out for 2007, analysis of average Federal tax rates showed that the top 1 per cent earned 40 per cent more *in one week* than the bottom 20 per cent earned in a year, the top 1 per cent received in *a day and a half* what the bottom 90 per cent received in a year. The richest 20 per cent of income earners received after tax more than the bottom 80 per cent combined.[8]

This is staggering and the situation has become considerably more accentuated a decade later.[9] The reason why it is a problem is that the wealth that works its way to the top of the food chain does not come down again. The old idea was that wealth should 'trickle down' and that everyone will benefit. The mantra sustained economic and political discourse for a generation or two, most famously expressed by John F. Kennedy, that a rising tide will float all boats. To change the metaphor from boats to pies, in theory it should not matter if those below get a comparatively smaller share of the pie as long as their slice is growing because the pie is enlarging. All fine in theory but in practice it does not happen. In the six years following the global banking crash, the number of those in India with disposable assets of a million dollars or more rose from 127,000 to 200,000. Trickle down economics failed to translate this growth into benefit for the rest of society.[10]

Should anyone be concerned with the *difference* between what they have and what others have? Why isn't such a concern at heart a question of envy? Harvard philosopher T. M. Scanlon offers four reasons why we should object to economic inequality.[11] His reasons are worth noting.

1 **Economic inequality can give wealthier people an unacceptable degree of control over the lives of others.** If wealth is very unevenly distributed in a society, the wealthy control of many aspects of the lives of poorer citizens: over where and how they can work, what they can buy, and in general what their lives will be like.
2 **Economic inequality can undermine the fairness of political institutions.** If those who hold political offices must depend on large

contributions for their campaigns, they will be more responsive to the interests and demands of wealthy contributors, and those who are not rich will not be fairly represented.

3 **Economic inequality undermines the fairness of the economic system itself.** Economic inequality makes it difficult, if not impossible, to create equality of opportunity. Income inequality means that some children will enter the workforce much better prepared than others. Those with few assets find it harder to access the first small steps to larger opportunities, such as a loan to start a business or pay for an advanced degree.

4 **Workers, as participants in a scheme of cooperation that produces national income, have a claim to a fair share of what they have helped to produce.** What constitutes a fair share has been much debated. According to the Difference Principle espoused by John Rawls, inequalities in wealth and income are permissible only if these inequalities could not be reduced without worsening the position of those who are worst-off. All those who participate in producing these benefits – workers as well as others – should share in the result.

Creating wealth does not result in a more equal society. Thomas Piketty argued in his magnum opus that when the rate of return on capital exceeds the rate of growth of output and income, as it did in the nineteenth century and seems quite likely to do again in the twenty-first, capitalism automatically generates arbitrary and unsustainable inequalities that radically undermine the meritocratic values on which democratic societies are based.[12] The distribution of wealth is less equal than the distribution of income: it tends both to accumulate and concentrate.

The tour de force of this modern Marx was heavily criticised on many grounds. Was this resurgent concern not just a cultural phenomenon of the moment that would soon pass? Were the statistics correct? Could his thesis be seriously advanced when there is been a rising tide of democratic freedom and prosperity for most? Does it matter if the rate of return on capital aggregates faster than the rate of return on labour as Piketty argued? Capital is not usually static. After all, investments help pay for everything else. Yet a world where the wealthy succeed in protecting their returns, never minding the effect on the downtrodden workers, is not really true to life. Politics changes, tax rates change and financial regulation has varied fortunes.

A raft of reports from international bodies draw attention to income inequality being pernicious. The International Monetary Fund backed economists who argue that it is a drag on growth. Right wing theories that emphasise efforts to redistribute incomes are self-defeating. The IMF argued:

1 More unequal societies tend to redistribute more. It is thus important in understanding the growth-inequality relationship to distinguish between market and net inequality.
2 Lower net inequality is robustly correlated with faster and more durable growth, for a given level of redistribution. These results are highly supportive of our earlier work.
3 Redistribution appears generally benign in terms of its impact on growth; only in extreme cases is there some evidence that it may have direct negative effects on growth.

Thus the combined direct and indirect effects of redistribution – including the growth effects of the resulting lower inequality – are on average pro-growth.[13]

Trawling through the literature, it is hard to avoid the impression that the so many of the objections to inequality based on economics are in fact about fairness, or rather the unfairness and social consequences of some groups in society having so much and most having so little. In other words, it is egalitarian arguments against capitalism that are really at issue. How researchers try to capture and measure inequality affects the political messages people want to send. There are, however, two sets of economic objections that stand out that are not arguments about fair shares per se.

1 One strong reason for reducing disparities of wealth is rooted in self-interest. When capital is funnelled to those at the top without coming back down again (as Piketty demonstrates), there is less demand in the economy. The rich can only buy so many pairs of trousers. When income is tight for a growing majority, they are less likely to buy consumer products. If wealth is concentrated among only a small group of people, it might spur increases demand for imported luxuries and handmade products. Since demand is the key factor in economic prosperity that will have major implications. After all, the point of such anti-austerity measures as quantitative easing is as a stimulus, as was

Keynesian demand-management. The great economist himself viewed economics as primarily studying the satisfaction of demand in conditions of scarcity.

2 The other primarily economic argument is about 'rent-seeking'. In the hands of economists, the idea of 'rent' goes beyond charges to property to include any form of fee and payments accruing from position power. Income from inheritance among the very top echelon is extensive in advanced economies such as the United States and sustains inequality.[14] Monopoly capitalism by dint of wealth suppresses the diffusion of economic clout that could bring real benefit. Stiglitz contends that the reality of the 'rentiers' greatly exacerbates the problem.

Practical Arguments

The poor getting poorer and having so little wealth causes profound social strain and economic insecurity, as the US elections of 2016 amply demonstrated. Decent jobs requiring a few skills are disappearing rapidly. The polarisation of the labour force results in social worlds moving apart. For the lucky few, their standard of living is running away into fantasy land compared with those for whom it is declining. We have looked in Chapter 1 at the social disparities where so many can hardly meet the necessities of life. Now we must note a second explanation of why inequality matters; that it has serious practical implications that hold people back.

The lack of opportunity is profound. What are the chances of young people making it to the top? As was commented on by someone from the north in a debate about poorer life chances in the north of England, 'I don't have a cat in hell's chance of becoming someone like a doctor or professional!'[15]

Joseph Stiglitz argues in the context of America, 'we are no longer the land of opportunity that we once were'.[16] The evidence for this is disturbing because in theory, what has been so central in America's self-understanding is a narrative of rags to riches, of equality of opportunity. Fed by the occasional success story and family memory of second or third generations from immigrants, it has been a persistent myth. But now, it is simply not the case either side of the Atlantic that just anyone can get on. The barriers are significantly against it. Those at the top will most likely stay there as will those at the bottom.

Lack of economic and social mobility results in an entrenched link between parental education and social location and the life outcomes of their children. The key to all this is education; the education that can widen the horizon of possibility for young people beyond what they thought they could do, the education that gives people a stake in the system.

New OECD research shows that when income inequality rises, economic growth falls. One reason is that poorer members of society are less able to invest in their education. Tackling inequality can make our societies fairer and our economies stronger. The OECD argues that inequalities in access to education are the most important factor behind the connection between inequality and growth. Data from 15 OECD countries shows that, at age 30, people with the highest levels of education can expect to live, on average, six years longer than poorly educated peers. The report on the strong connection between inequalities and education concluded that:

> Inequalities which surface in the job-market are often entrenched during education, which puts those at the bottom at a serious disadvantage. Poorer students struggle to compete with their wealthier classmates and go on to lower levels of educational attainment, smaller salaries, and most strikingly, shorter lives.[17]

According to the OECD, 'One key channel through which inequality negatively affects economic performance is through lowering investment opportunities (particularly in education) of the poorer segments of the population'.[18]

It is clear that the level of social inequality prevents prosperity being shared equitably across the population. It is also clear that the level of education within a country has a strong bearing on its economic potential for growth and prosperity. Correlations between the distribution of numeracy skills in the population to measures of economic prosperity suggest that a higher numeracy skills spread is related to higher social inequality.[19] Education cannot be separated from it.

Nevertheless, the life chances of the poorest in society are framed, though not determined, before children even start school. All too often, patterns are set that will be very hard to break as exposure to difficult social settings and lack of accordable housing and healthy food take their toll. Grammar schools have more middle class children with motivated parents. In the current state of social mobility, this is how things are. Yet in developed countries as everywhere, it is going to school that makes the difference between the social location people are born into and remain – against a new horizon of options.

Surprisingly, a driver of inequality turns out to be lack of access to credit. The economic theory saying that some inequality is no bad thing should run like this. A world where a few people have most of the wealth motivates others who are poor to strive to earn more. And when they do, they'll invest in businesses and other areas of the economy. However, a study of 21 OECD countries over more than a 100 years shows income inequality actually restricts people from earning more, educating themselves and becoming entrepreneurs. In turn, businesses invest less in things like plant and equipment. Inequality makes it harder for economies to benefit from innovation. However, if people have access to credit or the money to move up, it can offset this. As Doucouliagos, argues, from 1870 to 1977, inequality measured by the Gini coefficient fell by about 40 per cent. People were more innovative as productivity increased. Rising inequality more recently is having the opposite effect.[20]

Certainly, disability is a site of enormous inequality. Those who are disabled are being left behind, still being treated as second-class citizens. In many respects, opportunities have gone backwards. More disabled people are in poverty than non-disabled. A third of families where one member is disabled are in deprived households. They are less likely to be in employment; more likely to be excluded from school. Educational attainment is lower. Life expectancy is lower; health inequalities wider. And at the heart of these disparities lie attitudes – negative attitudes and devaluing.[21]

The result is significant barriers, disabling barriers such as loss of benefits, poor accessibility, lack of vocation, lack of employment prospects and lack of support. Charities such as Liveability are very active in promoting joined-up opportunities to participate in community life and break down social isolation – a particular problem among those who live with disability.[22]

Case Study[23]

The UK Disability Discrimination Act 1995 provided new rights for disabled people. It required greater access to jobs, goods, premises and services. Organisations had to make reasonable provisions to help disabled people overcome practical obstacles. The politics of disability are played out on equal access to public transport, for example the bus companies.

In the recent Supreme Court case between Doug Paulley and First Group (FirstGroup Plc v Paulley, 2017) it was argued that wheelchair users were being discriminated against because of the policies adopted by First Group in respect of the wheelchair space provided on buses. The problem is not however confined to wheelchair users, but all disability groups and elderly passengers.

Mr Paulley, a wheelchair user, was prevented from boarding a bus because a child in a buggy was in the disabled space. The Supreme Court found that bus companies must do more to cater for the needs of wheelchair users. For example, the driver should take firm steps to ensure a non-wheelchair user makes space for wheelchair users rather than just accepting that a non-wheelchair user cannot move. Bus companies should have clear policies in place and give training to drivers to help them to remove any barriers which wheelchair users face.[24]

The problem is not however confined to wheelchair users, but all disability groups and elderly passengers. The cause of the problems faced by key vulnerable groups is not the policies adopted by the bus companies per se, but the failure of government policy to account for the commercial interests of bus companies. At heart is the concept of centrality of power. Who has control of a network; and, who allows access to that network?

At least 60 per cent of those in the world who have to live with disability do so in countries where there is often little help available apart from that offered by relatives or friends. Most of those have little opportunity for employment. Some will end up begging on the streets.

In 1971, the United Nations set out rights of people who are mentally disabled and did so in 1975 for the rights of physically disabled people; 1981 was declared to be the International Year of the Disabled. Its motto was 'full participation and equality'. Objectives were laid down to secure equal value of people who live with disability such as:

- To help those with physical and mental disabilities be fully adjusted to society
- To educate people to lead as normal a life as possible – the equal right to full employment
- To encourage shops and public places to make access easier

Late capitalism recruits its subjects by requiring those who will succeed to keep up, fit in and look good. In reaction to this, the disability movement has followed a similar trajectory to other disadvantaged groups. The main solution is to remove discriminatory treatment and prejudiced thinking. This is not going to equalise the situation for people in a post-industrial society. The strong social model of disability proposed that people are disabled by society and not by their bodies (this is fuelled by 'welfare reform' which has cut disability provision disproportionately). Social attitudes are not the only reality, however. Human subjects are disabled by the way they are treated but also by barriers to being part of society that prevents their being able to fit in by dint of their health impairment. The health problems generate limitations (interestingly, 38 per cent of those with disability agreed with this in a recent survey while 46 per cent thought the way their disability generates health problems was the major issue they had to deal with).[25] Anecdotal evidence supports this balance.

For centuries, people have devalued or depreciated the Other because of race, class and gender. But human devaluation also occurs when those who are fit and healthy write-off those who have a disability who need to insist on taking a sense of pride in themselves. Disability has also been a system of social write-off rooted in the kind of people that are valued; in this case able-bodied. Negative attitudes towards the construction of subjects with disabilities have been a site of profound devaluation. To the practical problems that often come with everyday life, prejudicial attitudes by others place even more barriers in people's way and serve to undermine self-esteem.

Other forms of practical outworking of inequality abound. In a country like Malaysia, one-quarter of the people are Chinese, though constituting the backbone of the middle classes. Ethnic Malays control the levers of power. Indians are in even more of a minority, being fewer in number but lacking less power. Minorities of ethnic groups have felt excluded. The poor are also excluded from the New Economic Policy embarked upon a generation ago to raise living standards for Malays by giving preferential treatment to correct an imbalance. Now there are no poor Malay or poor Indians, just the poor.[26] The price is too high. Exactly equal treatment inevitably denies different identity.[27] As I write, there is immense concern about the pressures on the Rohingya Muslims of Myanmar. For centuries, Burmese Buddhism prevailed. No other citizenship was possible, at least in its full version. In August 2017, thousands of Rohingyas poured over the Bangladesh border to escape harassment by security forces endorsed by the State. Legal barriers remained with no pretence to equal citizenship.

Inequality matters because it has practical impact on people's lives. Ask the Jews of medieval Europe!

9

The Argument from Intensified Social Comparison

It is being claimed increasingly that lack of equality places palpable strain on the social fabric. The Centre for Labour and Social Studies, in its pamphlet *Why Inequality Matters* argues that the scourge of inequality had a major role in the financial crisis and that 'greater inequality seems to lead to general social dysfunction'.[1]

Although the direction of causal relationships is not always clear, there is little doubt that inequality is bad for society, associated as David Cameron argued in the Hugo Young Memorial lecture for 2009, with doing worse according to every quality of life indicator. Wilkinson and Pickett described the 'pernicious effects that inequality has on societies: eroding trust, increasing anxiety and illness, [and] encouraging excessive consumption'. They show that for each of 11 different health and social problems, in areas of: physical health, mental health, drug abuse, education, imprisonment, obesity, social mobility, trust and community life, violence, teenage pregnancies, and child well-being, outcomes are significantly worse in more unequal rich countries. An index they compiled of these health and social problems showed that they are definitely worse in unequal societies. These effects, they contend, are most prevalent *within countries* and not merely *between them*.

The crucial question, however, is why? It seems to be not a question of average income. Statistics they adduce show that the link between health and social problems and average income is at best weak. The well-being of children is greater in more equal countries but again is unrelated to average income. What are the mediating factors, the pathways, by which rates of imprisonment, homicide rates and teen pregnancy rates, affect society? The prevalence of mental illness and so on is clearly worse in unequal societies? Something(s) must be driving it. Which way round causality flows is not entirely obvious. It is a fundamental statistical mistake to confuse cause and correlation. For this and other reasons, such recent arguments for an egalitarian society (and by implication a bigger role for the state), have been widely critiqued. Snowdon, for example, argues that the case made by Wilkinson and Pickett lacks empirical support and is pre-disposed towards the need for more government intervention.[2]

What is the evidence that it is levels of inequality per se that is shaping these effects? If equality is defined in terms of where people stand on the income distribution bell curve, they might not be overly concerned with their relative poverty per se matched by society generally. What concerns people most, it may be, is the daily reality of having to pay the bills. To be sure, others looking at the bigger picture would be perfectly entitled to make overall claims about their position in the social league tables. But is this uppermost in the minds of those who have to struggle with income inequality?

The case studies and examples we noted in Chapter 1 might suggest that this is indeed the case. The pressing reality of lived experience is such that the practical barriers individuals and groups in society face of getting access to the same conditions of jobs, education and health care bothers them far more than a general concept of equality, or its lack, applied by those on the outside looking in. If the argument is made that it is where people stand in the pecking order that drives the adverse outcomes that are being widely discussed in the resurgent equality debate, it must be asked 'what are the mediating factors that engender such results?'

The argument by Wilkinson and Picket probes why more unequal societies seem to have higher levels of social ills. Differences between whole populations or countries do not matter for negative outcomes so much as differences within the same population.[3] This raises the question of 'who it matters for?' or not. Negative outcomes could arise from the absolute levels of poverty within each country rather than how they stand in relation to others.

The steeper the social gradient within a society, the more strongly issues such as children not doing well at school will be linked to inequality. They shed light on how inequality shapes the very fundamental outcome of people's lives, their health, the mind and the way people see the world and behave towards one another. Status and how people perceive themselves compared with others is crucial. It seems to be about how people perceive their sense of value and worth. 'If there is this big difference, with some people worth everything and other people worth nothing, where do you come?' So asked Wilkinson in the trailer for the documentary based on *The Spirit Level*.[4] In his view and that of Michael Marmot, it was looking more and more that social status *itself* was a really important determinant of health.[5] Those who feel subjectively lower on the social ladder, or who are objectively poorer, who experience all the negative outcomes.

It is worth examining these claims in more detail. Health and social problems, the authors argue, are linked to the extent of inequality within a country rather than average income levels.[6] 'What matters is where we stand in relation to others in our own society.'[7] Wilkinson and Pickett agree that living up to the prevailing standards and wanting to keep up affect more than just the poor within a society. Yet while societies are endlessly recreating social ills (such as education failure), these problems are more common in the most deprived sections of a given population. Health inequality affects the poorest neighbourhoods, not because of the inequality within them directly, but because they are unequal – or deprived – in relation to the rest of society.[8] Marmot argues in similar vein, that where one stands in the social hierarchy is intimately related to one's chances of getting ill or to life expectancy. For him, the higher the social status, the healthier people are likely to be. These findings cause immense surprise. Why should people with good stable jobs be more prone to illness than someone with slightly higher education or social status? Social status is not an accidental footnote to patterns of health within a society; it is the heart of the issue.

What, however, is the driver behind these observations and statistics? What might be the reason why low status employees have greater risk of heart and other diseases? Marmot is quite clear that 'an important cause of the social gradient in health is that people in different social groups are exposed to different social and economic conditions.'[9] The way that differences in social ranking translates into health outcomes is due to where we stand relative to others. Relative income is a more important determinant of happiness than absolute income. This is where, according to Marmot, happiness research is a window on this distinction. Happiness equates to relative position.

Marmot's earlier groundbreaking study of the effect of health inequities examined health differences among civil servants in Whitehall, London.

There were large differentials across the social scale; a three-fold difference in mortality rates between top and bottom of the scale amounting to a social gradient. Those at the bottom were neither poor nor unemployed yet there was a relationship between hierarchy and health.[10] It seems clear that one person's health may be made worse by another person's wealth. This analysis requires us to stop thinking of wealth simply in material terms. Once there is enough to assure the basics of life for all, wealth is not harmful because it reduces the amount left for another, but because it raises the wealthy person to a higher rank. As social status rises, so do health prospects and life expectancy.

The answer to the puzzle of social gradients, Marmot suggests, is the competition for status and the psychological effects of awareness of its erosion. The relative comparison is between those whose wealth or income has more direct impact upon us rather than billionaires or celebrities who are far removed from our lives. The reason why relative position is important for health and well-being is, he argues, that it is fundamentally about power. It is built into us.

As The Centre for Labour Studies booklet argued, *Why Inequality Matters* comes down to the way that humans are very much affected by their relative position in the social hierarchy. This links into a raft of studies showing the connection between lower status and stress.[11]

Loss of status seems to be a particular killer because it fosters loss of control of one's life and a loss of value. A growing body of research points to economic inequality as having a profound impact on the health and well-being of populations. Life expectancy, crime rates, levels of addiction, obesity, infant mortality, stroke, academic achievement, happiness and overall prosperity are all adversely affected as economic inequality widens. The healthiest and happiest nations are not necessarily the most prosperous, rather they are where wealth and income are unevenly distributed. Generally, the greater the difference between richest and poorest in society, the greater levels of health inequities. It was responding to increasing concern about these persisting and widening inequities, that the World Health Organization established the Commission on Social Determinants of Health (CSDH) in 2005 to provide advice on how to reduce them. The Commission's final report was launched in August 2008, and contained three overarching recommendations – improve daily living conditions, tackle the inequitable distribution of power, money and resources, and measure and understand the problem.

The World Health Organization convened a global conference in October 2011 in Brazil to build support to implement action. Participating Member States adopted the Rio Political Declaration on Social Determinants of Health. It is clear from wide studies on this that distribution of money, power and resources at global, national and local levels are closely linked to economic status. Stiglitz suggested that widely unequal societies do not function at their optimum; their economies are not sustainable because, for instance, disposable income does not get ploughed back into the economy. The rich end up paying a steep price for the invisible costs of inequality.[12] As always the question in social analysis is what is the possible mechanism behind defined effects? Wilkinson and Pickett's analysis in *The Spirit Level*, proposed that economic inequality affected the quality of social relationships. The greater the inequality, the more competitive were the social relationships. There was greater status competition: relationships were degraded and trust eroded.[13]

It is now common knowledge among epidemiologists that status affects health. In the UCL's The Whitehall 2 Project following 17,000 civil servants through time, employment grade has been confirmed as a powerful predictor of premature death. It is not just a question of cholesterol – that low-ranking workers eat in a less healthy way and smoke too much:

> The Whitehall studies have gone some way towards unravelling the mystery of why someone in the middle of the social hierarchy should have worse health than those above them and better health than those below them. There is a social gradient in smoking, in lack of physical activity, and in obesity [...]. The poorest people had the highest mortality rates, while the mortality rates of people in middle income groups were intermediate between those at the bottom and those at the top.[14]

How far people choose between absolute and relative standing has been the subject of experiments. Would participants choose less income if it meant being better off than those around them? It turns out that most people would opt for a better relative position than an absolute level of income.[15]

Psycho-social pathways most important influencers in population health are being better understood. Psycho-social effects of status and inequality go beyond entirely physiological causes. The most important drivers of outcomes seem to be where they concern social relationships. The most common theory among happiness researchers is that people care predominantly about their relative income; that is, how their standard of living compares to people around them. As Oswald and De Neve point out, in a paper presented at the Royal Economic Society's 2012 annual conference at the University of Cambridge, economists do not think hard enough about human beings' need for status. Medical researchers, in contrast, have been making interesting discoveries. They have found that it is rational for people to be obsessed with rank and hierarchy. Success has profound consequences for how well your body functions.

> If you want to live to be 100, get promoted to the top at work. Higher status makes people healthier and gives greater longevity [...]. Even factoring out all these influences, a person's seniority at work remains the single best predictor of long life.[16]

In ways we are just beginning to understand, social comparison shapes lived experience markedly.[17] Conspicuous consumption means that things become the norm and relative gains are neutralised. Relative-income effects matter profoundly.[18] Wilkinson and Pickett seek to show that individuals are affected by the social structure not because they have an income distribution per se (something that is only observable from outside) but because they have relative position. To be sure they argue that it is the scale of inequality that must be changed rather than individual psychology. Nevertheless, sensitivity to inequality comes on account of shared psychological characteristics.[19]

The cognitive turn in social sciences endeavoured to take account of the interaction between mind-emotions and our social experience. It is a commonplace of the cognitive sciences that there are different realities. Rooted in the phenomenological tradition of Husserl[20] and Merleau-Ponty[21] the embodied mind and emotions are a dynamic and plastic way of knowing and as a formative root of one's selfhood and subjectivity.[22] How someone else perceives the world is different to my perception. Experience of reality is not 'a one-size fits all'. Reality is something that is created inside our heads. Every brain gathers together the fragments that come to us every day and from it constructs a narrative. Reality is whatever our brain tells us it is. Routinely, may seem to people misconstrue the social and economic reality they inhabit. But does that matter? Who is the social scientist to deny the subjective sense of reality they lay claim to?

Both poverty and higher status wealth and power have ambiguities that are masked by a formal attribution of where people stand in the social hierarchy. It is an observable fact in the Parish or consulting room that not all those who are poor by comparison have an equal sense of being poorly off. Those who experience what Oliver James labels 'affluenza', often experience an obsessive, envious, 'keeping up with the Jones' that makes apparently better-off people twice as prone to depression, anxiety and addictions than those in many other countries.[23] They can experience the advantages that seem to accrue to them as bars in a 'gilded cage', to use Max Weber's phrase.[24] Affluence can demoralise as vigorously as poverty.

The proposal here is that relative standing and positioning matters because it is a question of value and worth. It is our sense of personal value that is compromised if we have less relative position.

Perhaps in troublesome reaction to this un-brave new world, intensified social comparison is creating serious harm. Proposed by Festinger, a fundamental impetus within the human psyche is that we make constant self-evaluations based on how we measure up against others.[25] Our own frame of reference is continually shaped in a larger field in which social actors perform. How people measure their self-worth is not a question of private judgment but this bigger frame of reference. Necessarily, social actors compared themselves to others for the purpose of self-evaluation. The more someone is different from you, argued Festinger, you are less likely to compare yourself with others. The importance and relevance but also the attraction of a reference group determines the pressure towards uniformity.[26] What then are the motivations towards such referential evaluations? As the theory developed, the drives towards social comparison were seen to be those of self-enhancement and maintenance of a positive self-evaluation. Downward comparisons are more likely when self-esteem is lower to begin with.[27]

Invariably, the consequences are deeply pernicious; 25 per cent of young people, according to a UK study by the Mental Health Foundation, suffer from anxiety and depression, attributable in no small measure to intensified social comparison. There is for instance a well-documented rise in distress among teenage girls arising from social toxins such as models of idealised body shapes, the pressure to look good, consumerism – all of which feeds relative deprivation that others are ahead in the high stakes game of life.[28] If so many 15-year-old girls *of all classes* are emotionally distressed to a significant degree, this phenomenon highlights how we must look at negative social forces in a less fixed way.

Within inter-personal and intra-personal life, social anxiety disorder is well documented. It is the most common type of anxiety disorder and the cause of much limitation. Despite it being common human experience to know what it is like to feel shy or lacking in social confidence, social anxiety is under-recognised and under-treated. Feelings of nervousness or dread in relation to feared social situations might come out as physical symptoms such as trembling, rapid breathing, sweating or blushing. Panic attacks are common. Sufferers tend to be very self-conscious and worried about whether others might be evaluating them negatively.[29]

The idea of social comparison as social dynamic is nothing new. Hobbes had placed as being central to human conflict the passion that proceeds from the imagination or conception of our own power above whoever contends with us.[30] Istvan Hunt points out that Adam Smith, rather than write two contrasting books as often supposed (*Theory of Moral Sentiments* vs *Wealth of Nations*), had a unified view. Crucial to his single project is the notion that social relations depend on the capacity to compare ourselves with others and to have good standing in their eyes. This may be benign, in the sense that self-regarding desire is suspended in favour of impartial assessment of the valid needs of others. But it can also be malign in giving us the motive for greater status; that quest for greater status becomes a spur for us to demand otherwise useless commodities. Hunt argues that although Smith critiques Hobbes' view of conflictual life, our moral sense as well as striving for superiority emanates from this same social dynamic of comparison.[31] Rousseau also, far from being in hock to the idyll of a non-commercial society, saw the human capacity to compare ourselves with others and see ourselves through their eyes as being the driving force for both good and evil in society. While it is true that Rousseau, in his *Discourse on the Origin of Inequality*[32] opposed the harmful effects of *amour propre* (that leads to fierce comparison and emulation), he also believed that social comparison can be channelled into a positive constituent of human relations.[33]

What is new is the effect of both print media and social media. For example women's magazine's 'do not simply mirror our own dilemma of beauty […] they intensify it'. Advertisers, photo features and beauty copy in the glossy magazines 'make up the beauty index, which women scan as anxiously as men scan stock reports'. As Naomi Wolf remarks, in *The Beauty Myth*, what 'men want from women is actually what their advertisers want from women'.[34] In *The Equality Illusion*, Kat Banyard quotes studies showing that just five minutes exposure to thin and beautiful images of women leads viewers to feel more negatively about their body image in comparison to more neutral objects.[35]

Adolescence has always generated anxiety, at least since its discovery in the 1940s. Social media is amplifying a particular self-consciousness, however. Charm, looks and popularity are paraded, weighed in the balance and found wanting. This is an image-saturated environment where there is a disproportionate emphasis on appearance; there is unsophisticated anxiety about rivals in any department and bullying is rife.[36]

It is the impact of the social media avalanche that has given a tornado twist to comparison. Having to cope with peer pressure among many hundreds of young people around you at school daily is hugely magnified by social media. For anxiety is now framing social space, not only inter-personal exchanges. According to qualitative data from the Deloittes sixth annual edition of the UK Mobile Consumer survey analysing the current trends in the mobile industry, almost half of 18–24-year-olds check their phone in the middle of the night.[37] Increasingly, within the general population first thing in the day we spend more time checking emails than eating breakfast. Jean Twenge has analysed how teenagers are more depressed and isolated than ever because of smartphones which may be destroying a generation of young people. They go out less, date less and feel more depressed and suicidal. There is a strong link between the amount of time they spend looking at screens and how sad they feel.

> Around 2012, I noticed abrupt shifts in teen behaviors and emotional states. The gentle slopes of the line graphs became steep mountains and sheer cliffs, and many of the distinctive characteristics of the Millennial generation began to disappear. In all my analyses of generational data – some reaching back to the 1930s – I had never seen anything like it.[38]

In 2012 the proportion of Americans who owned a smartphone surpassed 50 per cent. As Jean Twenge observed, rates of teen depression and suicide have skyrocketed since 2011. It is not an exaggeration to describe this 'iGen' as being on the brink of the worst mental health crisis in decades. It is deeply linked to the vitriolic multiple-personality world of social media.

It was a new and disturbing development. Twenge had already found an upward trend in anxiety. Two meta-analyses find that Americans have shifted towards substantially higher levels of anxiety and neuroticism during recent decades; both college student (adult) and child samples increased markedly. The average American child in the 1980s reported more anxiety than child psychiatric patients in the 1950s. Correlations with social indices (e.g. divorce rates, crime rates) suggested that decreases in social connectedness and increases in environmental dangers may be responsible for the rise in anxiety.[39] Twenge discovered a trend that was linked with that – a rise in narcissism, an unhealthy form of self-esteem. There are similar studies showing a rise in anxiety and depression in many developed countries. Depression among people in their mid-20s was found to be twice as common in a study of some 10,000 people born in the 1970s.[40] A review of studies from 12 industrialised countries found that adolescent girls are increasingly depressed and anxious about their looks. Peggy Orenstein argues that this pernicious self-objectification comes at a cost.[41] It is the fall-out from the wider cultural pressure for women to reduce their worth to their bodies – and this is probably the point. Intensified social comparison devalues human beings.

Very likely, our brains are already beginning to work differently and we are being re-programmed by social media: coded with the expectations of others as Laurence Scott puts it in *The Four-Dimensional Human*.[42] Technological innovations affect how we connect and interact with one another and as a collective, where newer generations are leading the evolution. The broader cultural consequences are just beginning to be felt.[43] 'Your device is learning every day more about who you are and what is important to you. Your life is being downloaded.'[44]

The stress of overwork is fuelled by social comparison and the need to keep up and never switch off. Today's workers are shaped by the high-stakes drive for performance, raised to be equipped to compete. Fuelled by tech firms, the war for talent that generated such huge rises in CEO remuneration has created inequality within companies. A highly anxious workplace became the norm. The social comparison of relative performance becomes a driver of inequality. Many companies have a rating system that can in some cases sack people. Data is collected on staff, on everything they do from the start to the end. Productivity and activity level is measured by algorithms, the new bosses. This will be fuelled by automation and forces an identity crisis. Teachers, doctors and lawyers are seeing their professions change as much as the physical labour of yesterday. How did work go from what we do to who we are? You have become your job.

Everywhere lurks the dark side of the social evaluative threat. Chronic social self threats are integrally linked to the persistent experience of shame-related cognitive awareness. It is causing considerable stress.[45] Indeed, Scheff remarked that shame (in the sense of looking stupid) was *the* social emotion.[46]

The rise and rise of intensified social comparison is underlined by Wilkinson and Pickett in the context of inequality. Rising inequality, they contend, is strongly associated with social status. Inequality accentuates the importance of social comparison.[47] Some will seem to have all the positional goods that desire can cast with envy. Others lack – and are all too keenly aware of it.

Intensified social comparison is therefore a strong reason why inequality matters. It will take us to the core of the thesis in Part Three of this book, that inferiority and superiority are transmitted through relative positions in comparison with others. To end here, however, in *The Spirit Level*, Wilkinson and Pickett remark that one reason why the effects of inequality have not been properly understood is because of a failure to understand the relationship between internal and external factors. It is to this that we now turn.

10

The Psychodynamic Argument: Marx versus Freud

'Domination always involves the objectification of the dominated; all forms of oppression imply the devaluation of the subjectivity of the oppressed.' – Patricia Hill Collins[1]

'Individual psychology and societal inequality relate to each other like lock and key.' – *The Spirit Level*, Wilkinson & Pickett[2]

Inequality matters for reasons that are religious as well as philosophical, practical as well as economic. We are here going to consider briefly another major reason why inequality affects people so profoundly; namely its impact on the human psyche. This represents what might be described as a psychodynamic reading of inequality. Do we have the analytical tools to account for the way that inequality dents the value individuals and social groups might lay claim to inside themselves?

We are going to examine this through two representatives of what is by now the classic tradition of the sociology project and that of the psychological lens on human action. The impact of external social forces upon the lives and consciousness of people was articulated very forcibly by Karl Marx. The way that human beings sought to come to terms with their loves and hates was expressed by Sigmund Freud. Both were well aware of the forces that constrain people. Freud saw civilised society as taming human impulses and squeezing the life out of the psyche. Marx saw ownership of the means of livelihood by others as squeezing the life out of the dignified worker. The former described repression; the latter oppression. But they came together ingloriously within the subjective self.

The esteem in which we perceive we are held by others distils into our own self-esteem. Interior and exterior lives have never been seen as incommensurate. Take the dichotomy between structure and agency. Social actions and social structures are reciprocal and inseparable. As Marx observed, people make their own histories, but not in circumstances of their own choosing. Yet it was an exercise in angry curiosity why people colluded in their own oppression. No less was it for Freud an analytical puzzle as to why people acquiesced in their own repression to the extent of recruiting the ego and superego so it on their loves and their hates. *Libido* and *thanatos* are far too dangerous. Both thinkers repudiated unthinking conformity.

Consider the internalised dynamics of social class, referred to in Chapter 2. 'Where I come from, it was all put-downs. "You'll never amount to anything, it's no good teaching you lot!"' remembers someone growing up in the East End.[3] Class consciousness took centre stage in Marx's analysis of workers' attitudes. He drew attention a false sense of supporting the status quo. Since then, there has been recognition that class (and indeed other identities) do not just lie not on the surface. They go into the fabric and fibre of people. Class and other identities are rooted in ways of thinking and feeling, what Diane Reay describes as 'the psychic landscape of social class'.[4]

Elizabeth Bott suggested in *Family and Social Network* that when an individual talks about class, he or she is trying to say something, in symbolic form, about his or her experiences of power and prestige in social relationships.[5] In an era that proclaimed the death of class consciousness, it is problematic. What it means to be 'classed' or indeed inhabit other identities, is easier to address than the more politicised or socio-economic understandings. Class runs deeper than how far individuals demonstrate politicised awareness of their social positioning. It goes deep into the unconscious. As Diane Reay perceptively notes, class identity is lived on a conscious and unconscious level. It pervades inner worlds and outer practices: 'beneath socio-economic categorisation, underneath class practices, lies a psychic economy of class that has been largely invisible'.[6] Beliefs that sustain injustice and inequality are endemic across the board. They transmit and shape the value and worth of people.

Psychic responses contribute powerfully to the marking of inequalities. Bourdieu's work contributed to the affective lexicon of class. *The Weight of the World* charted the despair and misery that came from lack of recognition and low social standing.[7] Some American studies have mapped the affective dimensions of social class.[8] Yet for the most part, the unconscious dimensions are individualised. Marginalised Feminist studies have been an exception, showing that gender is implicit in everyday social processes, that ambivalence, inferiority and the markings of taste are vital constituents of identity.[9] The psychic economy feature in psychoanalytic insights of race and ethnicity describing racialised identities formed in relational dynamics of fear, power and desire.[10]

Class, gender and oppressive inequalities is deeply etched into our psyches. Sayers gives an account of a psychic landscape of class, one that brings together the static descriptions of social class with unstable, internal dimensions of affect.[11] The account of moral responses to social class includes a combination of arrogance, satisfaction and pride within middle-class 'egalitarian' positions in contrast with the resentment, envy, pride and anger which often constitutes communal solidarity in working classes or the mix of deference, envy or shame featuring in more individual conceptions.[12]

Post-material identities based on ethnicity, disability, gender, age or sexuality that today represent stronger drivers for collective action than just say class, do not just lie on the surface. They go into the fabric and fibre of people. The age of austerity through which we are passing underlines how economic pressure constrains a sense of worth. The psychic hinterland of recession is highlighted when youth unemployment or the low wage economy dents what people feel they are worth. Economic distress is experienced subjectively. Poverty too is not just a description of constraint; it is internalised: scripted on the interior life. So too are forms of value based on external systems that differentiate between categories of people. Inequality matters because it is profoundly subjective. The comparison with others is too compelling.

The repressive effects of power on the interior life are well illustrated in Danny Dorling's magnum opus *Injustice* which traces the deleterious effects of toxic contemporary beliefs on the way human beings are stunted.[13] For example:

- **Elitism is efficient and natural** – the children of the lower classes obviously have less ability despite being portrayed as lying along bell curves (as if such things are natural and real).
- **Exclusion is necessary** – it is justifiable that one in six households in rich countries are excluded from social norms as well as being poor in at least two ways we count poverty.[14]
- **Prejudice is natural** – disdain and fear by those at the top towards those lower down the social ladder is maintained by inherited wealth and the deep social polarisation that ensues.
- **Greed is good** – a society that places such salience on consuming leaves casualties; a quarter of households are out of the equation by dint of not having access to car or to internet.[15]
- **Despair is inevitable** – depression and chronic anxiety is a fact of social life that is becoming more obvious in a society constrained by the injustice embedded with prevailing norms.[16]

Such continued beliefs in the tenets of injustice are, in Dorling's view, the contemporary equivalent of the five social evils that defined injustice – lack of education (ignorance), lack of money (want), lack of work (idleness), lack of comfort (squalor) and lack of health (disease). They are endemic within the ideological structure of society in the same way that holding slaves or withholding the vote from women was once considered 'natural'. Certainly elitism has made a strong come-back from the more egalitarian 1970s. In *Dream Hoarders*, Richard Reeves argues that the 'opportunity-hoarding' US upper-middle classes are making it far harder for everyone else to climb the economic ladder. Reeves defines the upper middle class as those whose incomes are in the top 20 per cent of American society. Income is not the only way to measure a society, but in a market economy it is crucial. Access to money generally determines who gets the best quality education, housing, health care and other necessary goods and services. Reeves argues that the growing separation between the upper middle class and everyone else can be seen in family structure, neighbourhoods, attitudes and lifestyle. This is self-perpetuating. Those at the top of the income ladder are becoming more effective at passing on their status to their children, reducing overall social mobility. The result is not just an economic. Upper-middle-class children become upper-middle-class adults.[17] This matters. Legitimate resentment inevitably arises if birth counts for more than brilliance. High-income parents pass on their class status to their children, threatening American ideals of equal opportunity and social mobility.

Marx's March

Karl Marx would not have raised an eyebrow at such fracturing of American society along class lines. It was how the system worked. 'Twas ever thus. His analysis of social evils was that it came down to who owns and controls the productive forces in a capitalist economy. Marx's 'The German Ideology' inveighs against the notion that thinking alone produces social distress.[18] What is needed is to change the system and hierarchies that imprison men and women within a class bound society.

The question in social analysis is how one defines the forces that constrain people. It is the standpoint of this book that external social forces constrain human life by transmitting value and worth in a way that shapes internal psychic forces that react against them – 'you are worth less'. External social value impinges upon internal, personal value (or its lack) with marked effects, leading to internal strategies of switching positions. These are the psychosocial dynamics of inequality.

The intriguing Marxist 'Frankfurt School' sought to expand its analysis beyond class in order to come to grips with the failure of a German revolution after World War I and the terrifying forces on the march in the 1930s. Its then director, Max Horkheimer, proclaimed in his inaugural lecture that the Institute must address 'the question of the connection between the economic life of society, [and] the psychological development of individuals'.[19] The contemporary need he said:

> is to organise investigations stimulated by contemporary philosophical problems in which philosophers, sociologists, economists, historians, and psychologists are brought together in permanent collaboration to undertake in common that which can be carried out individually in the laboratory in other fields.[20]

Worker alienation could produce a revolutionary sense of class consciousness, Horkheimer believed, but it could also produce worker disenchantment and resignation.[21] When it comes to inequality, an issue that loomed so large in the Marxist lexicon, the question in social analysis is why it can go either way? Above all, the Frankfurt School sought to grasp capitalism not just in its materialism but in its psychological condition and effects. Hence the interest in Freud.

It was a question of human beings, essentially workers who produce their value and rise to self-consciousness through meaningful labour, interfaced with the material substructure of life – the economy. Amid the twists and turns of the Institute's engagement with Critical Theory, a young psychoanalyst joined the Institute, Erich Fromm, later to be a poster-boy for the public face of revisionist psychoanalysis. Fromm's work was a blend of Freud's account of psycho-sexual development and Marx's insistence on the material substructure as experienced through economic and technological transformations. The classic Oedipal complex was linked to the underlying state of the economy. Neither parental stables reacted well to the melding of Freud and Marx. The former considered it constituted no realistic programme for the transformation of society while the latter regarded it as heresy. Intriguingly, Freud himself had just published *Civilisation and its Discontents* arguing that society would always be repressive, though not because of class domination.[22]

In fact Fromm was not really working with orthodox Freudianism in anything else but name. It was his way of bringing Marx into his own emerging account of oppressive regimes. The apparatus of child development and human instincts were modifiable, Fromm thought, by economic conditions.[23] Melding social forces with desire and its dilemmas was all very dialectic.

Perhaps his best known work, *Escape from Freedom*, Fromm had shifted ground to believing that human instincts were not so much shaped by the familiar psychoanalytic categories as social conditions.[24] But then that was 1941 and Fromm was endeavouring to explain (as did the rest of the Frankfurt School) the dark phenomenon of Hitler and why if humanity cannot stand freedom, it will probably turn Fascist. Democracy brought into existence a society where human beings feel isolated from others, where relationships in an industrial age are impersonal and where insecurity replaces a sense of belonging. It is this isolation that may compel people to seek escape in blind devotion to a leader or into a barbarous and sadistic program of aggression against minority groups.

Deeply relevant to the spirit of our times, and more relevant perhaps to our enquiry here is Fromm's contention that other entities can act as causes but the cause of their acting is external. The human person is a subject in that he or she possesses interiority, self-direction and creativity. Fromm made a pertinent observation about the relevance of this to resistance.

> There is hardly a psychic state in which man cannot live, and hardly anything which cannot be done with him, and for which he cannot be used [...]. Despots and ruling cliques can succeed in dominating and exploiting their fellow man, but they cannot prevent reactions to this inhuman treatment [...]. Whole nations, or social groups within them, can be subjugated and exploited for a long time, but they react.[25]

The seedbed of reactions to inequality? It was later, in 1955, that another leading member of the Frankfurt School, Herbert Marcuse, would challenge Freud's pessimism that repression (or oppression) would always be with us. Unbridled gratification will always be at odds with society's need for discipline and conformity. Marcuse disagreed.[26] Marcuse himself was developing the powerful critique of both communism and consumer capitalism, *The One Dimensional Man*, that was to position him within the decade of radical political change we call 'the sixties'.[27]

The power of consumption has advanced in terrifying measure since either Marx or Freud, eclipsing productive forces as being key to how contemporary societies function. Consider, for example, the way that if people find themselves at the bottom of the pyramid, to then value their 'intrinsic selves' when others are so materialistic requires either great tenacity or requires them to borrow extra money to supplement their pay. As Dorling comments, 'you borrow it to buy things which others like you have because "you're worth it" and you want to believe you are like them, not inferior to them'.[28]

Or if you believe that a valuable person is a well-paid person, Dorling goes on to remark, it becomes especially important to accrue debt when income falls in order to maintain self-esteem. Economists since Adam Smith have after all noted the mortifying effects of social downgrading.

A Greek Morality Play

In Freud's exploration of the inward nether regions that was by turns archaeological and geological, his belief that he had come to the crux of the human situation was reflected in the Oedipus complex; a fundamental description of primeval exchanges cast in the form of a Greek morality play. Freud regarded dreams as the royal road to the infernal realms of unconscious life. He was surely mistaken. The unconscious is not as Freud supposed a dark, primeval place of unruly impulses but is sophisticated. The possibility of a first person perspective requires a strong defence of the uniqueness of the human person.

The 'I' is my consciousness of myself as a person, able to intend, to act and to give a reason for what I do. As individuals we recognise ourselves as human persons. Yet we are also inescapably social. As Susan Sontag insists, the Freudian perspective is also inescapably body-centred. Although people such as Eric Fromm in his revisionist Frankfurt School Freudianism posed the worthy claim of fulfilment through love, love does not only mean comfort and protection, it encompasses the claims of sublimation. 'Freud insisted on sex, he insisted on the body [...] but as he himself declared, when he used the word "sex" he might as well have used "love".'[29]

This was psychic determinism in full throttle. By contrast, Sartre considered that 'the fundamental project', the notion that each of us a basic purpose to fulfil, was a more satisfactory way of understanding the subject than the Freudian unconscious with its panoply of subterranean forces that surfaced and disturbed.[30] Where Freud said, 'I cannot', Sartre wants to say that what is really meant is 'I will not' – in other words, assertion of personal responsibility rather than determinism.

It was much less hydraulic. As in every dialectical scheme, the question is what supplies the energy for generating the opposite to an original state. The dialectical method, central to Marxist politics, especially in the writings of Lukács and members of the Frankfurt School, was the most celebrated pattern of action and response to inequalities and social injustice.[31]

Using the dialectic analysis of Hegel, Marx proclaimed the working class as the instrument of the final revolution of history. Famously, Hegel had argued that each stage of social processes is the product of contradictions inherent or implicit in the preceding stage. The whole of history is a progression from self-alienation as slavery to the self-unification of free citizens. For Hegel, a doctrine of negation was vital to this movement. Something is only what it is in relation to another, but by the negation of the negation this something incorporates the other into itself. The opposite is overcome.[32] The usual formulation is that of thesis, giving rise to its reaction, an antithesis, which contradicts or negates the thesis, tension between the two being resolved by means of a synthesis. (Hegel himself never used that specific formulation, ascribing terminology of the model to Kant.[33])

Critics have observed that the Hegelian dialectic cannot be mechanically applied to any particular thesis. The selection of any antithesis, other than the logical negation of the original position, is subjective. If that is so, selection of a synthesis is also arbitrary and the resulting contradiction rhetorical rather than logical. Nevertheless, Hegelian dialectic has had a strong outing historically. Most famously, in the hands of Marx, dialectic was wedded to historical materialism in the form of the primacy of economic conditions explained the inevitability of socialism as the final resolution of internal contradictions in social development.

> The mystification which dialectic suffers in Hegel's hands, by no means prevents him from being the first to present its general form of working in a comprehensive and conscious manner. With him it is standing on its head. It must be turned right side up again, if you would discover the rational kernel within the mystical shell [...]. With me, on the contrary, the ideal is nothing else than the material world reflected by the human mind, and translated into forms of thought.[34]

The whole sociology project is an endeavour to account for linking the social system with the cognitive dimension of human action. Functionalism, a very influential paradigm, looked at what happens when people interact; that is, linking the social system with the cognitive dimension of human action.[35] Goffman, for instance, proposed models of organising social reality – what he called frames – in the form of 'an interaction order' of things, akin to rules of engagement.[36]

All this has echoes of the German philosopher Jurgen Habermas, second-generation leader of the Frankfurt School in its resurrection after the Nazis shut it down. Communicative action, he suggested, is a rational process whereby two or more people interact and co-ordinate their action based upon agreed interpretations of a situation.[37] Habermas argued that mutual search for understanding and the compelling power of a better argument based on inter-subjective rationality makes communication and action possible. The function of the agreed rules is to keep social interaction going. The problem with these ideas is that there is no power-free human interaction.

Habermas ignores the way that the rules of social engagement merely reinforce the status quo and keep down marginalised groups.[38] And it has to be questioned how far human action is framed by people sitting around in coffee houses. It is surely events that shape action and reaction. The theoretical challenge is to explain the responses within our cognitive function that generates social systems. 'It must have something to do with the fact that social systems are made up of human beings who produce such social structures in their interaction.'[39]

It was drawing on Hegel's earlier work that Axel Honneth, third generation director of the Institute of Social Research and student of Habermas, suggested that failure of recognition constitutes a kind of insult or threat stimulating a struggle to overcome the attack which in turn brings about a positive development.[40] Honneth's emphasis throughout his writings is the importance of inter-subjective relations and not just economic relations. It is lack of recognition that undermines the solidarity of oppressive states. Whether or not social injustice or even violence are perpetrated because those with power misread the ontological status of others – or just simply oppress them – is a vexed concept. To this we will return briefly.

The proposal in this book is that inequality matters profoundly. Social experience is shaped by the value that is placed on people. Personal value is impacted by social worth. The question is, 'what happens when such collision occurs?' Oppressive regimes have been described in different ways, some internal, some external. How do they overlap? How do external forces reach into the psyche?

It depends upon how we categorise the forces that constrain human beings. Borrowing these two leading thinkers as eponymous representatives of whole traditions of thought, Marx and others saw human action through the lens of *oppression* or class pressures that sit on top of men and women and crush the life out of them. Freud and co. saw *repression* as playing the vital role. As Frankfurt scholars were well aware, these regimes of constraint are configured very differently.

- **Marx** – ownership of productive forces by a minority bourgeois that exploit alienated workers, obliged to see their surplus labour value creamed off.[41] Human beings should be considered social and are essentially producers, not just rational animals as Aristotle and subsequent philosophers argued. It is capitalism that sees people as isolated individuals.[42]
- **Freud** – human beings are ambushed from within by dark forces arising from the unconscious. External constraints combine with internal awareness of guilt to keep in touch with primitive, passionate libido and aggression; our loves and hates.

> The discontents to which all societies are susceptible [...] entailed the most drastic interference with the passionate desires of the individual, the

> suppression – and repression – of instinctual needs, which continue to fester in the unconscious and seek explosive utterance.[43]

A division between external (the sociological) and internal (the psychological) has always been artificial. These two sources of constraint are experienced in a unified way in the lived experience of human beings. We do not pick out the source of external pressures from their inner impact. Social anxiety or status that people feel keenly as an internal failure very often emanate externally but then locks on to cognitive and emotional structures in a pernicious way.

Freud's analysis left out the social dimension of inequalities. Marx left out the psychic economy. The view of equality espoused is very different. Marx and classic theorists of oppression described the impact of being *classed* in terms of political positioning and a false consciousness that should be repudiated. But a crucial dimension is the effect that being relegated has on the psyche.

If we accept that a psychodynamic reading of inequality makes sense, against the background of the grand narratives of social theory, what theoretical framework should we find helps to clarify such social dynamics? Foucault, for instance, focused on issues of power. It is not a matter of either you have or you do not; power circulates through social life in subtle ways. We are all enmeshed, everyone implicated. Forms of power are mediated through the state and its institutions whereby technologies of social discipline have a profound effect on human consciousness and the sociology of emotions.[44] Words are weapons. Language and discourse are central to the practical outworking of dominant ideas. Power has a lot to do with value and how different forms of value are exchanged and operate within a given society. As a recent analysis of the power structures in south-east Asia makes clear, your life is worth far less if you lack power. Competition for power is life and death for life and the psyche.[45]

A major route through which power relations and oppressive categories of inequality shapes inner subjectivity, is, I propose, the effect of socially assigned worth that de-personalises humanity and devalues us. However, this comes up against what has to be a major drive in human action, the inner need to be of value. Specifically, it is the collision of external value with *value-in-oneself* that channels socially assigned worth into inner worth or its lack.

Unequal social relationships are characterised as the exercise of power relations. Value is imposed or imparted according to the nature of the relationship (most obviously family or economic). Someone else makes the shape you have to fit into. Although Marx did not use the notion of social value, he did have a great deal to say about surplus value as being the output and expression of the worker that was creamed off by the bosses and owners. An exploitative capitalism could be none other than a system that entrenched inequality and social divides. The alienation of workers from their work emasculated their humanity.

Several generations separate Marx and Freud. What they shared was a common cultural tradition, a coercive social order where oppression and repression had become synonymous and where self-repression was self-abuse. Herr Docktor Freud seemed to have little sense of the value and worth of people. As the curtain opened on the psychological century, Freud's *The Interpretation of Dreams* was a drum-roll, not just for a method of psychological treatment but a new way of looking at human beings.[46] Freud's hagiographer Ernest Jones remarks, 'starting as a theory of certain illnesses of the mind, it went on to become a radically new and momentous theory of mind itself'.[47] Freud quoted Virgil – 'If I cannot bend the gods above, then I will move the Infernal regions'.[48] We have to become aware of how our neurotic responses derive from the inner depths, notably the way that desire is at the heart of the earliest relationship. Life is about managing two major dynamic forces motivating human personality from the Unconscious, the reification of sexual energy, and the urge towards death – *eros* versus *thanatos*. Before we can respond to life without fragility, we have to become aware of how our neurotic responses derive from unconscious primary processes in the inner depths. We have to recognise that we are in ourselves a site of resistance as well as a building site.

Freud saw little inherent value in people. 'I have not found much "good" in the average human being', he wrote to his friend Pastor Pfister. 'Most of them are in my experience riff-raff.'[49] An inconvenient rabble persisted in finding their way to Bergasse 19 in Vienna, reinforcing his belief that few patients are worth the trouble he spends on them.[50]

Nevertheless, the effect psychoanalysis had on the culture of the West is incalculable, 'offering a kind of secular salvation, comparable in its totality to that which had been offered in the literal sense'.[51] Psychodynamics focus on unconscious processes that by-pass conscious activity. The task of Freudian psychoanalysis is the recovery of the unconscious and to bring drives to the surface. Although the idea of the unconscious came to be superseded by research into how the brain functioned, what Damasio calls the embodied mind, key assumptions became part of the currency of our time.[52] 'The unconscious nature of mental processes, the peculiar mechanisms they obey and the instinctual forces that are expressed in them' are concepts that became taken as read.[53] We later grasped that matter and energy are not to be put into different boxes as Freud supposed.[54] Nevertheless, Freudian psychodynamics does provide a roadmap of all the right questions – the kind of questions that personality psychologists have been asking ever since.[55]

But if psychodynamics offer a mind-map of the human, where is the need to be heard, to feel worthwhile, to be taken seriously? This is a silence in the psychoanalytic discourse.[56] And where are their opposites and the reaction that funnels humiliation and the put-downs into mental defiance? What is the mechanism that can explain what happens in the mysterious depths when it is *we* who seem to be attacked and not just what we *do* that is on the line? Does such a recognisable peculiarity attach itself to the noisy unconscious world or the landscape of conscious existence and its meanings?

> Self-esteem has not been a major content area for psychoanalysis […]. Lack of genuine self-esteem is the result of personality problems, however, not the cause of such problems and analysts do not treat esteem problems directly.[57]

Psychoanalysis did nothing to value women. Freud indeed famously characterised women as being subject to envy – damaged creatures with a lack instead of whole persons in their own right. In *Neurosis and Human Growth*, Karen Horney disagrees. If some women want to be like men, it is because they perceive men as being freer to act.[58] Early psychoanalytic politics is riven with envy, jealousy, paranoia and ambition – a hothouse of charismatic egos and an odd situation for those who claimed that to experience their therapy was to embrace a more exalted state![59]

Nevertheless, Freud had struck a cultural moment. Second-generation neo-Freudians went on to describe the inner world in terms of object relations, attachments as well as the curiosity of the orgasmatron – Wilhelm Reich's combination of science fiction and sex in a box.[60] The French psychoanalyst Jacques Lacan proposed a rather different formulation of our psychic structure, the *real* (roughly corresponding to Freud's 'id'), the *symbolic* (superego) and the *imaginary* (the ego).[61] From a Lacanian perspective, Parker describes the revolution in subjectivity to do with the politics of the subject, subverting the link between therapy and capitalism, objecting to 'the bio-political management of populations and individuals in which medical psychiatric practices compatible with late feudalism inform the psychologisation of individual subjects under capitalism'.[62]

The approach taken by Freud's one-time associate, Alfred Adler, carves out a little more space for the value of other human beings as well as oneself.[63] It was configured as a problem of inferiority. Adler argued that individuals are motivated to attain equality or superiority over other people to compensate for organ inferiority. The typically masculine need to act and become powerful to compensate for feeling inadequate undergirded Adler's Masculine Protest.[64]

There is therefore little scope for the role played by a dynamic concept of social versus personal value in the dramatis personae of psychic forces any more than in the usual line up of social forces of which Marx is prominent exponent. This creates a problem, a lacuna. It is to do with value-in-oneself and how that is translated into the forging of new subject positions as sources of action. The impetus to realise our worth is a neglected topic in social psychology or psychodynamics. It is fundamental to why inequality matters. Why has this not been an active dynamic in accounts of human action?

As we will now see, there is an internal impact of inequality which does not come just externally but which finds an answering echo from within. Inequality (diminishing), is the politics of reduction, of insult, of a denial of a full measure of humanity. Being belittled or placed in a passive position sustains dependence and vitiates against walking with heads held high as a free and equal participant in social relations.

The relationship between forms of power and forms of value warrants investigation. To this we now turn in an endeavour to bring a conceptualisation as a lens on the inner dynamics of inequality.

Part Three

Clarifying Social Dynamics of Inequality: Notes on a Theory

11

A Theory of Social Relativity

'When you wake up in the morning, you do not think about triangles and squares and these similes that psychologists have been using for a hundred years, you think about where you are in relation to your peers.' – Michael Gazzaniga, neuroscientist[1]

'A rich man is one who earns $100 more than his wife's sister.' – Henry L. Menken[2]

Inequality matters because of internal effect; that is, it is not just a question of how it affects people externally through lack of income or access to equivalent resources, jobs and places. Inequality impacts on the person, and in particular, his or her sense of inner value. Social worth impinges upon interior value.

We will explore the proposition that behind the various ways that inequality purports to get under the skin lies, not so much questions of *status* or *power*, but questions of *value* – in particular the value of people that economic or social worth conveys. We will go on to give a psychodynamic reading of this in terms of relative position versus an absolute sense of our identity. Society perpetrates a category error.

The proposal here is that relative standing and positioning matters because it is a question of value and worth. It is our sense of personal value that is compromised if we have less relative position.

Relative Poverty

It is in recognition of relative effects that social scientists coined the notion of 'relative poverty', in which people lack the minimum amount of income needed in order to maintain the average standard of living in the society in which they live. The concept of relative poverty is considered the most meaningful way to measure the level of poverty in an individual country as it is defined relative to the members of that society and, therefore, differs across countries. People are said to be impoverished if they cannot keep up with the standard of living as determined by society; in the case of the United Kingdom, 60 per cent of the average income. In 1965, Peter Townsend developed a definition of relative poverty. Anyone with an income below 140 per cent of a household's entitlement to National Assistance, which was the main means-tested benefit in the United Kingdom from 1948 to 1966, was living in poverty.[3] Even those above the National Assistance level were regarded as still in poverty. It is of course arbitrary. Why 140 per cent at that moment? It could be regarded as so generous as to conceal the real nature of poverty. This definition would result in many millions being 'in poverty'.

In time, Townsend concluded that a definition of poverty based solely on income was inadequate.[4] A garden or allotment, decent housing, good working conditions and caring friends or relatives are also important in maintaining a lifestyle that is half-way decent. Poverty created exclusion from the accepted lifestyle of a community. Households deprived of a significant number of indicators of deprivation were deemed to be poor. It did then mean that a deprivation index was an objective measure of relative poverty. Critics said that what Townsend really had in his sights was inequality.

Relative poverty also changes over time. Lack of private, indoor toilet facilities would not have seemed odd to our great-grandparents. Now it is a mark of poverty. An 'absolute' definition of poverty, as compared with a definition in terms of relative income, is arbitrary. As a society becomes more affluent, the 'poverty line', as popularly perceived, will also move upward. Minimally adequate food, shelter and clothing will be available to most members of western societies.

The concept of relative poverty – based on the customary index for relative poverty of being under 60 per cent of median income – is intended to explain why people's views of their own economic well-being are inextricably intertwined with the idea of equality. A sense of relative deprivation is probably more about social justice or fairness ('to each his due') than equality per se. Relative poverty can mean a race to the bottom. Median earnings can fall and therefore relative poverty falls. Poverty measured by how everyone else is doing is only part of it. People do respond on a relative scale but from their absolute measure of what they afford.

In *The Price of Inequality*, Stiglitz points out that economists talk a lot about the importance of 'relative income' and 'relative deprivation'. What matters for an individual's sense of well-being is not just absolute income but income relative to others. 'Individual's concerns with their consumption relative to others – the problem of "keeping up with the Joneses" – helps explain why so many Americans live beyond their means – and why so many work hard and so long.'[5] Spending seems to increase among those who live in a community with higher income inequality, though so too do bankruptcy and self-reported financial distress. This is not helped by credit being available – often at extortionate rates of interest.

A field of research has opened up, 'trickle-down consumption', that probes whether rising income and consumption at the top of income distribution since the early 1980s induced households in the lower tiers of the distribution to consume a larger share of their income? Using state-year variation in income level and consumption in the top quintile or decile of the income distribution, Marianne Bertrand and Adair Morse of the US National Bureau of Economic Research found good evidence for this. Middle income households would have saved between 2.6 and 3.2 per cent more by the mid-2000s had incomes at the top grown at the same rate as median income. Additional tests argue against permanent income, upwardly-biased expectations of future income, home equity effects and upward price pressures as the sole explanations for this finding. It was rather that middle income households' consumption of more income elastic and more visible goods and services seemed particularly responsive to top income levels, consistent with status-driven explanations.[6]

Economists have little doubt that the relationship between GDP growth in more developed countries and subjective well-being is an open question. It is far from settled.[7] Indicators of subjective well-being (SWB) go beyond the scope of this essay as this is an industry in itself. Reported SWB consists of two distinctive components: an *affective* part, which refers to both the presence of positive affect (PA) and the absence of negative affect (NA), and a *cognitive* part. The affective part is an hedonic evaluation guided by emotions and feelings, while the cognitive part is an information-based appraisal of one's life for which people judge the extent to which their life so far measures up to their expectations and resembles their envisioned 'ideal' life.[8] Ed Diener and his associates produced a scale of human flourishing that has been well-used, as has his earlier scale of Psychological Well-being.[9] Their related Satisfaction with Life surveys probed questions such as:

In most ways is my life close to my ideal?

- The conditions of my life are excellent.
- I am satisfied with my life.
- So far I have gotten the important things I want in life.
- If I could live my life over, I would change almost nothing.[10]

A definite critique can be mounted of this happiness industry – that it is far too individually conceived and offers little criticism of the injustices in society. Comparison income and status matter profoundly.[11] So why does it matter it matter that countless numbers in society perceive a sense of relative deprivation that others are ahead in the high stakes game of life?

A Conceptualisation of Relative Effects

The consensus among happiness researchers is that people care predominantly about their relative income – how their standard of living compares to people around them. Paradoxically, if we all get to own BMWs, those cars are not much worth having. There is only so much rank to go around.

As we are seeing, it is vital for debates in society about lack of equality that understanding is developed about relative effects, whereby social actors see themselves as not getting on relative to others or being held back.[12] Lack of fairness will affect the moral relationships that bind society together but there is a reality that must also be taken into account; the internal worlds that people inhabit and what inequality does to them on the inside. Devaluation is the real culprit – the sense of being of less worth relative to others.

A hundred years ago, Albert Einstein published a famous paper applying the General Theory of Relativity to model the structure of the universe as a whole. The General Theory was seemingly at odds with a universe that is eternal and unchanging. This type of universe is not consistent with relativity. To fix this, Einstein modified his theory by introducing a new notion, the cosmological constant. With a positive cosmological constant, the universe could remain conceived as a static sphere that had always been. Einstein's publication of his modification of general relativity in the paper 'Cosmological Considerations of the General Theory of Relativity', marked the birth of modern scientific cosmology.[13]

Frames of reference were the subject of Einstein's special theory in his *annus mirabilis* of 1905 amid a trio of breakthroughs. Both time and space could no longer be regarded, as in the Newtonian model, as absolute containers within which bodies moved so as to change their location over time. Einstein's special theory abandoned an intuitive description of the world in terms of absolute space and time in favour of a counter-intuitive four-dimensional spacetime. Hence observers moving at different speeds got different answers when measuring lengths and durations. Einstein was, in his General Theory, only extending the relativity principle to any accelerating system of reference.[14] The special theory described the implications of local frames of reference as a general postulate that reshaped absolute conceptions of space and time. An inertial system at rest has its own frame of reference.[15]

An extrapolation of the relativity principle into the social sphere was provided by Alan Parducci in his seminal work on judgmental relativism. Parducci used psychophysical scaling techniques to model subjective judgment through a range-frequency model. Total happiness can be represented as a weighted average of all positive and negative experiences. Judgments of individual episodes depend on comparisons with an entire set of episodes that may be relevant (especially the most extreme ones).[16] Parducci asked his readers to consider an outing on either of two ships: a low-speed sailboat or a yacht capable of a high top speed. Since the value of any experience is computed, in part, as the experience itself *relative* to the peak experience (i.e. top speed), greater satisfaction will be provided by the more leisurely sailboat consistently travelling near its top speed than the faster yacht that rarely reaches its peak (a relationship described as the sum of each boat's observed speed divided by its maximum speed). Within the context of a distribution of judgments in a given frame of reference, Parducci concluded that 'The average level of happiness can be raised by arranging life so that high levels of satisfaction come frequently, even if this requires renunciation of the opportunity for occasional experiences that would be even more gratifying'.[17]

In his book *Falling Behind*, the economist Robert Frank argues that if you had a 3,000 square foot house when everyone else had one of 4,000 square feet, you would feel uncomfortable about it. Yet if we had to choose between living in an area where the latter was the norm, even if it meant a long commute to work, we would choose that over a 3,000 foot square house.[18] The impact of inequality and social comparison is clearly context-sensitive. This affects patterns of consumption. Context matters. Against this background, I conceptualise as follows:

- How inequality affects people is to do with their subjective experiences; these will vary. It is their internal affect and thought processes that will shape whether they are demoralised or just get on with their lives. Practical barriers to equality will affect people at this level. Larger patterns of injustice and concern can be discerned and it is at this higher order thinking level where economic and moral arguments matter.
- Relative position within the same frame of reference matters; which leads on to intensified social comparison in which social media is but the latest symptom.
- The experience of subjects.

The subject position that people inhabit is crucial for how far lack of inequality is a strong concern and source of distress to them. It profoundly affects how they will react to the broader pressures that bear down upon them. Social participants have sufficient agency, I contend, so that they can respond from a different position than the location that might be the consequence of that pressure.

Economic, social and environmental indicators do indeed matter at the larger 'system level' and field of behaviour where national and international trends can be discerned. The concept of subjective well-being is able to capture's people actual experience in a direct manner, while broader indicators do so only indirectly. What is experienced does not of course have to coincide with objective conditions. For many that is why SWB indicators are useful complements to objective indicators.[19]

Viewing the higher order thinking about overall trends within which individual lives play out, the point is, however, that the bigger picture constitutes different magnitudes of systems and it is at that broader system level that the concern about social injustice and proceeds not being shared out evenly weighs most heavily. Moral and philosophical objections to inequality per se (as distinct from pernicious individual experiences of poverty or discrimination) apply most obviously here. This social field of national or international arenas might be described as a 'second level' account of economic and social experience. This is not to decry the importance of the patterns which social historians can discern over a wide field of activity.

Constituting the Frame of Reference

We will return in the next chapter to the 'first level' issue of subject positions that social participants adopt and switch from in the way they experience these broader pressures that shape their lives.

Here let's note that the frame of reference applicable to the way people experience inequality will be drawn differently, according to the referent group.

When it comes to our social standing, attitudes and aspiration, both positive and negative, are shaped by the frame of reference within which they are situated. 'Reference groups are groups that people refer to when evaluating their [own] qualities, circumstances, attitudes, values and behaviors'.[20] The frame of reference leads to social actors feeling aggrieved, if for example they are denied promotion at work. If they hope for more than can be achieved, they will be discontented. The concept of relative deprivation has been used to describe the psychological effects of when A, who does not have something, compares himself or herself with B, who does. The group which provides a standard of comparison is the normative group that is in contrast with those that look-on. It is the context of inequality in which a perception of relative deprivation is engendered.[21]

As Runciman notes in an older text, *Attitudes to Social Inequality in Twentieth Century England*, relative deprivation depends on how one chooses to delimit the boundaries between groups. 'All inequalities which give rise to feelings of relative deprivation must be treated as inequalities between and only between the membership reference group and comparative reference group.'[22]

Reference group theory is familiar in social sciences. Reference groups act as a frame of reference to which people always refer to evaluate their achievements, their role performance, aspirations and ambitions. Merton and Rossi stress that 'some similarity in status attributes between the individual and the reference group must be perceived or imagined for the comparison to be applied'.[23] The term 'relative deprivation' was coined by the authors of *The American Soldier*, a large-scale psychological study of the American Army undertaken in World War II. Looking at how soldiers viewed their chances of promotion, it was clear that such opinions 'represent a relationship between their expectations and their achievements relative to the others *in the same boat with them* [my emphasis]'.[24]

Though I wish to re-conceive this as a question of inner value in dialectic relationship with social value, this topic is usually conceived of as a question of status and the referent group for the purpose of social comparison. Both within the brain and also behaviourally, social participants set considerable store by status. It matters profoundly.[25] Human social hierarchies are prominent in different domestic, professional and recreational settings, where they define implicit expectations and action dispositions that drive appropriate social behaviour.[26] Gaming this, it has been shown that players earning money in a simulated computer game and told they could thus boost their status, reacted very markedly to the status of fellow players.[27] Comparisons between oneself and an individual of higher status underlie an important role for hierarchical rank in achieving accurate self-knowledge and self-improvement, particularly when it comes to upward social comparisons.[28]

The question is, however, what constitutes a frame of reference? It is known, for instance, that poor people living in richer neighbourhoods die sooner.[29] Perceiving a discrepancy in social status can cause stress that provokes a range of health factors. This suggests that the frame of reference needs to be proximate in order to feel the weight of inequality effects. It might be the disparity between those in the same neighbourhood where one family is worse off and might have a second-class car parked outside that triggers a sense of them being second class.

The applicable frame of reference might be the disparity between those earning more within the same company for doing broadly the same job. This situation reflects gender inequalities or those based on other forms of discrimination. It matters more if those whose face fits and have a higher value (reflected in being higher up in the wage economy) are working in reasonably close proximity.

It might be a school where students and staff are placed together in close proximity and might feel obvious differences between them in terms of being of slightly higher or lower worth.

In an internet age, the frame of reference might be those with whom one is bound by being in an electronic peer group who have been given power over you (imagined or not) to ridicule and trash. Here the frame of reference that constitutes a local nexus of social forces is being given influence, not by geography but through emotion rooted in electronics. As with most forms of discrimination or communal attitude, such social forces are generated by broader cultural trends, potent in framing expectations and norms of the standard issue people. I might not be made to feel unequal to a celebrity earning vast sums or might not be subject to relative poverty living in a poorer area or country. By comparison with those nearby, I may carry an invisible load of a weighty freight.

What is going on though with these relativity effects taking place within a social force field? What form of explanation might be driving the very impetus to respond with social comparison?

One candidate could be status anxiety, an anxiety about what others think of us; about whether we're judged a success or a failure, a winner or a loser. As Alain de Botton describes in *Status Anxiety*, we care about our status for a simple reason. Most people tend to be nice to us according to the amount of status we have; hence the loaded first interrogation of new acquaintances is 'What do you do?' or secret dismay at the success of our friends.[30] We suffer – to a greater or lesser degree, usually privately and with embarrassment – from status anxiety.

It is true that we worry about what others think of us. Status anxiety might help to describe social comparison of occupation, possessions or wealth but that might not explain gender social comparison; for example, that women in the United Kingdom do 60 per cent more housework than men due to gender roles being loaded with expectations.[31]

Status is not a straightforward matter. Within a social hierarchy, status can be brought into focus through such vehicles as uniforms, the honorifics of carpet thickness in an office and explicitly the kind of car one drives. The concept of status anxiety is a descriptor rather than explanatory. What is it that makes for concern and consternation about the comparisons in the first place? In short, the concept does not seek to explain why agitation arises.

Social envy is another possible driver. Chapter 81 of Rawls' *A Theory of Justice* addresses 'Envy and Inequality' and refers to Nietzsche, who placed envy at the centre of social relations and psychology.[32] Rawls, however, did not regard envy as an intrinsic part of human relations. In Nietzsche, *ressentiment* is given the form of the relation of master and slave, which reduces the slave to *ressentiment* in the powerlessness which prevents the execution of revenge against the master.[33] *Ressentiment* clearly translates from French as 'resentment' and as it contains the word 'sentiment' brings in strong overtones of feeling itself. Nietzsche regarded the animal which can feel consciously as the animal which has a consciousness structured by *ressentiment*. In Nietzsche, that refers to the desire for revenge frustrated and turned into an impotent obsession with imaginary punishment. It is suggested that time itself produces such a reaction, as time places the past outside the power of consciousness. The realisation of the relation is a major dramatic and structural element of *Thus Spoke Zarathustra*;[34] and is discussed in *On the Genealogy of Morality* in a relatively discursive manner.[35]

The conceptualisation I wish to advance here is as follows. The effect of inequality upon human beings is shaped by the dynamic of what I will call 'switching positions'. Whether we are discussing inter-personal exchanges where individuals might feel diminished, or wider influences and unconscious systems of society bearing down on people, the move between absolute and relative frames of reference does much to determine both the impact of inequality and the capacity to move from a different position to what might otherwise be the case. It is to this move that we now turn.

What enables the self to switch positions from socially assigned value to value-in-oneself?

12

The Politics of Positions

'Life was about the different stands you could make.' – Cosmo Jarvis, song-writer and film-maker speaking of music being a response to very difficult life experiences[1]

'Everyone is born ok [...] there is a profound difference between the intimate worth of our existence and any evaluation of our behaviour. Our being is unquestionable, our actions may not be [...]. Whatever we do, every life has its own unique value. Clients are helped to restore this belief in themselves as intrinsically worthwhile.' – *Humanistic Approach to Psychotherapy*, Eric Whitton[2]

At the heart of social processes is an unconscious strategy of switching positions. As we will see, society perpetrates a category error. Social participants often take what could be seen as a comment or even an assault on their position relative to others – and make it something far more serious. It is an attack on *them*. Central to the way people experience perceived unequal treatment is that it digs down into a sense of themselves. The frail self engages in a strategy of responding from a different place from what may have been intended or from perceptions of others. People move from a different subject position than that of relative status. They respond from an absolute view of themselves that is now under assault. Hence a psychological reading is essential. It is especially in the field of inequality that internal psychological dynamics are the logic of social processes. The way that equality or its lack affects people on the inside cannot be separated from the collective impact on whole groups of people being left out in the cold. The psychodynamics of inequality are central to its corrosive impact.

We are going to consider here a fundamental pattern of response to forces that bear down on the individual and inner life, a response that could help to clarify social dynamics. A driver of human action that seems fundamental to inequality's inner impact is that of the capacity people have to move from at least two subject positions.

1 An *absolute* sense of their value and of themselves – who I am
2 A *relative* sense of themselves in relation to other points of comparison, be they wider societal groups or inter-personal players – what I am doing

In response to social forces or situations of discrimination that generate inequality, human beings tend to oscillate between these two polarities. They will often react from an absolute subjectivity, even where a given context was not intended to generate such a sensibility.

In societal contexts, social comparison is not necessarily intended as a fundamental attack on identity. But it will often be taken that way. Social media can trigger an absolute sense in someone that *they are on-the-line.* It can trigger an existential moment when it is not what they do or how they look that is under review, their very identity is no longer secure and indeed is being laid siege to.

In the inter-personal arena, a difficult situation might be might be a job interview or appraisal, it might be facing those whose frames of reference pose an anxiety or source of fear or it might be a situation that is now radically re-constructed. Instead of a constructive comment, the occasion is construed as destructive. It is not our purpose to explore this inter-personal dynamic in this essay so much as to note it as a window on social processes. Our contention here is that the pattern of pressure and response in individual life that is evident in the consulting room or in the parish can illuminate wider social dynamics.

Different subject positions are available to human beings responding to perceived pressures they experience. Within inter-personal life, Eric Berne's *Games People Play* was a text that became the foundation stone of transactional analysis (TA).[3] TA described the different positions people adopt – parent, child and so on – in terms of the stance to which they retreat and from which they engage in different forms of exchanges.

Relationship trade takes place within a force field of complex patterns that is always subject dependent. How we come to a true understanding of the human person is fraught with complexity. It may be answered philosophically, from the ontology of our being, yet be tripped up by social sciences when that human essence makes a foray into the world. The human is not a mere phenomenal being, to be assimilated into community or state. He or she is not the product of impersonal forces. It is the essence of phenomenology that the human person is not only to be known empirically from the outside but as an intuition from inside.[4] Yet the outside observer seeking to analyse the forces upon and within the human person is entitled to ask how deep does it go? Do the various subject stances analysed by Eric Berne and his school cohere with a substratum of interior tectonics?[5] Or is the knowing subject choosing unknowingly from a menu of options that has no fixed abode?

This does of course imply that humans have sufficient agency to take up those positions. Of great conceptual clarity here is Michel Foucault's proposal that individuals respond to different situations and issues by adopting subject positions.[6] Because every situation is unique and is rooted in expectations and contexts that mould us profoundly, subject positions are in flux and fluid. Different positions can be maintained. Foucault showed how the social discourses that are so immensely powerful in society are laden with various subject positions: that is, specific positions of agency and identity relative to particular forms of knowledge and practice. For human beings to become subjects of a particular discourse and therefore bearers of the power/knowledge that goes with the territory, we must locate ourselves in the position where that discourse makes most sense. It is worth pointing out that Foucault's postmodernity invoked the impersonal play of forces that replaced the dynamics of action advocated by Sartre amongst others:[7] Nietzsche also in his espousal in his *Genealogy of Morals* of the slave and the master (in which the slaves join forces to undermine the master's moral regime).[8] However, Foucault did argue that we are the subject of discourse, its meanings, power and regulations but also subject to the discourse if we put ourselves within it. This is not then full-blown social determinism in which we are shaped by the play of impersonal forces that subjectivise us; we have the agency to relocate.[9]

The potential for us to move back to a position where we do take things personally does pre-suppose agency and the freedom to liberate ourselves from oppressive forces that constrain and devalue. Personal responsibility militates against the sense of victimisation and 'being done to' that is so pervasive today. In some modern or post-modern philosophy that has rejected the notion of the subject, this is illusory. The death of the author means that the third person vocabulary has replaced the first person way of looking at ourselves. Yet there does seem to be a first person position and he or she can be activated. The existentialists insisted that we understand what we are in the world through our own choices.

As Davies and Harre, suggest once having taken up a particular position as one's own, a person inevitably sees the world from the vantage point of that position and in terms of the particular images, metaphors, storylines and concepts which are made relevant within the particular discursive practice in which they are positioned.

> A subject position incorporates both a conceptual repertoire and a location for persons within the structure of rights for those that use that repertoire. At least a possibility of notional choice is inevitably involved because there are many and contradictory discursive practices that each person could engage in.[10]

Like the flux of past events, conceptions people have about themselves are disjointed until and unless they are located in a story. Since many stories can be told, even of the same event, many possible coherent selves are available. Often, class positions are characterised by resentment, defensive, guilt and shame, 'the balance of these feelings and the ways of handling them are likely to vary according to class positions'.[11]

A reactive model of inter-personal change is inherent to the social psychology of G. H. Mead. The intuitive sense of human individuation is a developing process by which the person can form an identity through interaction with others who recognise that identity and offer approval and the means for expansion of the circle of social environment. As consciousness of human identity grows, the subject is dependent on conditions for recognition afforded in that social environment. It is because every individual needs constant reassurance by significant others, the experience of disrespect threatens an injury that could cause the identity of the individual to be at risk or even to collapse.[12] The self is compelled to reassure itself that it is autonomous and a distinct individual, forced to assume the standpoint of a 'generalised other' from whom inter-subjective approval is needed.

Within the social field, various other stances of action and reaction are available. Essential to the strategy of resistance, for example, is a stance, a move that can dissect, distance and differentiate. Those defined by lack or invisibility discover through the re-valuing of themselves expressed through the Protest that they are more complete and visible. Identity needs to be expanded beyond an identifying mark inscribed on the surface. *My Name is Not Dementia* expresses this strategy well, a report published by the Alzheimer's Society affirming the on-going humanity of those who can still enjoy life, despite their condition.[13] Those engaged in a move of re-valuation reject the dehumanising labels that have defined their condition in the eyes of others, removing words like 'handicapped' that set up cultural norms.

How the Theory Works

With these considerations in mind, the notion of 'moving from A' translates as follows.

Someone experiences pressures in certain social situations that press down upon them and threatens to 'depress them' or leave other marks of collision. It might be a comment on what they do, how they look, or a reminder of social status within the power-laden inequalities of society. This person might:

1. Handle the devaluing situation in a way that places them relative to others but without the absolute attack on identity. Resilience in that setting means it is not 'core'; capacity for perspective is engendered and quickly.
2. Handle the potentially devaluing situation in a way that constitutes a temporary attack on him or her. The human subject of such action is on the line; on trial; not for their life but for the equally serious existential crisis of demoralisation of identity. The trial might persist for a short-time or be a trial of some length in which the human subject is weighed in the balance and found wanting. For as long as the trial persists, within that context, the person is 'moving from A' (i.e. responding from an absolute sense of their identity feeing that it is at risk).

The point is that social pressures that engender inequality *are being experienced at an absolute level* – not just from a position relative to others.

Those who experience what it is like to feel shy or lacking in social confidence do so relation to others yet experience as an assault on their inner self. A theory of social relativity as considered in the previous chapter might lead us to think that frames of reference in relation to other entities are the determining subject position from which responses are made. However, when it comes to an existential moment triggered by situations that are felt as pertaining to core identity, the frame of reference shifts. It is no longer the distancing mode implied by social comparison that the subject might be resigned to. Rather, an absolute frame of reference is highlighted.

The kind of human experiences where these sharply differing reactions might be played out are seen most obviously within the social settings that frame individual life. To be sure, it is notoriously hard to separate such inter-personal actions and responses from the pressures of wider social systemic operations. When does a comment about what one is wearing or saying that engenders inferior status remain as strictly between the social actors involved and become a specific translation of trends and forces that are shaping society at any one time? Appearance or anorexic anxiety is social; there is hardly an inter-personal frame of action and response that is not.

Nevertheless some human experiences might be classified as broadly inter-personal. A client has a marked tendency to take everything as a slight, a comment about the client directly that lays siege to his or her identity. For reasons that are rooted in the client's psychopathology, the client responds from this subject position. It is extremely hard work to promote the perspectival shift that could delimit the numerous incidents that represent 'moving from A' and re-cast the various dramas as occurring within a relative frame and thus gaining the perspective of distance from the client's own inner core.[14]

Within the more directly social side of the boundary line that reflects the classifications of social psychology rather than intra-psychological processes, the kind of experiences rooted in comparison with others that seem to be readily convertible into an absolute sense of self rubbished include:

- Locating a sense of value in *the appearance 'stakes'* – obsession with size zero. Medical technologies to improve appearance are now routine in a society where people work on their bodies rather than their souls.[15] Bodily insecurity rules.[16] The global marketing of such discontent results in restless personal renovation and self-improvement. Fascination with the celebrity super-class co-inhabits with alienation from attractive norms. Obliged to live in two worlds, the subject dwells in ideals that are far-out of reach. Distancing carves a place where people live out their fantasy.

- *Status and class anxiety* – a study showed that putting someone into a weak social position impairs his or cognitive function. Participants in an experiment were divided at random into 'superiors' and 'subordinates'. The latter group were told that the superiors were directing them and that their evaluation would determine the subordinates' payment. The subordinates were sub-divided into the 'powerless' and the 'empowered', feelings which were intentionally reinforced. It became clear that 'empowering' people (raising their sense of value?) sharpened cognitive function.
- Parents who experience *empty-nest syndrome* as an erosion of worth. Parents experience their children growing up. They are not needed as they once were. The empty nest beckons and then where shall they be? To compensate, they end up spending more and more time in a voluntary capacity above and beyond their paid work. Or someone else is working later and driving himself harder.[17] This too is a source of significance – home and inter-personal life are difficult areas today.
- *Performance anxiety* – why it is that women have particular susceptibility to eating disorders and the way these forms of self-harm relate to feminine identity and cultural obsession with bodily imperfections?[18] Society's obsession with the shape and size of women's bodies has helped shape a generation of anorexics. Being thin has come to signify qualities of character such as self-control and strength as well as beauty, success and happiness. Anorexia is about control, using a strict attitude to weight is a defence, arguably the only one the anorexic has, against chaos. Rather than helping anorexics to accept and befriend their bodies, the hospital may view they body as a problem, an enemy. As Lucy Johnstone claimed, 'treatments which focus solely on weight gain are falling into the same trap as the anorexic herself; they are treating her body as an object, as something separate from her.'[19]

The position of women, especially women with children, is affected by this.

These demoralising effects arise because they go beyond relative comparison. Relative effects translate into an absolute sense of self being weighed in the scales and wanting. Take performance anxiety in children generated by high-earning, high-achieving parents who want their offspring to be outstanding. Average is just not good enough. Performance is valued by the parents because at stake is the deadly business of status symbols. The impact on their highly pressured sons and daughters can be demoralising. Children from affluent homes are three times more likely to suffer from anxiety and depression than the average teenager. This places them at greater risk from drug abuse, eating disorders and self-harm.[20] Children who are not allowed to express themselves or be themselves will rarely believe they are loved for themselves.

Eating disorders are often linked with low self-worth. As with anorexic girls, it is 'where I stand in relation to others doing OK' that can exacerbate demoralisation and constitute a profound challenge to one's personal value. People give up and accept that a lowered sense of a valuable self is here to stay. The effect of ageing or unemployment often brings this kind of reaction. The client reports feeling written off and that is intensely de-stabilising, contributing often to depression among the elderly or newly retired. These effects are more than social evaluation. They arouse an underlying sense of self that feels devalued relative to others, affecting negatively a sense of value-in-oneself.

These responses translate into identity – who we are. They constitute a core challenge since relative social and economic valuing is experienced as an absolute sense of identity. In effect, society inflicts a category mistake. Social attitudes can generate a perceived lack of respect surrounding bodily gestures, inappropriate words or actions. They dig down into a substratum of the value of persons. The result is a taking of offence that evokes an absolute sense of a valuable self being trashed. An insult, a non-negotiable affront, has been made.

Inequality as Category Error

We are developing a framework for understanding the psychological impact of relative poverty and inequality. Arguably, it is value-in-oneself that is under assaulted in the range of psycho-social impact of relative effects such as unemployment, anorexia or status anxiety. Effects relative to other's place in social life are being experienced as an absolute threat to our being. They may purport to be about how we look, what we do or what we are not now able to do. Yet it is far more serious than that. So too are some forms of inequality and their impact upon people. This is why inequality matters. It engenders social distress for many that is harmful precisely because it assaults core identity whether temporarily or longer-term. The inferior status thus conferred creates certain effects.

These effects are potentially lethal because they are the politics of value. Social and economic life as well as inter-personal transactions continually shape and mould what might be termed 'self-worth'. Nevertheless, individuals and groups continually function from another subject position that of value-in-oneself, derived not only from external valuing but from inner capacity. Arguably, it is this switch of subject position that functions as a psycho-social driver, I suggest, in high value society.

In the hands of later post-modern philosophers, such as Deleuze, what we see is not the politics of reactive possibilities so much as the panoply of impersonal forces.[21] Many of the French philosophers of his generation had in their sights the grand figure of Jean-Paul Sartre. The notion of an alternative agency from which human beings can respond is basic to Sartre's philosophy of freedom and responsibility. Sartre's friend Levi-Strauss attacked him on the grounds that structuralism provided a more satisfactory view of the human consciousness. Different societies had anthropological structures that varied.[22] How could universals be valid if the consciousness of an indigenous ethnic group in South America differed so profoundly from that of a Northern European? In short, some strands of philosophy were not fertile ground for the notion of some kind of response or even 'mechanism' patterned into the human mind. The post-modern mood music has been to reject the rage for unity, the totalisation, so central to the western philosophical tradition.

Is it really a category error though? Questions must be asked if such experiences of inequality or pressures are intentionally diminishing – and whether that is the point? The proposition then can be expressed as follows: social actors can and do move from different subject positions than external value conveys.

Forms of human devaluation such as unequal treatment can also trigger a response, a dialectic that tells us a lot about how we function. We will dignify this reaction with a capital letter and call it, the 'Protest'. The heart of the Protest is the response to devaluing individual human transactions, family or social systems, a reflex that asserts, 'I'm worth more than that!' The pursuit of a high value for ourselves runs deep into the psyche. It emanates from interiority but is in sharp collision with the external factors of social life. It is this collision, I will be arguing, that is a major driver of social life. The Protest is precisely this bid for autonomy, for resistance and self-governance yet is more than that. It is a turn towards a more valuable self. It is not a single act but a mood. Yet while experiences of devaluation can trigger a range of demoralising psycho-social effects via an absolute sense of ourselves as being worth-less or inferior goods, another response is possible and indeed happens constantly in social and personal life. We will now examine this more closely.

What shapes people's experiences in contemporary life is the value that society places on them. As a determinant of social experience, this emerges when its contrast pole is evoked. To discern the pivotal role that value-in-oneself plays in social and personal life, it is necessary to track the response to human devaluation. We propose that this arises in response to three factors:

1. *Inequality (diminishing)* – the politics of reduction, of insult, of a denial of a full measure of humanity. Being belittled or placed in a passive position sustains dependence and vitiates against walking with heads held high as a free and equal participant in social relations. This is conceived of as the internal effects of inequality.
2. *Indifference* – not being seen or heard or given attention; being disregarded, set aside or left behind. People become invisible products, dependent on recognition, seeking significance.
3. *Indignity* – the politics of invasion, of violation of sacred space that is the essence of violence.

In response to these factors, the subject will make bids, bids that need to be listened and validated for the underlying theme playing. The notion of 'switching positions' seems to be an important strand of how we understand the struggle for value. When a client consistently responds to the pressures and threats of everyday life as a core challenge rather an issue relative to others, it is a reliable indicator that devaluation has taken place that has gone deep and created wounded history.

The challenge of an approach to address the motivation towards human value is to stimulate self-awareness about both causes and processes of devaluation, offering options to individuals to act and react differently to the impact of the constraining influences upon them. It highlights the need to elaborate one's own theory of human action before applications can be developed. Are human beings free to respond differently to the discourse that has shaped their lives and the social processes within which that discourse is embedded? Against the background of debates about agency and structure in social sciences, I suggest that stimulating reflexivity around one's own struggle for human value can engender a first person perspective that is the birth of a valuable self.

A giant category error is generated by social life. Faced with being devalued externally, people respond on the basis of value-in-oneself. External valuation collides with interiorised value (or its lack). The effect of the category mistake is to perpetrate ontological misrecognition. Comparison with how others are doing is just too important to be taken relatively and with a healthy dose of perspective. It eats away at our underlying value and worth and for that reason can triggers a core challenge and existential crisis. Arguably, class, gender and all forms of difference are responded to as if statements are being made about their absolute value and worth, not relative worth.

> The point about economic and social inequality is that people thereby perceive themselves as being of lesser worth by comparison with others, divorced from the good life or the good times everyone else seems to be having. Yet people can often respond from an absolute sense of their worth. Social value is thereby translated into personal value. In their effects, social structures have been translated into behaviour patterns that are a stone's throw away from being pathological.
>
> I don't feel ok about myself [...]. I believe I'm not worth very much [...] not a good person [...]. Don't talk to me about being told I don't count for anything. I've lived with that for 40 years![23]

Something has been impaired at a profound level when we agree with our critics. A sense of a valuable self has difficulty growing under such circumstances. A corner-stone of how to delineate the psychodynamics of human devaluation is what can be termed, 'moving from A' – an *absolute* sense of our own worth when that feels under attack. Certain experiences result in a client changing subject position. It is not just what they do or say by comparison with others that has been devalued: it is what they are that is at stake. How this triggers demoralisation may illuminate how some relative effects become translated into threats to our absolute or intrinsic value. Experiences of devaluation can trigger a range of demoralising psycho-social effects via an absolute sense of ourselves as being worth-less or inferior goods. A regular tendency towards 'moving from A' is a sign that earlier devaluation has occurred. Someone has been consigned to being second-class goods or written off.

'Moving from A' means that clients shift to a subject position (which may be their default position) of reacting as if they themselves are in court. Being has taken the place of doing. A category mistake has been made. There is an intriguing aspect to this category mistake, a propensity to switch to a default position of a devalued self. If a child feels that its worth has been measured by what it does, rather than what it *is* (i.e. unconditional love), the result is likely to be a readiness in adult life to take criticism of what one *does* as a personal attack. Being and doing changed places.

Differentiation is replete with messages about who are high-value people or who are of lesser worth. These texts of social and inter-personal life are demoralising because they assault an absolute sense of worth people need in order to flourish. They also stir up reactions of Protest, rooted in secret knowledge of value-in-oneself. This mechanism leading to a reflex of 'I'm worth more than that' is fundamental to social life. We also find this social mechanism in inter-personal life.

At the core of this dynamic is a strategy for role switching. Whether intended or not, factors in social life that seem to assault the absolute sense of inner value that people have will often accomplish demoralisation. Yet that is not the last word. For there is a response that can be stirred, which asserts a valuable self in the teeth of demoralisation. This mechanism switches position back to a stance relative compared with others which enables people to cope with the slings and arrows of outrageous life. It reverses the assault.

Arguably, it is value-in-oneself that has been assaulted in such situations of distress as it is in the range of psycho-social impact of relative effects such as unemployment, anorexia or status anxiety. Effects relative to other's place in social life are being experienced as an absolute threat to our being. They may purport to be about how we look, what we do or what we are not now able to do. Yet it is far more serious than that. Such experiences threaten us, rob us and mug an inherent sense of a valuable self rendering us 'worth-less', or even 'worthless'. Factors in social life that seem to assault the absolute sense of value-in-oneself will often accomplish demoralisation.

An effect relative to others is experienced as an absolute threat. A core challenge has been triggered. It may be as a result of labouring under the pressure of expectations about the life led as a woman in a developing country, as one of an ethnic minority group or subject to class-based poverty of aspiration. Being different from standard norms or made to feel unequal has huge potential for engendering anxiety and low-self esteem precisely because it strikes at an absolute sense of a valuable self. Inequalities engender an absolute assault – not just that which is relative to others. It digs into value-in-oneself with certain effects. Those effects we are about to conceptualise.

13

Understanding the Triggers: Indifference, Indignity and Inequality

'Attention must be paid – even to a salesman.' – *Death of a Salesman*, Arthur Miller[1]

'I don't see why I should carry the can when I'm treated as rubbish.' – Anon[2]

'I am an invisible man. No I am not a spook like those who haunted Edgar Allen Poe; nor am I one of your Hollywood-movie ectoplasms. I am a man of substance, of flesh and bone, fibre and liquids – and I might even be said to possess a mind [...].That invisibility to which I refer occurs because of a peculiar disposition of the eyes of those with whom I come in contact.' – *The Invisible Man*, R. Ellison[3]

'You treated these young people as if they had no dignity and were not entitled to any respect.' – a judge sentencing seven men in a case of sexual exploitation in Manchester, UK[4]

This proposal is for a social theory based on the idea that much of our experience as individuals or in groups is shaped by the value society places upon its participants. It is intended to start a conversation about how questions of human value shape our lives and how the erosion of value is a category that clarifies social dynamics. The aim is to challenge usual approaches to how social value moulds human action by suggesting that it collides with a felt sense of inner value and evokes a response, resistance rooted in assertion of dignity and intrinsic worth. The previous chapters outlined a working assumption that the value of persons plays a major role in modernity; indeed that contemporary life would be unthinkable without this as an aspiration.

Now we are to examine the social transmission of value before considering how this impacts upon personal worth. In the way the world used to be run, to be high born, to come from a higher status profession, or to be born a white Anglo-Saxon male was enviable while their contrasts were of lesser account. Human devaluation both transmits the inequalities of the world but it also reproduces them. Fundamental to the social transmission of difference is that this is achieved not just by reproduction of material factors but the reproduction of scales of value. We have theorised three circumstances in which disvaluing is generated in personal life. How do these play in wider society?

The Politics of Indifference

Issues of value are not just aspirations; they are key narratives in human functioning. The first pivotal point in which human value is either eroded or enhanced is through not being heard, seen or given voice. This is a strategy of persistent lack of sensory response by those without eyes or ears. To be heard rather than ignored; to be seen rather than disregarded are actions that generate strong positive feelings of personal value rather than a denial of our full humanity.

To be shown face or to offer face is a fundamental human need. Is this, for instance, why there has been a shift from a top-down model of international development to a bottom-up model?[5] The issue of welfare dependency offers a parallel concern. Where there is an impersonal system without face that renders people passive, participants are robbed of agency and have no opportunity to do facework and return the gaze.

Often, teachers and professionals are heard, saying of children, 'it's all about attention-seeking!'[6] Such a reaction ought not to attract disdain. This is what humans do. Those same professionals would complain strongly in their field if they were not being heard.

Such responses are often framed in terms of such social psychology theories as self-verification.[7] People want to be known and understood by others according to beliefs and feelings grounded in how the self is viewed by itself and through consequent self-esteem. It is because self-view plays a key role in making sense of life that people are motivated to maintain them through self-verification.

To be seen (noticed) and heard communicates that I am worth listening to. In Adam Philips' psychoanalytical study of excess, *On Balance*, he explains excess as a desperate search for limitations by a parental figure who will say, 'no'. Exaggeration is a strategy for gaining attention, to know that somewhere there is a restraining hand and someone to care for us.[8]

'Please validate me, hear me,' cries a young woman constrained by mental illness. 'Say it's OK to feel like this.'[9] It echoes the vital need to be heard. Unacknowledged distress is profoundly devaluing. It strikes a blow at the human subject, not just the words he or she is uttering or the angst with which those words are expressed. The need to be heard, to be seen – this is an Emporium of the senses.

Race was a composite concept, built from such an Emporium of the senses. How African people sounded along with the the European belief that their skin was rougher and their hair coarser and that they smelt different played important roles. But above all, it was visual appearance that was the most important marker of race, especially skin colour.[10] The status of sight became predominant in communicating disvaluing. An African looked different.

The gaze is fundamental. Winnicott proposed the concept of the 'good enough mother', who looks her baby in the eye and by mirroring the child's face shows the child that he or she is known, safe and seen.[11] The most essential parenting psychological function, Winnicott suggested, is 'eye-love'.

Disvalue and value are communicated by acts of gazing. How we treat someone results from how we see them. The unformed self is called into explosive being through parental gaze – whether smiling eyes that sustain secure attachment or indifferent eyes that disappoint a baby looking up. It is a century since Charles Cooley formulated the idea of a 'looking glass self'.[12] Neuroscience has since confirmed that we are made in the mirror. The new-born infant endeavours to regain eye-to-eye connection with its mother. It becomes expert in scanning facial expressions.[13] Language comes later – and with it the ability to name the world. A whole new branch of neuroscience has grown, dedicated to exploring how people come to know the minds of others and their own minds. Elegant studies indicate that infants know something about other minds by making inferences from their own experiences and their experience of others.[14]

Experiences of devaluation are generated along the lines of imbalance of power. Where someone or some group holds more power than another – and the other knows it, there is often a deployment of resources and a show of strength that values them over and against another. One party in a relationship, one social group, must rise; another must fall. It is a zero-sum game. Power imbalance is the raw material that shapes human interactions resulting in a lessening of worth. Yet such a reduction in value does not only arise from the exercise of power. Erosion of worth and dignity are also a matter of perception. Issues of value are communicated – or denied – through recognition.

What an amazing sleight of hand is conveyed through vision! The act of seeing magically transforms people and situations. Self-worth feeds self-identity – the way we perceive ourselves. An individual seeks to break free from the all-encompassing way he or she is seen.[15] A social group demands to be seen differently, to have a greater stake in the politics of attention. Perspective means a different way of seeing which counteracts the asymmetry of vision.

I write this in South India where homeless Dalits (untouchables) are regarded as being lesser individuals, not to be sited on the same street as Brahmin families, even in a poor village. A wall has been (literally) built so the Brahmin families do not have to look upon their underclass neighbours. Maybe the wall serves a dual function. Perhaps the Dalits feel they are being shielded from superior eyes. Devaluation is closely bound up with the gaze. Someone who does not think they are worthy of respect does so because they do not see themselves in that light. Value and worth are accorded through acts of vision. The gaze communicates either value or disvalue. The act of seeing transmits because it triggers. It reproduces what is perceived. The other rarely looks at the self from the perspective from which it sees.

The gaze triggers a reaction. Sartre insisted that a shared gaze generates a struggle over who is to be subject and who is to be object.[16] 'I felt I was repulsive,' says someone, who complains of being treated with disrespect.[17] His sense of himself as shameful arises because he perceives himself in the eye of those who disrespect him. It was an act of seeing – or so they thought – that triggered a temporary self-loathing. The client now sees himself in a certain way and that act of vision is intrusive. It intrudes, it molests, until the self is seen as worth-less or even worthless.

Meanwhile, in the Unite Kingdom, one of my clients has new neighbours, who are on benefits.[18] The neighbours become aware of those that live next door. 'What are you looking at?' is their belligerent assertion, provocative (or reactive) because no gaze was intended. It is rather in their perceived vision of superior eyes that they feel an affront. Their own gaze has misread, misperceived the vision of another, casting their own self-regard on to the perception of their neighbours who they see as 'looking down' on them. The internal gaze has somersaulted next door to attach itself to the face of the neighbour that in turn triggers a reaction. The gaze is devaluing because it is cyclical, interactive. It not only sees what is there; for better or worse it transforms what it sees. The human situation is one where the self is able to see itself. Projectors all, we take up a position outside of ourselves (or so we think) and look at ourselves. The problem is that such reflexivity (which is the essence of self-reflection) can reproduce false images. We see ourselves in the mirror. The capacity to be self-regarding is essential to the human condition yet sometimes, the gaze is too intense. A characteristic of some psychological conditions such as being bi-polar or paranoid is that sufferers are all too aware of the gaze to the point where eyes are everywhere, even to the point of being re-located in a split self. In a condition such as obsessive compulsive disorder (OCD), every action comes under the most intense scrutiny.

A sufferer of OCD comes to realise that his or her intense scrutiny of the body is greatly exacerbated by a fear of how others will see him or her as a contaminated person. Fear of dirt is fear of scrutiny. A dearth of smiling eyes and regular criticism has generated panic about how the person with OCD is seen. In turn, his or her self-regard has hijacked the vision of how he thinks others will perceive him. Distorted vision communicated by not feeling up to the mark has become a circular problem and a channel for transmission of disvaluing of self.[19]

This is the kind of raw human experience that has aroused considerable philosophical speculation. Hegel emphasised that we need acceptance by others as we work out our identities. If there is a 'Me' for whom the 'Other' is an object, this is because there is an 'Other' for whom the 'Me' is an object. 'The Other cannot act on my being by means of his being, the only way of that he can reveal himself to me is by appearing as an object to my knowledge.'[20] Two self-consciousnesses collide. A master–slave relationship for instance is colonised by power. It is not just the underdog that is affected. The master sees himself as the oppressor.

Recognition leads to the bifurcation of the world. In *Psyche: Inventions of the Other*, the French philosopher Jacques Derrida comments that the 'I' is never at home in the world, never at one with itself. The self includes the sense of a turning or swivelling mirror.[21] To locate oneself in the world requires the experience of a 'kind of vertigo of place', everything related to everything else (as in Derrida's 'distracted theory', there is no saturation of context).

Power is a fluid concept. It does not just arise from formal social relations but flows around them. Often the river is reversed. A client reports feeling de-skilled by her partner; her independence now but a memory.[22] This may exemplify the social forces of gender construction shaping the dynamic between them or inter-personal dynamics per se (as if these could somehow be separated). Yet the point is that subversion of this mini-social order within the family (resulting in her having not felt she was worth very much) began with fresh perception of herself (based on prior recognition of worth).

> The problem of recognition of our value, what in philosophical terms is a question of anthropology, emerges too in discussions about shame. Shame is, Sartre argues, by nature recognition. I recognise that I am as the Other sees me. 'The human being is not only the being by which negatives are disclosed in the world; he is also the one who can take negative attitudes with respect to himself'.[23] The Other has not only revealed to me what I was, he has established in me a new modality of being which, potentially, was not in me before the appearance of the Other. I need the Other to realise fully all the structures of my being. Sartre considers the phenomenon of shame, a mode of consciousness which is: 'a shameful apprehension of something and this something is me. I am ashamed of what I am. Shame therefore realises an intimate relation of myself to myself. Through shame, I have just discovered an aspect of my being.'[24]

Shame is important for what it reveals about ourselves.

In *The Struggle for Recognition,* Honneth argued that there are three distinct kinds of recognition, which support three distinct stages in the development of individuals, each with quite different social and political implications. Critics have pointed to his failure to even consider the significance of the dominant relationship of modernity, the commodity relationship.[25] Together with Nancy Fraser, his subsequent work, *Recognition or Redistribution?* argued for the priority of ethical categories such as recognition over structural social-political categories such as class redistribution.[26] Honneth's most recent work *Reification* reformulated this idea in terms of inter-subjective relations of recognition and power. For Honneth, all forms of reification are due to intersubjectively based pathologies and lack of recognition rather than the structural character of social systems such as class.[27] It may be doubted that the problem behind conflict and distress is ontological misrecognition but there is nevertheless an important topic to be investigated here.

The demand for recognition assumes that our identity can be distorted through non-recognition in a way that becomes internalised. Black people or feminists adopt a self-depreciation that then serves as a potent instrument of their own oppression. Due recognition is a vital human need. As Charles Taylor observed in *Multiculturalism and the Politics of Recognition*, 'democracy has ushered in a politics of equal recognition, which has taken various forms over the years, and has now returned in the form of demands for equal status of cultures and of genders'.[28] The notion of recognition was developed by Hegel as intrinsic to core humanity.[29] Following Hegel, Charles Taylor proposed that 'the struggle for recognition can find only one satisfactory solution, a regime of reciprocal recognition among equals'.[30] Taylor's *Politics of Recognition* explored what kind of human communities can be moulded from human diversity. What lies behind a politics of difference, he argued, was development of a modern notion of identity.[31] Receiving recognition from others is a vital human need. Our identity is partly shaped by recognition or its absence, often by the misrecognition of others.

Following this kind of analysis, it has become more common to talk about a politics of recognition (focused on securing equal respect for hitherto marginalised groups) rather than a politics of re-distribution. One is about social esteem; the other is to do with material goods and income. But there are questions to be asked. Is it superficial to see such social relationships as being about perceptions rather than power? The argument is not that humans have been deprived of resources so much as just recognition and it is this that reproduces inequality and oppression. The self is able to throw off the weight of history and rise, unencumbered, to profound empowerment and mastery of the future. Yet as Hannah Arendt observes in *The Human Condition*, 'nobody is the author or producer of his own life story'.[32]

Patchen Markell argues in his discussion of the dangers of recognition that there is no such thing as disembodied action or identity.[33] We all come from somewhere; we are not a person in isolation but a person-shaped by significant others. The lure and promise of recognition is, he argues, illusory and even stifling. But this is to go too far, such as saying that behind movements for reform and social change, it is not essential to change perceptions. A struggle for recognition may well be the prior shift that is needed in the minds of the powerful before laws are passed to affirm the powerless. I will contend that it is human devaluation that transmits the pernicious effects of social divisions. This is associated with social injustice rooted in practice and actions. The question is how these two aspects interact and which is prior. They are connected. 'I only get £40 per kilo for my shark fins because I am only a fisherman', complains a poor African coastal fisherman.[34] The lack of recognition goes hand in hand with the lack of reward that keeps him in poverty. From a wider perspective, the incessant hunting of sharks just for their fins that will provide a delicacy for soup-drinking Chinese is a different question of justice.

There is invariably a prior mindset. The decision to use African slaves was not about profit. Colonists in America could not imagine using European labour in this way. Africans were different. It was acceptable to enslave them. Africans were not fully human but if human, clearly inferior to whites in mental and spiritual faculties.[35] Once slaves were de-humanised, treated as objects, not 'people like us', slave trade helped build racism that became deeply embedded in attitudes to black people later.

But what is it that is being recognised? Is it that we see our fellows as equal bearers of moral status, awarding recognition of someone as a person or 'purely' as a rational agent? This is a pressing concern. Throughout history, most humans have been cloaked in invisibility. From the perspective of those who dictate the terms of recognition, the social experience of women, black people, minorities, the disabled, colonial subjects and so on has been invisible – or only partially seen. As Raimond Gaita, Professor of Moral Philosophy at King's College, points out, 'it is only when one's humanity is fully visible will one be treated as someone who can intelligently press claims to equal access to goods and services'.[36]

Sartre's phenomenology of vision is not the last word on the subject.[37] A shared gaze can establish shared humanity rather struggle and resistance, an ambiguity that confronts us in the present volume.[38] Yet the sensorium of disvaluing is only one social arena where issues of value are generated. There is a curious quality in self-respect. It has the ability to somersault to the social gaze of others so they come to witness (celebrate or be threatened by) this move. The act of self-valuing commandeers the vision of the other.

Diminishing, however, goes beyond the gaze of unseeing indifference we have just noted: it is about how the 'put-downs' of everyday life reduce and dwarf.

The factors that promote disvaluing are not to be seen in isolation. Someone who carries themselves with dignity will tend to earn greater respect than someone who is a walk-over.

The Politics of Diminishing and the Quest for Significance

'I am going to prove you wrong – they are not going to get away with this. I will not be put down.' – behind the story of the singer Susan Boyle's rise to fame is her mother, who believed in her daughter strongly against life experiences that had conspired to reduce and diminish her[39]

Diminishing is a strategy of reduction by those with power. Experiences of being belittled, put down, pushed down, insulted or disrespected lead readily to a sense of lost value. It is also the case that when people lose respect either by their own actions or the actions of others, to that extent they are diminished. By contrast, self-respect sets up a virtuous circle. Respect is sought and usually granted.

Disvaluing people is closely bound up with a strategy of reduction. 'He [or she] makes me feel small' is a complaint that often surfaces in client reports. The thesis we are exploring on this essay shows itself in its hot, true colours in the need for *affirmation* and significance, especially against demeaning talk and behaviour. Such careless talk or action is profoundly reductionist; it is belittling. The essence of such denigration is being made small.

A particular client is keenly aware that he is operating in a social environment where many customers and acquaintances in a superior position. It is in the background behind many of the statements and practices about how he sees himself in relation to others. This is languaged as 'they are above me' or 'they won't want to mix with me'. Identity surfaces as being a working man. Yet behind this narrative, another story is playing; one arising from personal worlds. One of my clients suffers from a strong sense of inferiority. His father systematically put him down and belittled him.[40] The point is, how do you separate the inequality apparently resulting from class from personal factors? Equality has various dimensions – equality of resources, of working and learning opportunities or of power relations. But among the strength of reaction against the forms inequality takes, the demand for respect and recognition is significant.[41]

Honneth argues that the act of disrespect could apply to a person's physical integrity; for example, rape, 'a degree of humiliation which, by comparison to other forms of disrespect, has a more profoundly destructive impact on an individual's practical relationship to self'.[42] There is for Honneth a hierarchy of forms of disrespect which someone experiences by being deprived of group or personal rights. This constitutes a violation of the inter-subjective expectation of being treated as responsible person, thus depriving that person of recognition.

To paraphrase William Butler Yeats, identities are in flux – the centre cannot hold. Barack Obama, for example, seemed to transcend racial identity. He made a deliberate choice to define himself as black and identify with the glory days of the civil rights movement. His bid for the summit, the Presidency itself, was clinched by a flair for mediating between strongly opposed views. If he lacked an ability to be proud of blackness without making whites uncomfortable, he could not have got where he did.[43]

In an era when difference dissolves, it becomes truly difficult to name the world. Feminists insisted that 'consciousness-raising' was a vital strategy to address the politics of reduction. Much lampooned by those who did not see the point, the argument gradually began to make sense. Language is not and cannot ever be, neutral. For a generation, it steadily seemed more appropriate to talk of 'those with disability' rather than 'the disabled'. The nuance is important, raising a division between having and being. Someone who *is* disabled is a different kind of being and always lesser. Language is as devaluing here as referring to 'under-developed countries'. The concept of richer versus poorer nations seems to do the heavy lifting these days as being more descriptive. Major shifts in society were responsible for minor terminological alterations. By the 1960s intellectuals had learned to say 'third world' but then became more hesitant about this.[44] Sexist language was frowned on.

Rooted in a growing realisation that language and terminology was not neutral, the quest to re-name the world drew heavy fire. Yet language can go inwards at the same time as the words go outwards and are externally expressed. To take one example, the UK National Director for Patients and the Public urged that doctors and health managers should be banned from referring to patients as 'crinklies, crumblies and bed-blockers'.

Pejorative terms describing elderly people reflect a climate of ageism. The term 'frequent flyer', describing older people at hospital regularly, was 'demeaning and trivialising […] we must not de-humanise patients. Hospital managers or professionals have responsibility to their patients which must include courtesy'.[45]

The realities of naming the world are complex. The third edition of the Diagnostic and Statistical Manual of the American Psychiatric Association (DSM) in 1980 re-biologised psychiatry through reclassifying mental illnesses.[46] Its influence was considerable, and some would say, heavy with inappropriate and pharmaceutically driven classification.[47] Or here is an American commentator writing about the contemporary struggle by Latino people for a better life in the south-east corner of California. William Vollman can cross the border southside into Mexico and walk 'like a lord'. Northside, the reverse is not true. Mexicans 'slink like fugitives'.[48] Is this diminishing, imposed by economic disparities, a way of talking, an example of social discrimination or a psychological exercise in unwitting collusion by Latinos? This too is a strategy of reduction; disvaluing through speech acts.

It is a strategy of power to start with the supposed superiority of men/the West/white people against which one can speak of women/the East/black people. It is only when women/the East/black people are defined as peripheral that men/the West/white people can represent themselves as the centre. The development of post-colonial theory demonstrates the validity of respecting and recognising the distinctive life experiences people have. Some analyses of 'third world women' speak of common linkages of 'dependency relationships based on race, sex and class, perpetuated through social, educational and economic institutions'.[49] This is like speaking of all African women as being economically dependent or compelled to use prostitution as their main source of livelihood.[50] Speaking of women as victims of male violence locks them into 'objects who defend themselves' and men as 'subjects who perpetuate violence'. It robs women of agency.

The devaluation that diminishes is sustained by language – crude, rude ways of naming the world that masquerade as descriptions. Critics that assault the notion of having something in common that transcends differences are often fighting against a metaphysical realism that holds on to the idea of humanity as 'an unmediated account of human essence as it is in itself'.[51] This is impossible. Without identity, there is lack of rootedness, of belonging. Labels we use such as class continue to act as markers for types of experiences by which people will not move very far from the womb of original experience. Shorn of our social location, we are not disembodied spirits. We all come from somewhere. Our views are embedded in a context. And language shapes that context. Men's talk about violence, for instance, 'is not merely descriptive, it creates social reality for men and women'.[52] Where we sit determines what we think and what we say.

But burglary of agency can also take place through well-intentioned subtlety which is profoundly diminishing. Paternalism involves those adopting a position of power (by dint of capacity for impartation) inadvertently disempowering those on the receiving end. By definition, dependency does not foster a community of free and equal partners. Whether it be welfare dependency or that arising from international aid, a 'helping' relationship creates position power which needs to be a temporary client alliance or face the restricting possibility of solidifying into permanence. When development is put into the hands of local people or communities themselves, there is a sense of ownership that constitutes a repudiation of top-down aid. New identities are fostered through holding the head high. Within inter-personal relationships, mutual dependence allows belief in the possibility of growth and value that contrasts with diminishing and disrespect negating my humanity.

The Politics of Indignity

'Our sense of indignity is the essence of our dignity.' – David Martin[53]

According to both contemporary abstractions and best practice, dignity must neither be defaced nor assaulted. But what is dignity? It is an abstraction in its Latin root, it is *dignitas*, worthiness, honour, height of excellence. Dignity at work is to do with policies to combat bullying and harassment. In health care, giving dignity to those seeking help and treating them holistically became fundamental to a vision of medical services and of the healing of the mind. In the United Kingdom, Care and Quality Commission (CQC) Reports have highlighted persistent dignity deficits. Some of CQC's findings have been alarming and show low rates of compliance with the essential standards, particularly by nursing homes and by NHS hospitals. In their 2011 Annual Report, only 51 per cent of nursing homes and NHS hospitals were compliant with requiring that people experience 'effective, safe and appropriate care, treatment and support that meets their needs and protects their rights'. When the CQC reported that a lack of 'kindness and compassion' was leading to the inadequate treatment of the elderly in half of all hospitals, it was shocking – but not surprising.

What is this invasion or dignity that generates such a strong sense of disvaluing? Rosen argues that 'dignity' carries three types of freight – dignity as social status, as inherent value, and as a mode of behaviour. Once, dignity was reserved for aristocrats and kings. In the Renaissance, all of God's creation – humans, animals and plants – had dignity. Later, only humans were worthy of the distinction. In modernity, dignity is cherished as a fundamental human right, the focus of our thinking about law and human rights. Its meaning is contested. The idea of dignity as the foundation for the universal entitlement to human rights represented the coming together after World War II of two extremely powerful traditions: Christian theology and Kantian philosophy. Not only is this idea of dignity as an 'inner transcendental kernel' behind human rights problematic, it has drawn attention away from the right to be treated *with dignity*. Rosen presents Kant as a philosopher whose ethical thought is shaped, above all, by the obligation to show respect towards a core of value that each of us carries, indestructibly, within ourselves.[54] In contrast, Kateb asks what human dignity is and why it matters for the claim to rights. He proposes that dignity is an 'existential' value that pertains to the identity of a person as a human being. To injure or even to try to efface someone's dignity is to treat that person as not human or less than human – as a thing or instrument or subhuman creature. Kateb does not limit the notion of dignity to individuals but extends it to the human species.[55]

The quest for dignity plays out in many social transactions. A male doctor examines a female patient; a male security guard checks a woman at an airport. This is an affront to dignity, not an act of belittling per se but a violation of something that is sacred to the person on the receiving end. At the interplay of indignation and dignity, there stands the struggle for assertion of a valuable self.

We have looked at three triggers that evoke disvaluing – diminishing (respect reduction), indignity (dignity invasion) and indifference (attention deficits). So what is that 'value-in-oneself' or 'us' that is essential for our flourishing and breached by such triggers? What does it mean for human action that we seem compelled to live as if we had high value and wither in its absence?

Responses to systemic pressures and oppressive constraints which operate continually in social life are often framed in terms of loss of value. Human devaluation both transmits the inequalities of the world but it also reproduces them. Social pressures cluster those with similar subjective experience into categories and fixed groups such as economic and occupational classes. In addition, social evaluation brings it with a host of stigmas, labels and normative judgments about who is standard issue and what type of people are of lesser worth. This is usually framed as a matter of agency versus structure – a continuing debate in sociology about how higher levels of social structures contain and mould the personal, conscious layer of human action. The key dimension is that of systems thinking; complex adaptive systems which shape devaluation and entrench inequality.

What is crucial to note from the perspective here is that such social valuing, inherently relative to other human subjects as communicating and shaping lesser worth or higher worth, digs into value-in-oneself. When aroused, this supplies energy for 'the Protest'.

14

Inequality's Inner Thread: Towards a New Social Category

Intersections

Sara Ahmed was an activist and academic who wrote about why she resigned from Goldsmiths College, London in protest against the institution's failure to address sexual harassment. 'I am to keep my words as close to the world as I can', Sara Ahmed wrote in *Living a Feminist Life* – a highly personal account of how patriarchy, feminism, racism and homophobia are not just theories. They are embodied realities, incidents and structures. The biggest bigots turned out to be self-styled liberals who could not see through the way the inequalities they condemn are maliciously entwined. A woman of colour challenging misogyny came up against entrenched attitudes and prejudicial blind spots.[1] In the personal positions she occupies, Sara Ahmed observes the intersection of feminist theory, queer theory, critical race theory and post-colonialism.

This is related to the question of intersection. The idea of 'intersectionality' is that multiple identities cross over to create a whole that is different from the component identities. The idea was coined by American feminist legal scholar, critical race theorist, and civil rights advocate Kimberlé Crenshaw.[2] The experience of being a black woman cannot be understood in terms of being black or a woman considered independently, but must subsume the interactions, which reinforce each other so often. Women of colour experience domestic violence and rape in a different way from how white women experience them. The customary depictions of oppression within society – such as racism, sexism, classism, disability discrimination, homophobia, transphobia or ageism – are not independent of each other. These forms of oppression are entwined, creating oppression that is systemic (within the systems of social life). A case can be made for saying that the notion of intersections undermines identities if there is no single aspect of identity that will be predominant.

The classic formulations of how the world is divided up have to do with class, ethnicity (as 'race' is usually termed now) and gender. These social realities overlap and intersect each other in complicated ways. Other forms of differentiation should now be put into the equation. Disability is now widely seen as shaping social experience. But attitudes are also moulded by such factors as age, sexual orientation and religion. These are not just ways of organising the world but are widely seen as reproduction of forms of prejudice and delivering discrimination for millions of people. What they have in common is that they are all forms of devaluation. The narrative of how these formulations came to be seen as primary determinants of social experience is relevant to the circumstances in which people react against being devalued. Arguably, devaluation is a key driver in social processes because it is fundamental to the way difference becomes hierarchical and pernicious. Issues of value are a common thread in the way subjects experience and report the effects of differentiation. Devaluation is inextricably linked to the reproduction of difference. Looking at the social world through this lens shows how forms of difference cannot be rooted only in class and economic location since those who dictate the terms of high versus low value, and thus set the terms of aspirational norms and discourse, are clustered in various social practices.

Social devaluation affixes labels on people, labels that are far from neutral in purpose, far more real and destructive than mere names. Devaluation operates through labels and the naming of the world. Labels become self-fulfilling prophecies, creating reality like the Empires of history, releasing terrifying possibilities for those who are not in our class or like us in age, gender, ethnicity, physicality or sexuality. Sticking labels on people who are different is intrinsic to experiences of devaluation.

The key proposal in this essay is that the conditioning effects of our social lives, that mould and communicate our value, come up against the inner sense of personal worth that is to do with the emotional side of life that social analysis so often ignores. Hence experiences of devaluation are mirrored by a second social reality, that of a capacity people have for revaluing themselves. This happens through getting a job, gaining a qualification, becoming upwardly mobile or adopting a strategy of more confident assertiveness and heightened consciousness. The result is a renewed (or new) aspiration and sense of value – being worth more because one is being worthwhile. Value is both empowering and motivating. A key issue is where the energy for this comes from within personal or social life.

All this matters profoundly.

Case Study

Leah is a young lady in the district who comes originally from Eritrea. Her family left there only to find themselves in the mess and the violence of South Sudan. Now she is being placed with a local family. Leah experienced multiple disadvantage. She is in an ethnic minority, she is financially poor, she is often labelled and taken advantage of by young males at the college where she is trying to get a belated education. Nevertheless, Leah aspires. Something within her wants to be a doctor. She knows from mysterious inner knowledge that somehow transcendence is possible.[3]

The classic struggles of the twentieth century tended to focus only on one form of oppression at a time – the struggle for emancipation of women, civil rights, colonialism, disability, homophobia, ageism and class discrimination. Yet the swirling sands of social change result in new patterns in inequality. It is now officially recognised that more of a growing ethnic middle class have their own homes and good jobs whereas some white working class can be faced with serial disadvantages.[4] We need to deconstruct the opposition between categories of hierarchy and stratification. For disadvantage is endemic to issues of class and poverty, not just race or gender. Behind the hot collective indignation that will no longer bow down before forms of domination is a demand for equal value. Pursue justice for all; all humans are fundamentally equal in worth! In this chapter, we explore the way cultures of devaluation operate in society. We will look at the way that identifying with different social experiences and social groups is constrained by identity and can only go thus far.

Things have changed. Amid the worst measure of inequality in the world, as rated by the World Bank (Gini coefficient), most black South Africans are poor. Most income still flows to a small elite. Economic growth still benefits the best educated. The difference is that a large part of the economic elite is black. South Africa's inequality is getting less racialised.[5]

Inequality constrains. It comes in many forms. The prime shape of inequality has been seen to be based on class. To that must be added inequality based on gender, ethnicity, able-bodiedness, age and sexual orientation. Yet another form of inequality clearly has a role in shaping human action; the role of inter-personal circumstances that demean human beings. Why should this not be among the types of inequality that oppress people, which is exactly how it is experienced?

A widely noticed educational text 20 years ago was *A Pedagogy of the Oppressed* by the Latin American educator Paulo Friere.[6] He suggested that the kind of education needed today was not knowledge parcelled up for those who do not know but a radical programme to foster liberated subjects. The fundamental human problem, he argued, is oppression. The educator is one who 'conscientises,' bringing out the key value of freedom in others through a model of Experience/Reflection/Action. This he sees as a process of empowerment. Paulo Friere went on to write:

> The question of social class empowerment involves how the working class, through its own experiences, its own construction of culture, engages itself in getting political power. This makes 'empowerment' much more than an individual or psychological event. It points to a political process by the dominated class who seek their own freedom from domination.[7]

The process of 'conscientization', argued Freire, enables the oppressed person to reject the oppressive consciousness which inhabits him, become aware of his situation and find his own language. He becomes freer, less dependent as he commits himself to the transformation and building up of society.

The idea of oppression has a strong resonance in Latin America. Hugo Chavez, Venezuelan President in his election campaign of 1999 declared himself champion of the people. 'I will not rest until we have broken the chains of oppression, of hunger and of poverty.'[8]

According to this kind of analysis, the fundamental human problem is 'oppression'. 'To oppress' is defined in the Oxford Dictionary as 'to treat or govern someone in a very harsh and unfair way'.[9] However, this does not encapsulate the experience of many who have had to fight for their place in the sun. Oppression is too oppressive; too one dimensional. Women may struggle in a way that men do not (which is unfair) but may dispute that social and sexual division of labour is inherently harsh.

Across the human ecology, forms of social injustice can be spoken of as being:

- Oppression
- Inequality
- Alienation
- Exploitation
- Social exclusion
- Deprivation
- Disadvantage
- Being downtrodden

These ways of naming the world are linguistic practices and conventions with a differing cachet of power and meaning. They are not equivalent. There is history attached to the use of each term. Karl Marx dwelt upon the 'alienation' experienced by the divorce of the workers from their work.[10] 'Social exclusion' is a more recent term originating in France to describe those marginalised by society.[11]

Drawing on the proposal by Amartya Sen and Martha Nussbaum that we should think of inequality and disadvantage in terms of lack of capability,[12] a more recent argument is that disadvantage is about lack of secure 'functionings'.[13] The most disadvantaged are those who suffer a cluster of important disadvantages, who cannot obtain a core of high-weight functions such as being well-nourished or being able to participate in society and make choices. The aim of public policy should be to de-cluster disadvantages so the position of the least well-off in society is improved. Identifying human devaluation as inequality's inner thread requires that some weight be given to the different dimensions of devaluation, what is known as 'the indexing problem'. It does not shape and mould people in the same way. It may be necessary to show that the disadvantaged are those that experience a number of forms of devaluation (race and class and disability perhaps) which need to be de-clustered.

Devaluation is central to the way group subjects are formed. It is this reduced value of those who are not standard issue that is the conditioning power experienced in the construction of subjects in the encounter with colonialism, ethnic discrimination, homophobia, ageism and disability discrimination. Human society constructed these differences in hierarchical ways, or by placing the speaker at the centre and relegating the 'other' to the margins. Social differences were based on processes of devaluation.

Cultures of human devaluation offer a lens on social and private worlds. They are the connecting thread behind inequality. Assigning whole groups of humans to a higher status or relegating them to second league can be a means of renaming the world. It opens up an immediate space for those who are dominated to find their worth and to re-value themselves. The old identity politics helped us make sense of ourselves, the formation of cultural-political identities and how they are mapped on to wider symbolic and political identification; how we saw ourselves in our own gaze in the mirror of the gaze of society generally. The Protest is about capability, of acquiring a voice that enables identity formation as a separate group. It brings a focus on subjective factors in the experience of being devalued.

A female client is very self-conscious of people who she construes as middle-class professional types who will look down on her. It isn't as if she lacks money or doesn't exhibit many apparently middle-class virtues herself. But she frames the encounter, how she thinks 'they' will see her, in terms of lack. She hasn't got what 'they' have. It tugs at experiences in her inner world that generate a resonance between being stigmatised for other reasons together with a positioning of herself in class terms.[14]

The statements people make to define worthy or less worthy people affect racial, gender and class boundaries. This affects which forms of inequality are to be spoken of and which are to have pre-eminence – an issue faced by governments in the face of new social movements of the past generation that have opened up political space. How we define and indeed re-configure equality is important in an era when identity markers are increasingly fluid. The old boundaries are less relevant. There are no hierarchies of inequality.

Many argue that social class is *the* factor that most defines where people are coming from. Yet class cannot trump all other factors. In the United Kingdom, data indicates that it is now poor, white boys who are doing worst in exam results at GCSE level. Yet there are greater similarities between black and white working-class children than between working and middle-class children from the same ethnic group.[15] Ethnicity and class interact in ways that bring about a complex and subtle picture. Neither factor explains achievement or opportunity by itself. A Communities Secretary, Labour minister John Denham went on to observe that the context of inequality had changed and that it was time to widen the focus and take action on both fronts. Class inequality must be challenged without losing the drive against racism. 'New trends that are linked to race, class and identity make the situation more complex [...] we will tackle both together.' Despite this, many young black people felt they were being discriminated against by police or in job applications.[16]

The working class used to be the universal subject victim. But has the restless energy of devaluation now largely moved to surround other categories in society? Ageism is perhaps the new class warfare. Equally, some feminist groups react very strongly against any attempt to represent men as victims of domestic abuse and not perpetrators. 'All men are bastards' is the strap-line on a 'man-zapper', a gadget obtainable online to deter men from aggression in the home.[17] Women's refuges are, thankfully, common and there is a presumption that a woman will be heard in cases of domestic violence and, increasingly, incidents of rape. But any suggestion that men might need similar protection does not meet with a polite yawn but hostility – as if any attempt to de-centre women as the universal subject victim of patriarchy undermines the script of a biased social order, a script to be staunchly defended. The reality is far more complex. Acknowledging the female capacity for aggression, violence and cruelty involves myth-busting, especially of a sentimental view of cosy motherhood.[18] Although in the United Kingdom one in four women will be targets of domestic abuse, it is also the case that one in five men will be badgered and battered by verbal, physical or financial abuse.[19] The history and sociology of rape is fraught with false allegations.[20] It is not about fixed, essentialist categories but human devaluation as inequality's inner thread. Power devalues and both creates and sustains pernicious inequalities.

What is needed is a far more fluid conception of power. Human devaluation may have clustered around the working class/women and ethnic minorities in the past. But tides of devaluation affects different social systems at various times, shaping and re-shaping the experience of individuals and of groups. So how do we develop a more integrative approach to the old way of mapping hierarchy and stratification that pays attention to the range of building sites where social divisions are produced?

A conversation about difference revolving around the idea of human devaluation might have a variety of meanings.

- Devaluation is a way of speaking about the effects of diversity as distinct from diversity itself. Forms of difference become conflictual when humans are graded on a scale of worth. Social injustice has to do with an act of malign writing: writing people down or writing them off entirely, causing some groups of humans to go second or third class or less.

- Re-configuring social injustice in terms of human devaluation is a way of speaking about forms of domination and oppression that brings out the psycho-social effects of oppression, exploitation and inequality that they have in common. Discrimination and inequality are species of human devaluation. It is devaluation that links racism to other 'isms'.
- By emphasising devaluation as the inner meaning behind such social injustice, we are relieved in part from the necessity to try to sort out which form of difference is primary and which factor underlies the rest.
- Re-configuring social injustice in terms of human devaluation highlights the way forms of domination based on difference plug into the sense of intrinsic worth that people feel. Conflictual diversity is inherently devaluing.
- Re-configuring social injustice in terms of human devaluation is not one dimensional, configuring the social divide into oppressors and oppressed, exploiters and the exploited but rather a fluid category. It points beyond itself to the reflex against itself.
- Re-configuring social injustice in terms of devaluation opens up that more fluid category as a tool of analysis. There is for instance a well-documented rise in distress among teenage girls arising from social toxins such as models of idealised body shapes, the pressure to look good, and consumerism – all of which feeds the feelings of relative deprivation, that others are ahead in the high stakes game of life.[21] If over 40 per cent of 15-year-old girls *of all classes* are emotionally distressed to a significant degree, this phenomenon highlights how we must look at negative social forces in a less fixed and more open way. Devaluation is the real culprit – the sense of being of less worth relative to others.
- On a global scale forms of difference fragment. The splintering of social differences makes the act of naming the world hugely fraught. As each form of difference is, when held up against a global mirror, shown to be not so essentialist and innate as we thought, what categories do we have left except some form of explanation that can act as a substratum behind all forms of difference? In other words, perhaps women across

the world have little in common except that many echo a common resonance of being devalued.

- We have entered a post-ideological age where classic forms of identity politics deployed by minority groups are based on an understanding of difference that applies less and less. The struggle for equality needs to be recast, perhaps in terms of affirming equal value and therefore equal status in the public square.

The struggle for social justice is inseparable from enhancing rather than diminishing the full humanity of our fellows. This is a focus on the subjective experience in being downtrodden, on the person who is on the receiving end. '"Treat me as a human being, fully your equal, without condescension" – that demand (or plea), whether it is made by women to men or by black to whites, is a demand or a plea for justice.'[22]

Feminism provided a critical gaze at colonialism, imperialism, race and power. Situating these struggles is complex. The white feminist consciousness-raising movement of the 1960s and 1970s sought to align itself with other women in contrast to a patriarchal society. Such a strategy did nothing for the concerns of black activists who wanted women to engage with men as partners in Protest. It also ignored the fact that feminism owed a large debt to the Black Civil Rights Movement. Black women objected to the hegemony exercised by the white feminist movement.[23]

Then came debates about post-colonialism. Post-colonial theory developed from colonial discourse argued by Edward Said in *Orientalism*, his analysis of representation of Orientalism and the present day legacy of imperialism.[24] It was contested, both in the idea that there was a single, homogenous 'East' and in the loaded assumption that all representations of the Orient, for example scholarship about India or China, were imperialistic in intention.[25] At the same time, feminism asked questions about the lack of an address to gender in post-colonial theory and about the universalising tendency in western feminist thought about what 'women' want. Post-colonial feminists attacked the idea of 'universal woman' as well as the idea of 'Third World Difference' that produces a monolithic picture of 'Third World Women'.[26]

Yet one can't help thinking that post-colonial feminism has landed the plane in a curious country. Attending to the specifics of each historical and social situation means we are reluctant to place experiences into broad categories of 'women' generally that look fixed. The closer you bring each group into the social gaze, the more groups dissolves into a myriad of experiences, each of deserving to be respected and recognised. 'You cannot speak for me. I cannot speak for us.'[27]

Back in 1976, members of the Combahee River Collective articulated an awareness that their lives, and their forms of resistance to oppression, were profoundly shaped by the simultaneous influences of race, class, gender and sexuality.[28]

There is now no single racism.[29] Racisms (plural), like multiculturalism are multiple, fluid and contested. Anti-black racism differs from anti-Asian, anti-Irish, anti-Gypsy reactions or that of the longest hatred, anti-semitism.[30] Individual identities piled up like layers but there was little sense that a complex interaction existed between these experiences or that there may be a commonality. In the contemporary arena, the categories of difference are themselves becoming contested, generating a number of dilemmas. It may be that difference has gone as far as it can. Certainly, feminism is no longer a stable place. 'Otherness [...] is not a stable place on which to build mutual identifications or communities of recognition.'[31]

Are the well-worn categories of differentiation now redundant? Perhaps we can speak again of the human in a way that gets us beyond difference, that we have gone as far as we can with the notion of difference and recognising equality of claim that each social groups sought to make in order to find an identity? These issues are highly complex minefields and beyond the scope of this essay but they are relevant to a serious proposal that social differences are constituted by human devaluation.

The Politics of Equal Identity

The restless energy of equality's search has moved now to a different location.

Identity politics has been around for a while. It puts the vulnerable at its centre. The identities of minorities should be voiced as overriding ways their concerns should be recognised. Policies and laws usually address one form of someone's identity. Multiple identities of those that are oppressed need to be recognised. So far so good. Yet identity politics does not evaluate people on the basis of the quality of their character or who they are but as a member of a group.

But how does that interact with the politics of equal worth? For example, there was an accord in Morocco in 1918 that guaranteed equal status for

Jews and Arabs as citizens (it did not last long).[32] Was Pierre Trudeau right in denying fellow-Quebecois their separate identity within Canada on the grounds of equality of worth?[33] As I write (October 2017) the Spanish government has just imposed direct rule on Catalonia to prevent a Declaration of Independence by this region.[34] Many of its citizens were keen to assert that their primary political identity is Catalan rather than Spain. And what about Scotland? Whose football team do people shout for?

Identity is hugely powerful on the contemporary agenda. A person's identity should never be up for debate. Or should it? What is the most important marker or distinguishing feature of who we are? We might be Scottish or English, a professional or a factory worker? But definitely a man or woman? All that is changing.

In the United Kingdom, for 50 years it has been illegal to discriminate against people because of which adults they have sex with. The freedom to express identities is gaining ground and legal protection. Now we have a new debate that is throwing everything up in the air. Forget LGBT. It is LGBTQQIAAP (Lesbian, Gay, Bisexual, Transgendered, Queer, Questioning, Intersex, Asexual, Allies and Pansexual) – any number of self-identifications.

There is growing indifference to overall binary categories in the name of 'just being yourself'. The focus on what might be termed 'micro-categories' is intense (gender neutral, gender-queer, gender fluid, gender questioning, agender, bigender and many others). As Josie Appleton observed in July 2017 in a talk at The Academy, the quest for the right category is the quest to establish a basis for the self:

> One formerly gender neutral man introduces himself: 'Hi, my name is Sam. My pronouns are "he" and "him", "how about you?"'.[35]

They *are* their identity box; they are their pronoun. And the content of this identity box is nothing but the violation of the commonly accepted category. It is an identity founded on the negation of the categories of social life, declaring them 'binary' and null and void. 'For two years I used "ze" and "hir" pronouns, and it's kind of a process of trying them out and having other people try them out to see how it feels and sounds.'[36]

Repudiation of traditional social categories we have been exploring, such as man or woman or class, was based on some generally accepted physical distinction or division in society. The new categories, by contrast, exist apart from someone's position in society or the social relations they enter into, as well as their physical reality. Identity box is independent of appearance. Enter Rachel Dolezal who claimed to be 'trans black'; identifying as black though biologically white. Dolezal, now Nkechi Diallo, a mixture of Nigerian Igbo and Fula, claims that her book, *In Full Color: Finding My Place in a Black and White World* was written partly 'to just encourage people to be exactly who they are'.[37] This comes two years after she was found to have deceived the people of Spokane, Washington, where she was a race activist and branch president of the National Association for the Advancement of Colored People. People have the right to call themselves whatever they want.

The 'express-your-real-self argument' appears reasonable enough on the surface, especially at a time when half of young people define gender on a spectrum. If people can transition from one gender to another, why not from one race to another if we feel another description better reflects our inner selves?[38] In a TEDx talk by Dolezal last year, she appeals to the predominantly white audience, asking: 'Is the identity that you were assigned at birth the best description of who you really are and what your purpose is for being in the world?' And she urges: 'What is life if we can't draw our own pictures and write our own stories?'[39] Some trans rights activists disputed Dolezal's argument on the grounds that gender reassignment is a matter of medical necessity rather than choice. But Dolezal's choice was flawed. 'The pick-your-own-race principle' works only for a privileged minority. It does not work both ways. A person of colour would be barred from entry into white society.

Everyone must be free, it is argued, to change their identity and not be constrained by the labels others impose on them. A new vocabulary has been invented for a new radicalism. Enter the new world of 'micro-aggressions, dis-invitation, no-platforming, safe-spaces, trigger warnings' (of possible controversial content).

The freedom of speech issue is clearly different for a new generation. Gradually there will be no critical discussion. The idea of the university is under assault. Identity is up for grabs. 'Identity politics' is both widespread and controversial. Are we to be defined by some marker of who we are?

What is doing the heavy lifting is a radical politics that is taking age-old debates about gender to a new dimension. Cultural trends towards the abolition of gender are pervasive. Fluidity is everywhere. The significance of the male-female dichotomy is eroded. The push-back has been against those challenging the notion of transgender, not willing to accept that, for example, trans-women are women. One focus for this move has been that the iconic feminist Germaine Greer has been given a 'no-platform' on many university campuses, because to her critics her position on transgender seems to say, 'you're not who you say you are'. Many feminists and former campaigners for gay rights are increasingly uncomfortable about non-binary identity. Are we in danger of re-labelling gay experience as transgender?

What is being hotly debated is the very notion of gender. If a man thinks he is a woman, all he does is say he is a female. There is nothing to prove. The proof is who you self-identify as, your experience of 'my body, my mind'. It is what goes on inside the head surely? The downside is that there can be a scale of moral merit based on their level of privilege (which is bad) and victimhood (that deserves applause).

A potent movement is under way to want to assert a non-binary identity. Thanks to modern medicine, without which none of this would be possible, gender re-assignment is taking place and is increasingly routine. To its advocates, the movement is welcome as it will help prevent suicides and mental distress among transgender people. To its critics, confused young people whose identity is not yet formulated towards a given trajectory are simply not mature enough to have hormone blockers that change gender. There are documented cases of people changing back. Besides, the possibilities for abuse are considerable by anyone who can wander into a female changing area on the grounds that, despite physiology, they are female. It is all in the name of equal identity.

Freedom to express identities are fundamental to contemporary life and gaining legal protection. There is a cultural trend towards the abolition of gender. Everyone is free to change their minds or love who they will. Fluidity of gender is the trope of our times. For the most part, religious belief holds to the binary distinction between male and female despite many voices who argue that gender is a spectrum. Such is the triumph of the equality idea that it seems self-evident that androgynous identity equates to ultimacy; anything else constitutes pernicious inequality that is deeply suspect.

Many argue that the future of gender studies takes us to the end of gender binaries entirely. Pushing the debate on gender identity to its limits, in *Beyond Trans* Heath Fogg Davis asks why we need to have gender labels at all? Individuals are classified according to sex differences. But why do we have such categories on bathroom doors or passports?[40] In an era when there are more than two sexes, when some men choose to become women and vice versa, when some want to be both or dispense with such labels completely, do the labels serve any useful purpose anymore? Whether human identity can be neatly parcelled out into two distinct sets of being is increasingly questioned. Of which more later.

Where is this all heading? Are we on the brink of a post-gender age? Should we not just abolish the whole concept of gender as obsolete? Unisex toilets are one thing as is being gender neutral but if gender is irrelevant, there are revolutionary implications for how we perceive ourselves.

There are massive questions about all this. The view until so very recently was that if someone is anatomically either male or female, their biology shapes their social status. If they look like a boy and function as a boy, they probably are a boy. The only basis for self-identifying otherwise is being regarded as being on the basis of feeling. 'I feel different.' Is that really sufficient to base whether or not males should go into female changing rooms? The feeling-based identification is highly questionable. Moreover it is highly confusing to young people who by definition are experiencing a turbulent adolescence. To be sure, bullying on the basis of transgender identity is inexcusable. No one wants to see the suicidal thoughts (and sometimes actions) that this leads to. But to corral such confusion through the prism of gender is to serve an agenda that may not serve long-term situations.

Renaming the World

In his travels through Europe in 1892, the great activist and writer W. E. DuBois witnessed the effects of 'the Jewish question', but for him it was completely separate from 'the Negro question' with which he was most familiar through insider knowledge and outsider status. It never occurred to him back then that race prejudice was really anything other than colour prejudice. Years later, he stood amid the remains of the Warsaw ghetto of 1945. Shaking, he could not conceive of how a civilised country with deep religious convictions could have done this. He knew that the colour line was a real and efficient cause of misery. But how to explain the holocaust? The conviction grew upon him that neither European anti-semitism nor civil rights in the United States were a species of harrowing provincialism, but were part of a broader struggle that had to be waged against oppression everywhere.[41]

Arguably, a unified idea of anti-oppression politics is emerging. Value or disvaluing is communicated through the social gaze as it manipulates our own internal perspective. It is also experienced through the crude, rude ways of naming the world. Central to that is the irrepressible instinct towards dividing the world into two. Difference agitates us profoundly. Yet difference can be construed in different ways. Our brains are always trying to divide things into two. The anthropologist Claude Levi-Strauss drew attention to the dual organisation that divides societies into two moieties.[42] The philosopher Derrida de-constructed the 'either/or' patterns that governed the world. Such binary thinking lay behind west versus east, north versus south, male versus female, culture and nature, the social and the self, agency and structure, knowledge as being split into arts or sciences, the economy as production or consumption. Derrida said, 'We are not dealing with peaceful co-existence of a vis-à-vis but violent hierarchy'.[43] Social pressure is often expressed in binary categories, oppositions that are usually set by the side with the most power.

The Western aesthetic tradition, for instance has prioritised the eye and ear over smell, taste and touch. In cultural appreciation, the appropriate response is one of detached contemplation which affords such special aesthetic experiences. These are the enjoyments of the leisured classes and do not begin to touch the scope of the sensibility experienced by ordinary people.[44] Other forms of binary divisions implying lesser worth could be:

- The city and urban life versus rural experience (encoding anti-urbanism or urban superiority)[45]
- Mind versus body
- Suburbs versus inner city
- Left versus Right
- Normal versus abnormal
- Public versus private sector
- Orient versus Occident
- North versus South

In this violent hierarchy, pre-eminent terms preserve their status by excluding and marginalising what they are not. Groups, individuals and ways of thinking assume they are centre; the 'Other' is marginalised or excluded from the circle altogether. 'By assembling the heterogeneous possibilities of meaning within language into fixed dichotomies, binarism reduces the potential of difference into polar opposites.'[46] Derrida's contemporary Michael Foucault emphasised that modernity moves not so much 'towards the never-completed formation of Difference' but 'towards the ever-to-be-accomplished unveiling of the Same'.[47] It is the unveiling of social difference that characterises modernity, especially the imaginative art that lay behind late twentieth-century struggles for emancipation. Foucault's re-conceptualisation of power emphasised that it is diffuse, fluid and subtle, not just concentrated into the hands of ruling classes. Difference is sustained by inequality in the balance of power.

In the twenty-first-century world, difference will be configured differently. Difference fragments into local descriptions operating in a smaller system. Yet the battery of 'race, class and gender' formulas[48] alongside attention to discrimination based on sexual orientation, age and disability suggests that there is something larger behind the scenes of which these forms are variant. These forms of social injustice are sub-species of the attitude and the practice of human devaluation. The same attitude that produces homophobia and racism will probably surface in gender discrimination. In June 2009, for example, a widely reported incident in Northern Ireland featured Rumanian families who came as migrant workers experienced disturbing hostility and violence from young people. They were hounded out the neighbourhood. It is curiously sad that a decline in sectarianism was followed by a rise in racist incidents – 1,000 in 2008.[49] It seemed as if attitudes of intolerance that resulted in devaluing others who were slightly different had merely changed seats.

Through the gaze and by means of naming the world, processes of devaluation drive social life. Difference can be seen as benign variation (diversity) rather than as conflict, by-passing power as well as history to suggest a harmonious, empty pluralism.[50] Emphasising our identity is a tribal response to uncertainty in our world. Yet interests we share as humans are more powerful than forces that drive us apart.

The conditions are available for resonance. Harriet Martineau, growing up in Victorian England, was conscious that life is a whole and that one can rarely escape from the emotional patterns of childhood.[51] As a child she brooded endlessly over her lack of feminine charm and sense of being deprived. Her early feminism made common cause with servants who were treated rudely; 'they, like children, were oppressed and denied status as human beings'.[52]

The world is waiting for communities and institutional forms to emerge that are aware of power differentials (it would be naive not to be) but whose cultures allow for the nurture of equal and non-oppressive social relationships; social spaces where the little people find a big voice.

15

The Effect of Inequality: Demoralisation, Resignation and the Protest

'We do not see things as they are. We see things as we are.' – Rabbi Shemuel ben Nachmani[1]

'Oppressive social orders, as a matter of routine operations cannot help generating the kinds of forces and desires which can in principle overthrow them.' – *The Ideology of the Aesthetic*, Terry Eagleton[2]

The socially corrosive nature of inequality is often attributed to jealousy or what Nietzsche called *ressentiment* as the slave–slaveholder relationship (or the master–servant ambiguity) is by turns felt and then reacted against. To be sure, a sense of injustice might be hardwired into what it means to be human – and not just human.

A 2013 experiment found that crows and ravens have a sense of fairness. People, other primates and dogs all react negatively when others get a better reward for doing the same work. Then some research indicated that some non-mammals dislike unfairness, too. Knowing which animals do and don't seem to notice unfairness helps scientists theorise how a sense of fairness might have evolved.[3] Then a 2017 study discussed how an innate sense of fairness often noticed among dogs could actually be eroded by human contact. It was thought dogs learned their sense of justice from their human 'best friends', but Australian tests on wolves show they have a stronger reaction to unequal treatment than their domesticated cousins. It is not therefore just a matter of social cognition. The point was that dogs have their own innate sense of fairness and did not learn this from humans as previously believed. In fact the research suggested the opposite may be true – that dogs have learned greater acceptance of inequitable treatment as a result of their close relationship with people.[4]

There is in human affairs an impulse which runs deep. It is the impetus to be valued, to be of worth. Like the wind, no one can say where it comes from. Through many avenues and multiples openings, we pursue this impulse. It is a key motivator in personal life. In wider society, it is a social driver.

This impulse seeps through many actions and interactions. Just as the sun in eclipse can be observed against its shadow, the impulse to be of high value is detected especially against the backcloth of its opposite, devaluation. It is not enough for this impetus that we are of worth; we must be of high value. Value-in-oneself requires social valuing and economic valuing to feed it but ultimately is not dependent on either.

In contemporary life, value is accorded to individuals and groups in a way that is unrelated to inner value or value-in-oneself. What someone is worth is awarded to social participants on the basis of the wage economy (economic value), identity badges (status value such as ownership or appearance) or identity boundaries (social value; being the right sort of person). A psychodynamic reading along these lines is fundamental to help explain why inequality matters. Freud is needed as much as Marx, it might be said. Psychology is, after all, the inner logic of sociology.

It is helpful to look at human value in two different ways than is usually conceived. One is to relocate the notion of human value away from an aspiration ('of course people should be valued'!) towards it being a social dynamic. It is not, in other words, an 'ought' but an 'is'; embedded in the human operating system. The other perspectival turn, I suggest, that clarifies social dynamics is to see the notion of human value in terms of its contrast pole, human devaluation.

The pursuit of a high value shows up in several ways:

- *Directly* – in personal life, when human beings flourish within equal relationships

- *Indirectly* – through experiences of being devalued that then react against them

The first relates to the role that the pursuit of value-in-oneself has in personal life, rooted in mental forces below the level of the radar. The second describes how the influence of society shapes the formation of human subjects in experiences and cultures of devaluation.

The social transmission of value is profoundly implicated in the formation of subjectivities. It is also an essential feature of the reproduction of the oppressiveness of oppressive categories. A case can be made that it is the erosion of value and denial of full humanity by those who hold more cards that constitutes the pernicious effects of social differentiation. Usually devaluation equates to difference.

Value per se is not an entity within psychic structure but the impetus towards being of high value is. Without it, we wither or we remain acting out the scripts that have been given to us. The struggle for a high value, in other words what we do to garner a sense of worth, becomes a way to scrutinise biographies. It was said, for example of the World War I poet Edward Thomas that self-respect dropped quickly when his depression set in.[5] Charting the ways people search for value through the pursuit of significance and self-worth reveals much about lived experience.

A good deal of human action is motivated by the pursuit of high value. Much of the real load-bearing work is done to establish, defend or build value-in-oneself. It shows up directly as we scrutinise social life and individual biography. It is revealed also indirectly through internal reactions to circumstances and cultures in which people are devalued. This essay suggests a different lens on the formation of subjects to usual perspectives. Forging of new subject positions as sources of action is part of the contemporary climate with its ensemble of dispersed positions. Subjecthood is, though, problematic.[6] The idea of the subject assumes an identity based on the basis of commonality with others and yet unique – sovereign. In the formation of identity, subjects come to place themselves in a force field of value-laden power relations; the site of dynamic struggle around human value.

The impetus towards high value does not take place in a vacuum. Subjective experience often shows an overlap of competing principles; external constraints and pressures rub up against an internal driver towards being of value. As an internal motivator, the drive towards high value constantly interacts with external systems. Deleuze sees subjectivities constituted by the internalisation of outside forces.[7] Here I want to observe that there is a psychological or psycho-social dimension to experiences of class, gender, ethnicity, disability, age, sexuality, religion or colonialism which converge on and either reinforced or subverted by personal experiences of being devalued. Traditionally, to be born on the right side of those equations was enviable while those born on the wrong side means that we are of negligible account. The connecting thread between the social and the personal is that of the systems in which we live and to which we are largely blind. Being devalued by society collides or colludes with value-in-oneself, a profound impetus in the psyche. Value-in-oneself is a crucial dimension to well-being. Put simply, being written off or devalued is bad for you; receiving a heady sense of being a worthwhile person with worthwhile tasks is good for you.

The idea of human value is a fundamental theme in social and cultural life and the motor behind many psychological and social processes. The notion of the (high) value of persons is associated with human rights discourse but these proposals indicate that it goes beyond the merely aspirational: value-in-oneself is fundamental to human functioning and motivation.

It is a 'taken for granted' assumption that has yet to be factored into theory. Indeed, the mystery of a human person cannot be grasped without invoking a construct of human value. The category of value-in-oneself acts as a helpful lens through which to observe human action and human reactions – both to difference and indifference. It has been well-understood that class or prejudice affects an individual's sense of identity and self-worth.[8] The sense of self is also a familiar face in psychology. But I am calling attention to the role that a sense, not just of self, but of a *valuable* self plays. In suggesting that issues of value arise repeatedly along power-lines of everyday transactions, it is important to remember that 'value' is here employed as a neutral term; entities can be accorded high or low value. The endemic struggle for our value in public and private worlds is an important dimension ignored in psychological and sociological descriptions of the world. It is a challenge to theory. Why has this not been an active dynamic in accounts of human action?

The indications are that there are three kinds of circumstances which give rise to reports of devaluation. Running through many encounters in inter-personal life is a reaction that proclaims, 'I count; I matter!' It is in response to being treated with:

- *Indifference* – the protest that echoes the need to be heard, to be taken seriously, to be involved and given attention
- *Indignity* – at the interplay of indignation and dignity lies the assertion of a valuable self: 'I am worthwhile'
- *Inequality (denigration or diminishing)* – the reflex against being put down, that calls for appropriate respect for a valuable self and affirmation

This is a proposal for a social philosophy exploring felt inner value as a major component of human action. It is rooted in two strands which offer an unusual vantage point in theory and practice in my own intellectual journey. Firstly, an empirical study in the consulting room in therapeutic contexts and developed through a process of 'reflection as research'. Secondly, post-doctoral work illuminated the author's own professional work and qualifications in the areas of public services and charity management, counselling and education.

For example, Malcolm Gladwell's book *Outliers* argued that tall trees matter less in the forest of human endeavour than the ordinary trees that work hard. Patience and perseverance and the magic number of 10,000 hours of hard slog pay off rather more than lucky breaks or those who somehow succeed beyond all expectations. For instance, 80 per cent of black children who are fortunate enough to be admitted to the Knowledge is Power Programme (KIPP) in the United States go on to college.[9] The real question is what helps them take advantage of the opportunity in a way that their inner-city peers, trapped in failing schools and economically depressed communities, do not. That is why unleashing aspiration is vital to tackling poverty. It requires a new focus, recognising the pernicious role of devaluation in the social processes that sustain it.

We are endeavouring to give an account of why inequality matters. Its harmful effects are not just because of the constraints that lack of equality imposes or the limitations on life. Inequality is problematic because of the impact on the inner person, whom it writes off and devalues.

There is a caution to be observed. The observation that devaluing operations within society can trigger their opposite does not imply some hydraulic understanding of social forces, as if, in a societal equivalent of a Newtonian universe, an equal and opposite reaction is produced. Neither does a reaction against oppressive operations based on erosion of value mean that there is a one-for-one and equivalent dynamic of Protest. Disvaluing builds up over a period of time. Could a biological model help here? In the conceptualisation offered by Parsons, in *The Social System*, reactive social systems contain the element of feedback mechanism to redress the balance and restore the system to equilibrium.[10]

These responses translate into identity – who we are. They constitute a core challenge since relative social and economic valuing is experienced as an absolute sense of identity – a form of category error. In effect, society inflicts a category mistake on many people. As we have seen, the way human subjects are constructed is bound up with processes of being devalued. At one level, this is social labelling. But the point is that it 'digs into' a layer of personal worth whereby what people *are* is called into question. A relative statement is thus converted into an absolute sense of core challenge.

Demoralisation

Steve Biko, the black South African leader and founder of Black Consciousness in South Africa, who died under Apartheid-era police brutality, diagnosed a submissive state of mind and lack of self-respect as illness. We collude with the definition of ourselves that others impose upon us. Biko defined its ideology:

> Evil-doers have succeeded in producing at the output end of their machine black man who is man only in form. This is the extent to which the process of de-humanisation has advanced [...]. All in all the black man has become a shell, a shadow of a man, completely defeated, drowning in his own misery, a slave, an ox bearing a yoke of oppression with sheepish timidity.[11]

The sorry litany of people who give up must include those with a history of abuse or maltreatment during childhood who are over twice as likely to have recurrent episodes of depression in adult life. Data from more than 26,000 people was pooled in a 2011 study which used various markers of maltreatment – rejection from a mother, harsh discipline, unstable caregiving, and self-reports of harsh physical or sexual abuse. Those who had experiences one or more of such markers were 2.27 times as likely to develop recurring depression than those who had not been maltreated.[12] Arguably, previous erosion of their worth has left them with a tendency towards life demoralisation.

Resignation

Resignation is a different response than demoralisation. Those who accept their lot in life in a passive sense seem capable of making life-affirming responses that negate miserable circumstances. This too is an affirmation of value-in-oneself. For millions, social life is heavily constrained by systemic patterns that assign a place in the social structure from which little escape seems possible. Reflecting on the few options available to him in his life as an agricultural labourer in nineteenth-century Kent, someone pointed out, 'people say why did you put up with it? Because you bloody well had to, that's why!'[13] The experience of millions surely is that they greet their lot in life with resignation. They cannot see any way out of their situation and it rarely occurs to change the conditions of life. The subject accepts the version of life in which it is formed. Gandhi, the inspiration behind the Indian Independence movement, believed India's shackles were self-made. He tried to instil new consciousness in the people. 'Prisoner, tell me who it was who wrought this unbreakable chain? It was I, said the prisoner, who forged this chain very carefully.'[14]

Where the borders are between resignation and Protest are contended. Martin Luther King referred to 'the ominous clouds of inferiority' in the mental sky of black people. Amid contemporary hagiography, it is easy to forget that Martin Luther King, colossus as he was, was a controversial figure, even among black communities. For some, it was the rhetoric of Malcolm X 'who seemed to speak with unabashed pride about blackness', that resonated more than Luther King's apparent acquiescence and non-violence.[15]

Steve Biko's narrative shows the extent to which there is unintended collusion between devalued and devaluers. It shows how human identity is created attitudinally, in dialogue and in symbolic interaction with others. The Protest is emancipation of the mind, the freedom to be who you are.

> Whites must be made to realise they are only human, not superior. The same with blacks. They must be made to realise they are also human, not inferior [...]. Blacks have had their noses rubbed in the dust by white racism, de-personalising them to the extent that they have [...] come to doubt the reality of their own personhood and humanity. They came to believe that the denigration of their humanity by those who oppress them is the truth about themselves.[16]

Such a sense of latent Protest does not only have deep roots in the personality, it has deep roots in literature and history. Here is a lady in waiting in eighteenth-century Britain, conscious that she is completely dependent on 'the compulsory Attendance and obligatory Dependence' that comes with her role.[17] The condescension of George III and Queen Charlotte is replete with a kindness that arouses the gratitude of Frances Burney but also tightens her velvet chains. But it is the Keeper of the Robes who is the real tyrant, a redoubtable woman who leaves Burney vulnerable to being 'No body'. Yet despite a constant attempt to subjugate her and punish resistance, tattered pride remains. Frances Burney has a secret knowledge that she is entitled to consideration and respect.

A high degree of value-in-oneself is essential for life. Yet unwitting collusion or demoralisation is not the only response to devaluing forces. Another script is possible, a stance that refuses to accept the script being handed out and which seeks another part in the play.

The essay has come to the core proposition, which is crucial to how identities are shaped and re-moulded. Devaluation triggers demoralisation when the absolute sense of a valuable self is assaulted. Without value we wither. There is another reaction, however. Devaluing forces engender their opposite. Oppressive formations create universal victim subjects, when people are not accorded the same validity. Being edited out of the picture can generate a response that calls forth Protest. This is because that very sense of a valuable self – whether individual or mobilised into the collective psyche of a group – seeks to assert itself. It is a strategy of re-valuing as individuals and groups feel more energised and hopeful about the future and their role in it. In this way, new forms of being can be constructed that transcend tradition.

We will look at several candidates for this strategic reaction and then ask if the response to being devalued is a reflex, a social dynamic that tells us something profound about human action.

It should be stressed, however, that for the thousands who join new social movements, there will be millions who seem resigned to their circumstances. This can look like collusion. Yet it would be mistaken to assess responses of resignation through the eyes of activists. The Protest need not be identified with politicised indignation. A life-affirming response is surely a legitimate reaction to miserable or devaluing circumstances, negating the straight-jacket of social forces bearing down on the individual through quiet Protest, getting on with life.[18]

Sometimes, indignation can be quiet, infused with dignity that has not been revved up. On a June Friday in 1953, two young boys were playing in the garden in New Jersey. They realise deep down that something awful has just happened and there is no one to call them in. Their country has just made them orphans. Ethel and Julius Rosenberg were executed by the US government as Soviet spies. One of their sons, Robert, went on to write that the best revenge is simply living a good life. It is one form of the Protest, quiet and unassuming.[19]

'I count for something!' is a reaction in some forms of anger against being devalued and put-downs. It has been pointed out that anger has a cultural element. How people express it varies from society to society.[20] Some anger can be a strategy by which to assert one's value. 'I'm not taking it!' we exclaim. 'I'm every bit as good as you are' – a signpost to a sense of pride in who we are, seeing ourselves in a new way. This is the possibility of a first person perspective that comes through the recovery of agency generally but it is also a powered movement towards a valuable psyche. Social agents acquire mobility and greater ability to re-invent themselves and construct new identities.

I suggest that how social actors come to the ability to the switch positions again is a lot do with the question of capability that we referred to in Chapter 6. We come lastly to re-visit this question.

16

The Politics of Equal Worth

'If I cut my hand and you cut yours, we both have red blood [...]. Do you not use the same bananas my caste grows to offer to your gods? Do you not use the flower garlands our women make to dress your deities?' – *Nine Lives*, William Dalrymple[1]

We referred earlier to the psycho-social dynamics of how inequality dents human worth. In Marx, the subject is told 'you are oppressed!' The subject might well respond, 'Am I? I didn't know that'. In Freud, the analyst tells the client, 'you are repressed!' 'Am I?' the analysand might respond. 'I didn't know that!'

In both cases, there is a process of awakening. The concept of 'awakening' is apt for what we are about to consider in this last chapter. We noted earlier that the dent that unequal situations make (whether externally or from within) evokes a reaction of causing the subject to move *from* a position relative to others. Instead, the response is far more serious. The subject moves from an absolute sense of their identity. A switch has been made.

'Switching back' is a strategy whereby there arises a reaction of 'I'm as good as you!' It is the sigh of aspiration turned into action.

The Protest is a capacity to subvert being devalued. In response to social groups claiming power as being higher value people, it sounds its trumpet call as, 'we will not be edited out of the picture!' In response to de-personalising encounters, organisational activity devoid of either name or face, the Protest cries out 'I am not an "It"!' This reflex underlies much of the contemporary search for dignity and respect from organisations. Finally, reacting to de-humanising or demonising forces that strip away human dignity and desecrate the sanctity of life, indignant protest of the victim (or those that mobilise on their behalf) is 'you shouldn't treat us like this [...]. We won't put up with this anymore'.

But how does this happen? How is it that psychic energy can be recruited into a stance that declares 'I'm as good as anybody else!' How, for example, does it arise that social mobility means the person can rise up the social ladder if they so wish and that is how they see things? What is the basis for the word that becomes politicised so easily – aspiration (as if there is something wrong or denigrating about the previous social and subject position?). Yet stories abound about how young people growing up in difficult circumstances, for example, have an aspiration to break out and do better. Stories abound about how people generally attempt social mobility – and succeed. What is proposed here is that the energy to get on in life emanates from the process of mimetic desire. Much inter-personal and social life stems from the politics of desire in some shape or form. Mimetic desire – a concept developed by Rene Girard – argues that imitation is a vital dynamic in social life.[2] Mimesis results in wanting to be like, to identify with, the desired object. This can be extended. I want to argue that it is desire aroused and extended in the direction of who is a high value person, to be emulated. Their persona becomes an object of desire; their worth becomes the basis for the self-worth of the desiree. Young people want to be a footballer, a skilled bricklayer or a professional person. Mimesis works by desire but the fuel is that of a valued status of someone else who is role model.

For some, music is their life. It is their escape from life as it is experienced. Laughter can also give vent to the same response. Jokes under communism were not just a contrast to dreariness in everyday life; they played their part in undermining it.[3] After World War II, eastern Europe saw a totalitarian campaign to regiment society and cripple critical thinking. A surreal reality of socialist enthusiasm was a smokescreen for complete submission to the Communist regimes. Yet through the grey concrete of life, the crushing of dissent and acts of rebellion, the Protest came through in personal and cultural life.[4]

For acts of mental defiance or collective indignation are central to resistance, witnessed in literature. One thinks of the gritty 'kitchen sink' dramas of the 1950s and 1960s, depicting the bleak realities of postwar Britain, allowing working-class heroes to have a voice, an angry voice against a social set-up that had dealt them a bad hand. The voices of 'a literature of resistance' became an alternative to the armed struggle by more militant Palestinians. Mahmoud Darwish, a poet from the one-fifth of Israeli society that was Arab, had been lionised abroad for refusing to leave his native land until harassment by Israeli security services became too constraining.[5] Satire was cut from the same cloth of resistance in the dissident Czech films of Dollacek, the plays of Havel or the self-immolation of Jan Polack in response to the Soviet invasion of Czechoslovakia in August 1968.

Or on a wider scale, the distinctive Negro spirituals and style of the Black church in America, evolving under conditions of slavery were the only forms of self-determination and resistance the slaves could experience.[6] Victors assume heroic status. They write the history but rarely write the songs. Those who are shunted to the margins have to draw on their musicals to keep the spirit intact. Rap enabled young black people to be heard, challenging authority, giving them a voice.[7]

In the psychology of human resistance, 'Excuse me! I'm a human being!' is the language of those who feel used, taken for granted or trodden upon. Behind this statement is concealed a statement of a healthy ego, a valuable self. This book is a proposal for how issues of value arise in the power lines of everyday life. The statement 'I'm worth more than that!' goes to the heart of the Protest. It is an uprising of assertive value. Assertiveness seems to be expressing the real you. The assertiveness training emphasis of the 1980s and 1990s recognised that instinctively.

'Consciousness-raising' became a key part of the feminist struggle for women to raise their position in society. For much the same reason, this is a key feature of the assertion of a valuable self by an individual finding its own worth. Behind narratives of depression often lies a suppressed energy of protest that can be released cathartically; the latent capacity to affirm that 'I am' marks the reflex reaction that seems to be embedded within our psychic structure. The woman who regains self-respect by learning to say 'no' is learning to value herself. Discovering that she can say 'No' for the first time in 50 years and being prepared to risk relationships has given her a liberation that is palpable. She wants to run and leap! Paradoxically, saying no has increased the respect people have for her as well as finding a well of self-respect that had lain deep underground.

This is not just about self-esteem, self-belief only, but value as an environment within which humans can flourish. It is powerful, heady stuff, guaranteed to evict the toxic messages we have downloaded. From nowhere, someone has made a glad and welcome discovery, their own subjectivity. It may happen slowly; it may take place with a sudden rush of heightened sensation. But in and through that discovery is a rising of confidence. With that ascension comes a discovery – a new valuing of self.

The Protest is a capacity, both a mechanism and a consciousness; a reflex against the depressive effects of devaluation in the form of an indignation. The Protest is a flower that has been downtrodden and is now springing up in freedom. This reflex does not happen automatically in inter-personal life any more than it does in social or political life. People do not always and inevitably react with indignation against the erosion of their value. There is, however, that which can be mobilised, that which can be aroused slowly into a new birth of consciousness. The idea of false consciousness featured in Marx's notion of working-class people deceptively feeling they were on the same side as the factory or land owners. Raising consciousness is a key feature of the assertion of a valuable self by an individual finding its own worth. The latent capacity to affirm that 'I am' marks the Protest.

January 2009. As Cuba prepared to celebrate the end of the Batista regime 40 years before, nostalgic revolutionaries remembered all too vividly the hopes stirred of building a better world. When Castro stood before the crowds in 1959 to launch Communist Cuba, the Havana square was packed with keepers of the flame. All things were possible. Hedonistic Havana, described by Graham Greene as a city 'where every vice was permissible'[8] now enjoyed a very different reputation.[9] Exploitation of the poor had been defeated. It was a People's Movement to change society. Then came controls, poverty, queues and the rigid system that defeated centrally planned economies across the globe. It all impoverished a prosperous Caribbean Island.[10] Che Guevara, a young doctor who had left Argentina on a motor bike in 1953 and had become radicalised by oppression and poverty, helped gain victory in the uprising.

> Because of the circumstances in which I travelled, first as a student and later as a doctor, I came into close contact with poverty, hunger and disease; with

> the inability to treat a child because of lack of money […]. I began to realise at that time that there were things that were almost as important to me as becoming famous for making a significant contribution to medical science: I wanted to help those people.[11]

Although Che Guevara died in 1967 in Bolivia, trying to export the social revolution in Cuba, his intense gaze and beret had become an icon of the twentieth century, used to sell everything from T-shirts to bikinis. Che Guevara's family were upset about this. 'We don't want money; we demand respect.'[12] It was a curious conjunction of the devaluing that is inherent in the oppression he fought against and those acts of disrespect perceived by his family that occasioned the Protest.

Once it dawns on people how far they have been downloading social programming without realising it, invisible forces can start to become visible. For most, blind spots abound and they do not realise they have been shaped by factors to do with class, gender, race and all the other dimensions that mould the lived experience of millions. The gift of self-knowledge opens up awareness of those blind spots so that the influence of unseen forces is brought into the open and the invisible becomes visible. Most of us are blind to the systems we live in.

Devaluation is implicated in all dimensions of social injustice. Yet cultures of devaluation not only shape the way the world has been divided up, they also evoke a reaction. It is a response that is addressed to those who seem to hold more cards. For there is throughout this essay an unresolved issue, that of the relationship between value as a social category and power. The cardholders of wealth and access to resources, of employment and leverage can seem to be gatekeepers to a controlling veto over the lives and options of others. They make the shape that others have to fit into. Yet there is always resistance and response that powers up the power-less. Within that empowerment, latent possibilities for re-valuing occur.

We have been exploring how human devaluation is central to the way subjects are formed. It functions as a social dynamic, shaping and moulding people in the inter-subjective field of social relations. The problem with such hierarchies of difference is that they generate psycho-social tension, tension that runs to the core aspect of an individual. They run up against value-in-oneself. Yet there is a response precisely because people reject the way society ascribes higher or lower value to them. This is the reflex to a dynamic of devaluation. The question is where the energy comes from to generate it.

As this analysis moves from inter-personal life to social life, there is another issue to ponder. How does the spring-loaded reaction of Protest become mobilised in social groups and collective formations?

The answer presumably is that what determines the scale and level of social response is radicalisation. The Protest needs to be mobilised in order to make that translation from individual to group reactions. This may require two strategies:

1. The gift of imagination so that participants can see a way to change things
2. Being spoken to in a way that creates and raises consciousness

Here a theory in linguistic philosophy called Status Function Declaration may be relevant.[13] The idea has its roots in the work of the Oxford philosopher J. L. Austin whose notion of performance utterance is a trick that creates a new state of affairs through uttering words.[14] Wedding vows – 'I take this woman to be my lawful wedded wife [...] I take this man to be my lawful wedded husband' are one such example. Speaking these words creates a new state. I suggest that latent indignation and Protest can be acted upon through external voices giving voice through speaking into the lives of those experiencing devaluing social effects and thus raising awareness of value. Someone must say to another, to declare, they are worth more than the script they were handed seems to suggest. Things change!

Dagenham, 1968, saw a raising of consciousness of women working at the Ford motor company plant, sewing and machining. The women downed tools when they are re-classified as 'unskilled'. This resulted in a confrontation, the outcome of which was a lasting blow for equal pay.[15]

Leadership and consciousness-raising are the tools by which groups emerge from a sense of low self-worth and implicit collusion in devaluation towards assertiveness in the public square. In movements of emancipation, individual women were recruited into a sisterhood they were not previously aware of; black people in the apartheid era in South Africa discovered a mobilised form of consciousness as the 'I' became 'we' and individual acts of mental defiance coalesced into collective indignation of Protest. Though the form of its expression assumes different shapes, with a slow fuse, the conditioning effects of social devaluation eventually engender their own dialectical contradiction.

The notion of resistance is of course well documented. In *Sharp's Dictionary of Power and Struggle*, an encyclopaedia of power and struggle presented by Gene Sharp, forms of resistance and Protest are catalogued. Yet questions arise about what motivates some to choose resistance against collaboration.[16] What is proposed here is that the energy of Protest is a strategy for revaluation. It is a reflex response to being devalued – especially where inequalities and injustice are infused with disrespect. For social processes of devaluation are, in the end, self-subverting. They result in radicalisation precisely because they assault a valuable self.

Social protest is not new to the twentieth century. In 1789, the French Revolution resulted in violent social upheaval. Political reforms quickly became too modest. What stirred was a mood; nothing less than war on privilege. As the aristocrats were guillotined and the women knitted, *egalité* was superseded as a banner by 'Get the rich!' Ruins of Empire' was a tract passed round in Jacobin circles in the 1790s when French revolutionary fever filled the air. Le Comte de Volney's dialogue occurs between two groups that highlights growing protest of populism against inequality.

> People [...] What labour do you perform in the society? Privileged Class: None, we are not made to labour. People: How then have you acquired your wealth? Privileged Class. By taking the pains to govern you People: To govern us! [...] We toil and you enjoy; we produce and you dissipate; wealth flows from us, and you absorb it.[17]

In Tolstoy's novel *Hadji-Murad*, peasant soldiers before the Russian Revolution objected to the familiar 'you' form by which they were addressed by their officers, normally reserved for children and animals.[18] The first thing a peasant had to learn was how to address his superiors – 'Your Radiance' for titled officers. Officers were allowed to use a wide range of abusive language like 'scum' or 'scoundrel' to ensure that peasants knew their place. A few years later, in the early stages of the upheaval in Russia, most workers' demands were economic. Some were emotional. Men and women were no longer victims of history. They had seized control of it and in that heady atmosphere there was a stress on the worker's own sense of dignity. In an atmosphere of growing self-confidence and political consciousness, they were now aware of themselves as citizens. They were no longer prepared to be treated with disrespect by foremen or managers. Waiters and waitresses in Petrograd marched with banners bearing demands: 'We insist on respect for waiters as human beings. Down with tips. Waiters are citizens.'[19]

Domestic servants marched to demand that they should be addressed with the formal 'you' as opposed to the informal 'you' previously used to address the serfs. Yardmen demanded that their degrading title should be changed to 'house directors'. Women workers demanded equal pay to men, an end to degrading body searches and an abolition of child labour. As expectations rocketed during the early period of the Russian revolution before they became heavily politicised by Lenin's version of socialism, aspirations reflected personal striving for dignity and individual worth; these aspirations were betrayed because the top-down re-engineering of society took no account of the empowering and motivating potential associated with personal value.

Britain avoided a similar convulsion against the *ancien régime*. The United Kingdom, the first country to industrialise, saw the emergence of a whole class of artisans and workers who experienced devastating loss of status and degradation through an industrial rather than political revolution. Yet the working class took part in its own formation and, in spite of the disturbing impact of industrialisation, managed to create political consciousness.[20] Movements such as Chartism flourished, characterised by great vitality and sense of dignity. Social protest of the sort that generated huge energies against injustice and privilege is encapsulated in Victor Hugo's *Les Miserables* on which the contemporary musical issues a rallying cry: 'Do you hear the people cry, it is the sound of angry men. It is the song of a people who will not be slaves again!'

The working movement in its classic historical form only really lasted from the 1830s to the 1950s. Through trade unions and the emerging Labour movement, workers developed dignity in the face of the brutalising factory conditions.[21] There was a strong feeling of banding together, of solidarity against an exploitative world. Behind the battle against class inequality lay a demand for respect, to be treated as being equal in value. Behind Trade Unionism, working class agitation and formation of Labour parties in the West was a Protest by 80 per cent of the people that the top 20 per cent should not have exclusive right to wealth and privilege. Class politics turned the place that people occupied lower down on the ladder into a site of resistance, saying in effect, 'we will not be constrained by your actions or collude with your discourse!'

Amid the reaction against class inequalities can be discerned the demand to be treated as being equal in value. Working class agitation, trade unions and socialist governments in the West raised class consciousness. Enter universal suffrage. Everyone had the right to vote and participate in the political community. Marx argued that the struggle between classes was the major motivation in history but as a Labour prime minister in the United Kingdom famously argued, 'My friends, the class war is dead. The true battle for equality is only just beginning.'[22]

The notion of devaluation links together that experience of conditioning by social rank with a personal reaction that may be felt by those involved. It links under the same theoretical roof the depressive effects of depreciating others and even writing them off with the reaction that can be mobilised of '*we are* worth more than that!' It is the end result of both moves – being aware you are less valuable to society on the one hand and discovering a consciousness-raising moment of being worth more than previously thought – that prevents us either regarding devaluation merely as a social attitude or subsuming all this under the rubric of status. What links these two social realities is that they embody a sense of value – be it positive or negative. This is more than social value or honouring more highly those who are higher in rank. When people are put in their place or conversely emancipated so they find a new sense of worth, they will often issue in effect some kind of statement about personal value. It tugs at the personal and does not merely shape social value.

For most historical accounts, the woman is a silent object. The native is also a silent object of history. The movements of Protest in the second half of the twentieth century were a form of historical consciousness that allowed such silent objects to stand forth and speak, to be the author of their own experiences. The Protest entails a symbolic process of self-representation and image bound up with a new narrative. 'I am now giving myself a value that was not therefore before' declares a client discovering new horizon of expectation and identity that comes with the this response.[23]

In Zadie Smith's novel *White Teeth*, Samad is a Bangladeshi waiter in an Indian restaurant. Poorly treated by his employers, he works until three in the morning and has to endure uncouth customers who reward him princely 15p tips for his services. Samad dreams of escape – escape from the consequences of his status, escape from the indignity and escape from the indifference of customers who barely look up when he takes their orders. He wants to wear a sign round his neck, a placard announcing to the world:

> I am not a waiter. I have been a student, a scientist, a soldier. My wife is called Alsana. We live in East London but would like to move north. I am a Muslim but Allah has forsaken me or I have forsaken Allah – I am not sure. I have a friend – Archie – and others. I am forty nine but women still turn in the street. Sometimes.[24]

Similarly, dismantling colonial structures and attitudes has involved the Protest. The 90-year-old Du Bois at the All-African People's Conference after the birth of Ghana in 1957 said to the assembled delegates, 'You have nothing to lose but your chains! You have a continent to regain! You have freedom and human dignity to attain'.[25]

It was when Asian nationals were able to distinguish between the white man's magic and his skin colour that the revolt began against imperialism.[26] When the twentieth century opened, European power was at its zenith. No nation could withstand its superiority of arms and its commerce. Sixty years later, only the relics remained. Between 1945 and 1960, more than a quarter of the world's population in 40 countries had revolted against colonialism and gained independence. As one historian suggested, 'never before in the whole of human history had so revolutionary a reversal occurred with such rapidity'. The revolt against the West represents 'the advance of the peoples of Asia and Africa – and, more slowly but no less surely, of Latin America – to a place of new dignity in the world'.[27]

After the famous salt march when Indian protesters had seemed to show up British rule as the upholder of race supremacy and exploiter of those outside her borders, that new consciousness gave Indians 'the conviction that they could, by lifting up their heads and straightening their spines, lift the yoke from their shoulders'.[28]

A story in the British and American press demonstrated a reaction of Protest against racism. A British family was banned from staying at a chain of luxury hotels after they had refused to be served by 'people of colour' at a Florida resort. The term had been lodged as a preference by the couple on the hotel computer. It went with a request not to be served by those with foreign accents. It did, of course, imply that the white couple were colourless. Others have a colour; white people do not. Their neutrality with respect to colour is significant for its claim to difference, distance and power. What is this category of whiteness that lays claim to being the norm? A hotel spokesperson emphasised that the hotel 'does not tolerate or condone discrimination of any kind by its employees or visiting guests'.[29]

Such defiance rooted in value is a form of identity. It enlarges the horizon of expectation. Freud was supposed to feel inferior because of his race. He had discarded this in 1873 in his first year at university. His response was defiance. He saw no need to bow to the verdict of the majority.[30] Human devaluation is rampant in anti-semitism, the longest hatred. The novelist Emmanuel Litvinoff grew up in the East End of London in the 1920s and 30s. Then, with the rise of fascism, 'the problem of identity' hit him in the face. Anti-semitism became an unwanted inheritance. You were lumbered with it. In parallel grew a self-contempt, a feeling that people were justified in despising him.[31] Devaluation became internalised but then comes the reaction of a valuable self, powered up to become a site of resistance. During the war, 'my Jewish neuroses vanished as I learned to turn the occasional anti-semitic remark against its perpetrator with nonchalant good humour'. 'Don't let the bastards get you down', was the advice given to a young Jewess facing hostility on the German street in the Third Reich.[32] It makes us human.

Some individuals with disability have always been able to achieve very highly – against all the odds and despite having to work twice as hard. Yet action was needed by governments to adopt anti-discrimination law to ensure the rights of disabled people. The reformulation of disability as a form of social devaluation as opposed to a medical or welfare model began in the 1970s. 'Disabled people began to self-organise to resist, among other things, their relegation to residential institutions, their exclusion from the labour market and the opportunity to earn a living wage and their enforced poverty.'[33]

'Don't write us off!' is the reaction by gay and lesbian groups against being devalued. This is the essence of dissent, claiming the right to author your own narrative. Behind the new social movements of the past generation lies a strong impetus towards minorities not to go second class any more, towards being re-valued.

> I've got a problem with men [...]. I would like to be comfortable with men as equals. Sometimes I want that so much I say, 'Give it to me [...]. Give me equality'.[34]

Progress in the West has been extraordinary. The position of women has been radically transformed as they demanded entry into the social mainstream.

The logic of liberal theory demanded what was a long time coming, the emancipation of women as well as abolition of slavery.[35] For early feminists as for advocates of racial justice, the goal was emancipation. Taking their place in the labour market, the women's movement raised consciousness. Alongside civil rights, it was the most important social change of the late twentieth century. In the light of history, it is astonishing that so significant a social change was accompanied by so little conflict. By and large, men welcomed it, partly because sexism was challenged profoundly; seen as unjust in liberal societies. Laws against domestic violence began to be passed, though not always enforced. Domestic slavery was out. Father was not always right. A woman should not just play Wife and Mum.

> This raising of women's consciousness has, for the first time in recorded history, brought substantial numbers of men and women to understand how patriarchal culture constructed and maintained male dominance and female subservience.[36]

But the trend towards more women working was not just about the politics of protest. Unseen forces were at work carrying it along, most notably demand for female labour in areas where women can compete. It was different in societies that needed brawn rather than brains. More than half the professional workforce in America is made up of women. It would seem that the rise of the service sector coupled with the decline of manufacturing in the West shaped the feminisation of the labour market. As a result of a social revolution, the gender wage gap is (partly) closed, educational attainment of women has risen and now surpasses that of men. It came with an unprecedented level of control over reproduction; much domestic drudgery was relieved through new domestic appliances.[37] For most women feminism was about choice and control over their lives, deciding their own fate, equal rights and control over sexuality and reproduction. 'It is also about feeling good about ourselves as women, recognising our worth and value in the contributions we make in every area of our lives.'[38] The Protest is at the heart of economic empowerment of women.

Peasant revival movements are going in a different direction to elites who advocate a liberalisation of women's rights. The movement of Muslim female professionals calling themselves 'Sisters in Islam' have emphasised the need to interpret the Qu'ran and Hadith in their contexts, criticising patriarchal practices such as dress codes, as 'mechanism of control' masquerading as norms protecting female modesty. In short, a veiled woman can be a symbol of oppression. But she can also represent a consciously chosen stance. Probably most Muslim wear the headscarf out of choice so Western governments forcing them to dress (or undress) against their wills seems an infringement of the individual rights their culture normally strives to safeguard. In a country like Malaysia, women demonstrated a range of responses to Islamic fundamentalism but also to modernity itself.[39] Professional women have been influenced by Islamic resurgence.[40] On the campus of University of Malaysia, 60 per cent of students wear the mini-telekung, a cloth that covers the head, hair and chest. A Muslim middle class is on the rise and this itself is a barrier to extremism.[41]

Many Islamic women are determined to become actors in their own drama, in spheres that are not defined by men.[42] Inscribing themselves into men's narrative as not just an idealised cluster of virtues but active interpreters of their own narrative is the essence of the Protest. To deny that a constructive response to the social order is possible is to deny agency. The Protest too is reflected in the thousands of organisations through the Muslim world dedicated to eradicating illiteracy and FGM or raising awareness of health issues.[43] Muslim women are in the forefront of campaigns for fresh interpretations of Islamic jurisprudence and calls for reform. It all demonstrates how Muslims are capable of the self-criticism needed to root out gender discrimination.[44–51] Struggle for women's rights in Islam involves using the same religious texts and doctrines that can be oppressive, driving reform. For some, there is no alternative battlefield.[41]

It is ironic that in the West, which largely criticises such practices, women undergo self-inflicted torture in submission to dietary regimes. Yet we live in a largely post-feminist era. Women in the West are less prepared to see themselves as victims, celebrate diversity rather than go for equality and are being empowered to choose their own way of life.[42] There is a post-modern challenge to refuse the way the world is split into binary opposites where all women are constituted as 'other'.[43] Or perhaps it represents the post-ideological challenge of what might be termed a Fourth wave of feminism in which the Protest is no longer reactive and largely loses its energy.

The reality of a movement from feminine consciousness (as a barricade from which to oppose being in a man's world) to being liberated subjects on equal terms in the workplace was often messy. The ideology of feminism militated against this but caught between career in a fiercely competitive corporate jungle and 'being nicely sabotaged by motherhood', paradoxically, working women were often left with little economic security.[44] A career break brings loss of momentum. Child care is hugely expensive. Part-time work can often represent economic marginalisation.[45]

In summary, political discontent and even radicalisation so often involves the reaction against being second class. To move from an 'I' to a 'we' involves a process of politicisation, of radicalisation. When it is mobilised, there is a psychological aspect to resistance rooted in the pursuit of value. Michael Foucault argued that power can only be understood in terms of resistance.[46] This can imply that those with less power adopt the subject position of victimhood. Yet empowerment lies at the heart of the Protest by working classes and peasants, by women, by the elderly, by LGBT groups, ex-colonial subjects, by those with disability and by ethnic minorities by those who wanted to change the system to being more inclusive of difference on equal terms. The range of responses cannot be reduced to 'resistance', a category that implies a stance and tactics of opposition. Self-valuation and self-definition are two ways of resisting oppression. Participating in approaches to preserve the self-esteem of the group that is oppressed helps them avoid any dehumanising outside influences.

'The Protest' highlights the person who has experienced social injustice. It focuses on the meaning of the action and the reaction, the transmission of lower value and the spring-loaded response to devaluation resulting in re-valuation. At first latent, it stirs towards beginnings of emancipation arising from a heightened consciousness of a valuable self. 'Hang a label round our necks! We are worth more than you say!'

Inequality will not always have the last word. The caged bird sings.[47]

Notes

1. Hardoon, D. (2015) 'Wealth: Having it all and wanting more', Oxfam Issue briefing, 19 January. Available at http://policy-practice.oxfam.org.uk/publications/wealth-having-it-all-and-wanting-more-338125.
2. Author's client notes – name withheld and used with permission.
3. Heaney, S. (1991) *The Cure at Troy: A Version of Sophocles' Philoctetes*. New York: Farrar, Straus and Giroux.

Introduction

1. Clark, M. B. (2017) *The Hate Race: A Memoir*. London: Corsair.
2. Luce, E. (2017) *The Retreat of Western Liberalism*. New York: Grove Atlantic.
3. Piketty, T. & Goldhammer, A. (2013) *Capital in the Twenty-First Century*. Cambridge, MA: Harvard University Press.
4. Hardoon, D. (2015) 'Wealth: Having it all and wanting more', Oxfam Issue briefing, 19 January. Available at http://policy-practice.oxfam.org.uk/publications/wealth-having-it-all-and-wanting-more-338125.
5. World Economic Forum Annual Meeting, 23–27 January 2013, Davos-Klosters, Switzerland. Available at https://www.weforum.org/.../world-economic-forum-annual-meeting-2013.
6. Christine Lagarde to Davos leaders: 'I warned about the dangers of inequality in 2013 and nobody listened'. Stéphanie Thomson (ed.) World Economic Forum. Available at https://www.weforum.org/.../world-economic-forum-annual-meeting-2017.
7. Scheidel, W. (2017) *The Great Leveller: Violence and the History of Inequality from the Stone Age to the Twenty-first Century*. Princeton, NJ: Princeton University Press.
8. Steed, C. (2016) *A Question of Worth: The Quantification of Human Value*. London: I.B.Tauris.
9. White, A. & Al-Othman, H. (2017) 'The PM says a new race disparity audit will reveal "uncomfortable" truths about Britain', *Buzzfeed*, 2 October. Available at https://www.buzzfeed.com/alanwhite/a-new-report-has-left-the-pm-vowing-to-fight-the-injustices.
10. Quoted by Roberts, A. (1994) in *Eminent Churchillians*. London: Widenfeld & Nicolson, p. 125.
11. Shapiro, T. (2017) *Toxic Inequality: How America's Wealth Gap Destroys Mobility, Deepens the Racial Divide, and Threatens Our Future*. New York: Basic Books.
12. Davey, M. (2017) 'Australian report finds disturbing evidence of gender inequality', *Guardian*, 7 March.
13. Hawking, S. (2016) 'This is the most dangerous time for our planet', *Guardian*, 1 December.

14. Nasr, J. & Escritt, T. (2017) 'Scuffles, water cannon at final anti-G20 march in Hamburg', *Daily News*, 8 July. Available at http://www.nydailynews.com/newswires/news/national/anti-capitalist-militants-front-anti-g20-demo-hamburg-police-article-1.3311309.
15. Morrison, S. (2017) 'Pride in London 2017: Celebration "best antidote" for recent terror and tragedy, Sadiq Khan says', *Evening Standard*, 8 July. Available at http://www.standard.co.uk/news/london/pride-in-london-2017-celebration-best-antidote-for-recent-terror-and-tragedy-sadiq-khan-says-a3583336.html.
16. HMIC and HMCPSI (2017) 'Living in fear – the police and CPS response to harassment and stalking', HMICFRS Publications, 5 July. Available at www.justiceinspectorates.gov.uk/hmicfrs/publications/living-in-fear-the-police-and-cps-response-to-harassment-and-stalking/.
17. BBC Radio 4 (2017) *The World Tonight*, 6 June. Available at www.bbc.co.uk/radio4/theworldtonight.
18. Ibid.
19. Mekhennet, S. (2017) *I Was Told to Come Alone: My Journey Behind the Lines of Jihad*. London: Virago.
20. BBC Radio 4 (2016) *World at One*, 24 August. Available at www.bbc.co.uk/radio4/worldatone.
21. Cf Fischer, L. (1997) *The Life of Mahatma Gandhi*. London: Harper Collins, Chapter 7.
22. Heber, R. (2012) *The Whole Works of the Right Rev. Jeremy Taylor*. Charleston, SC: Nabu Press, Vol. IV, p. 59.

Chapter One: A Tale of Two Cities

1. Gould, S. J. (1996) *The Mismeasure of Man*. New York: W. W. Norton.
2. *Independent* (2017), 14 June.
3. Kepel, G. (2017) *Terror in France: The Rise of Jihad in the West*. Princeton, NJ: Princeton University Press.
4. Available at https://www.rbkc.gov.uk/housing/regenyour-neighbourhood/grenfell-tower.
5. Snowdon, K., Sheriff, L., Bowden, G., & Rajan, N. (2017) 'Grenfell tower fire lays bare the "Tale of Two Kensingtons" – a borough of extreme rich and poor', *Huffington Post*, 15 June. Available at http://www.huffingtonpost.co.uk/entry/grenfell-tower-tale-two-kensingtons-borough-extreme-rich-poor_uk_594269e9e4b003d5948d5116.
6. Available at www.shelter.org.uk.
7. Demographia (2017) '13th Annual Demographia International Demographia International Housing Affordability Survey: 2017, Rating Middle-Income Housing Affordability', July. Available at http://www.demographia.com/dhi.pdf.
8. BBC Radio 4 (2017) *The World Tonight*, 14 June. Available at www.bbc.co.uk/radio4/theworldtonight.
9. BBC Radio 4 (2017) *The World Tonight*, 30 June. Available at www.bbc.co.uk/radio4/theworldtonight.
10. *Daily Telegraph* (2017) 'Grenfell Tower inferno a "disaster waiting to happen" as concerns are raised for safety of other buildings', 14 June.

11. European Commission (2012). 'EU Charter of Fundamental Rights'. Available at https://ec.europa.eu/info/aid-development-cooperation-fundamental-rights/your-rights-eu/eu-charter-fundamental-rights_en.
12. Tepperman, F. (2016) *The Fix: How Nations Survive and Thrive in a World in Decline*. London and New York: Tim Duggan Books.
13. Labour Party 'A more equal society', Labour Party Manifesto UK General Election 2017. Available at http://www.labour.org.uk/index.php/manifesto2017/a-more-equal-society.
14. Campbell, J. (2001) *Margaret Thatcher: The Grocer's Daughter*, Vol. 1. London: Pimlico.
15. Jones, D. S. (2012) *Masters of the Universe: Hayek, Friedman, and the Birth of Neoliberal Politics*. Princeton, NJ: Princeton University Press.
16. Kley, R. (1994) *Hayek's Social and Political Thought*. Oxford: Oxford University Press.
17. Plant, R. (2009) *The Neo-liberal State*. Oxford: Oxford University Press.
18. Yellen, J. (2015) *Perspectives on Inequality and Opportunity from the Survey of Consumer Finances*. Available at https://www.federalreserve.gov/newsevents/speech/yellen2014.
19. Richards, S. (2017) *The Rise of the Outsiders: How Mainstream Politics Lost its Way*. London: Atlantic Books.
20. Prime Minister's Office & May, T. (2016) 'Statement from the new Prime Minister Theresa May', 13 July. Available at https://www.gov.uk/government/speeches/statement-from-the-new-prime-minister-theresa-may.
21. Public Health England London Borough of Enfield, July 2017. Available at https://files.datapress.com/sport/dataset/health-profiles-2017/PublicHealthEnglandHealthprofilesEnfield.pdf.
22. Author's parish notes.
23. Information supplied to the author by Christians Against Poverty and based on their case studies.
24. Loopstra, R. & Lalor, D. (2017) 'Food, insecurity and disability', Trussell Trust. Available at www.trusselltrust.org.uk.
25. Centre for Responsible Credit (2017) 'The decline of crisis and community care support in England: Why a new approach is needed', 13 September. Available at https://www.responsible-credit.org.uk/decline-local-welfare-schemes/.
26. Marmot, M. (2016) *The Health Gap*. London: Bloomsbury.
27. Frey, B. (2008) *Happiness: A Revolution in Economics*. Cambridge, MA: MIT Press.
28. Ibid.
29. Marmot, M. (2008) *Fair Society, Healthy Lives*. London: UCL Institute of Health Equity.
30. Yeung, P. (2017) 'NHS abuse of mental patients "endemic"', *The Times*, 7 August. Available at https://www.thetimes.co.uk/article/nhs-abuse-of-mental-patients-endemic.
31. Buchan, I., et al. (2017) 'North-South disparities in English mortality 1965–2015: Longitudinal population study'. *Journal of Epidemiology and Community Health* 71(9): 928–36.
32. Christians Against Poverty (2017) 'Client Report Partnership; the key to transforming lives', June. Available at https://capuk.org/connect/policy-and-government/client-report.
33. BBC *News at Six* (2017), 8 August.

Chapter Two: Winners, Losers and New Class Divides

1. Gates Foundation (2008) About us. Available at www.gatesfoundation.org/AboutUs.
2. Channel 4, UK (2009) *Red Gold; the Story of the PDVSA Oil Company in Venezuela,* 10 February.
3. Oxfam. 'Inequality'. Available at http://policy-practice.oxfam.org.uk/our-work/inequality.
4. Bellah, R. N. (ed.) (1973) *Emile Durkheim: On Morality and Society, Selected Writings.* Chicago: University of Chicago Press. See also Giddens, A. (ed.) (1972) *Emile Durkheim: Selected Writings.* London: Cambridge University Press and Stedman Jones, S. (2001) *Durkheim Reconsidered.* Cambridge: Polity Press, for a more recent assessment.
5. Rushdie, S. (1981) *Midnight's Children.* London: Vintage.
6. Figes, O. (1996) *A People's Tragedy: The Russian Revolution 1891–1924.* London: Pimlico, p. 365.
7. Fournier, M. (2012) *Emile Durkheim: A Biography.* Cambridge: Polity Press.
8. Berlin, I. (1963) *Karl Marx: His Life and Environment.* Oxford: Oxford University Press.
9. Engels, F. (1984) *The Condition of the Working Class in England.* Chicago: Academy Chicago Publishers.
10. Figes, O. (1996) *A People's Tragedy: The Russian Revolution 1891–1924.* London: Pimlico, p. 114.
11. Ibid., p. 524.
12. Marx, K. (1969) 'The German Ideology', in Feuer, L. S. (ed.) *Marx and Engels: Basic Writings on Politics and Philosophy.* London: Fontana, p. 299.
13. Figes, O. (1996) *A People's Tragedy: The Russian Revolution 1891–1924.* London: Pimlico, p. 112.
14. Marx, K. & Engels, F. (1967) *The Communist Manifesto.* Harmondsworth: Penguin, p. 121.
15. Jackson, B. & Marsden, D. (1986) *Education and the Working Class.* London: Ark Paperbacks, p. 180.
16. Westcott, A. (1988) *Arthur's Village – The Somerset Childhood of Arthur Westcott 1900–1915.* Congresbury History Group.
17. Author's client notes – name withheld and used with permission.
18. UK Government (2016) 'State of the Nation report on social mobility in Great Britain'. Available at https://www.gov.uk/government/news/state-of-the-nation-report-on-social-mobility-in-great-britain.
19. Bourdieu, P. (1986) *Distinction: A Social Critique of the Judgement of Taste.* London: Routledge.
20. Savage, M. (2016) *Social Class in the 21st Century.* London: Pelican.
21. BBC Radio 4, 13 April (2014) discussion on the British Sociology Association Conference, London, April 2013.
22. Taylor-Gooby, P. F. (2009) 'Is education the key to combining growth with justice?' Lecture, 25 November, Royal Society. Available at www.alphagalileo.org.
23. Lamont, M. (2000) *The Dignity of Working Men: Morality and the Boundaries of Race, Class and Immigration.* Cambridge, MA: Harvard University Press, p. 97.
24. Holton, R. J. & Turner, B. (1989) *Max Weber on Economy and Society.* London: Routledge, p. 194.
25. Beck, U. (1992) *Risk Society: Towards a New Modernity.* London: Sage.
26. Crompton, R. (1993) *Class and Stratification: An Introduction to Current Debates.* Cambridge: Polity Press, p. 11.

27. Goldthorpe, J. H. (ed.) (1984) *Order and Conflict in Contemporary Capitalism*. Oxford: Clarendon Press.
28. Lash, S. & Urry, J. (1987) *The End of Organised Capitalism*. Cambridge: Polity Press.
29. Hanly, L. (2016) *Respectable: The Experience of Class*. London: Allen Lane.
30. Mommsen, W. (1992) *The Political and Social Theory of Max Weber: Collected Essays*. Chicago: University of Chicago Press.
31. Bruun, H. H. & Whimster, S. (eds.) (2012) *Max Weber: Collected Methodological Writings*, translated by Bruun, H. H. London: Routledge.
32. Weber, M. (1948) 'Class, status and party', in Garth, H. & Mills, C. W. (eds.) *From Max Weber*. London: Routledge, p. 181.
33. OECD (2015) *In It Together: Why Less Inequality Benefits All*. Paris: OECD Publishing.
34. Myles, J. & Pierson, P. (2001) 'The comparative political economy of pension reform', in Pierson, P. (ed.) *The New Politics of the Welfare State*. Oxford: Oxford University Press.
35. *The Economist* (2017) 'The new old: The economics of longevity', Special Report, 8 July.
36. European Commission (2015) *The 2015 Ageing Report – Economic and Budgetary Projections for the 28 EU Member States (2013–2060)*. Luxembourg: Publications Office of the European Union. Available at http://ec.europa.eu/economy_finance/publications/european_economy/2015/pdf/ee3_en.pdf.
37. Darvas, Z. & Wolff, G. (2014) 'Europe's social problem and its implications for economic growth'. Available at http://bruegel.org/2014/03/europes-social-problem-and-its-implications-for-economic-growth/.
38. Arulampalam, W. (2001) 'Is unemployment really scarring? Effects of unemployment experiences on wages'. *Economic Journal* 11(475): 585–606.
39. Bonoli, G. & Natali, D. (2012) *The Politics of the New Welfare State*. Oxford: Oxford University Press.
40. Hemerijck, A. (2013) *Changing Welfare States*. Oxford: Oxford University Press.
41. Boeri, T. (2011) 'Reducing youth unemployment and dualism', Thematic Review Seminar on the Reduction of Labour Market Segmentation Addressing the Needs of Young People, Brussels, 27 June.
42. Begg, I., Mushövel, F., & Niblett, R. (2015) 'The welfare state in Europe: Visions for reform', Chatham House. Available at https://www.chathamhouse.org/publication/welfare-state-europe-visions-reform#.
43. Quick, A. (2017) 'We need to talk about wealth', *New Economics Foundation*. Available at http://neweconomics.org/2017/06/need-talk-wealth/.
44. Office for National Statistics (2017) 'Household disposable income and inequality', 10 January. Available at https://www.ons.gov.uk/peoplepopulationandcommunity/personalandhouseholdfinances/incomeandwealth/bulletins/householddisposableincomeandinequality/financialyearending2016.
45. Gardiner, L. (2016) 'Votey McVoteface: Understanding the growing turnout gap between the generations'. Available at http://www.intergencommission.org/publications/votey-mcvoteface-understanding-the-growing-turnout-gap-between-the-generations/.
46. Smith, Y. (2010) 'Indefensible men'. From the December 2009 edition of *The Baffler*. Available at https://www.nakedcapitalism.com/2010/03/indefensible-men.html.
47. D'Arcy, C. (2017) 'Why wealth is the enemy of the young', *Guardian*. Available at https://www.theguardian.com/inequality/2017/jun/21/why-wealth-is-the-enemy-of-the-young-resolution-foundation.

48. OECD (2013) *Pensions at a Glance 2013: OECD and G20 Indicators*. Paris: OECD Publishing.
49. Doidge, S. & Drabble, D. (2010) *The Construction, Maintenance and Deconstruction of Older Worker's Identities in the Workplace: The Role of Anxiety*. London: Tavistock Institute.
50. *The Economist* (2017) World in Figures.
51. European Commission (2012) *The 2012 Ageing Report*. European Commission. Available at http://ec.europa.eu/economy_finance/publications/european_economy/2012/pdf/ee-2012-2_en.pdf.
52. The Chatham House London Conference (2015) 'Overcoming the risks and contradictions of globalization', Chatham House. Available at http://www.chathamhouse.org/london-conference-2015/background-papers/overcoming-risks-and-contradictions-globalization#.
53. UCL (2017) 'Inequalities in health in an ageing population'. Available at https://www.ucl.ac.uk/hssrg/studies/inequalities.
54. Help Age International (2013) 'Ageing, discrimination and inequalities in the post-2015 agenda'. Available at http://www.helpage.org/blogs/portia-reyes-14421/ageing-discrimination-and-inequalities-in-the-post2015-agenda-524.
55. Boycott, R. (2006) *The Times*, 29 March.
56. Sabadish, N. & Mishel, L. (2013) 'CEO pay in 2012 was extraordinarily high to typical workers and other high earners', Economic Policy Institute. Bivens, J. & Mishel, L. (2013) *The Pay of Corporate Executives and Financial Professionals as Evidence of Rents in Top 1 Percent Incomes*. Economic Policy Institute Working Paper 296. Available at http://www.epi.org/publication/pay-corporate-executives-financial-professionals/.
57. Hopkins, K. (2014) 'FTSE bosses earn 120 times more than average worker', *The Times*, 13 October.
58. Blair Smith, E. & Kuntz, P. (2013) 'CEO pay 1,795-to-1 multiple of wages skirts U. S. law'. Available at https://www.bloomberg.com/news/articles/2013-04-30/ceo-pay-1-795-to-1-multiple-of-workers-skirts-law-as-sec-delays.
59. Institute of Public Policy Research (IPPR) (2016) 'Future proof: Britain in the 2020s'. Available at https://www.ippr.org/publications/future-proof-britain-in-the-2020s.
60. Manyika, J., et al. 'Harnessing automation for a future that works'. Available at https://www.mckinsey.com/global-themes/digital-disruption/harnessing-automation-for-a-future-that-works.
61. WEF (2017) 'Donald Trump's inauguration: What they had to say at Davos'. Available at https://www.weforum.org/agenda/2017/01/donald-trumps-inauguration-what-they-had-to-say-at-davos.
62. Royal Society of Arts (2017) 'Machine, Platform, Crowd', public event, 11 July.
63. De Tocqueville, A. (2004) *Democracy in America*, translated by Goldhammer, A. New York: Library of America.
64. Mason, P. (2015) *Post Capitalism: A Guide to Our Future*. London: Allen Lane, p. 76.
65. Williams-Grut, O. (2016) 'Mark Carney: "Every technological revolution mercilessly destroys jobs well before the new ones emerge"', *Business Insider*. Available at http://uk.businessinsider.com/bank-of-england-mark-carney-technology-jobs-market-fourth-industrial-revolution-2016-12.

Chapter Three: Global Divides

1. *Guardian Weekend* (2006) 'Untouchability', 6 May.
2. Oswald, A. (2002) 'One per cent, not 33 dollars', *CCH Daily* (formerly *Accountancy Live*). Available at https://www.accountancylive.com/andrew-oswald-one-cent-not-33-dollars.
3. Global Justice Now. Available at www.globaljustice.org.uk.
4. OECD (2014) 'Focus on inequality and growth'. Available at http://www.oecd.org/social/Focus-Inequality-and-Growth-2014.pdf.
5. World Economic Forum (2017) *The Inclusive Growth and Development Report 2017*. Available at http://www3.weforum.org/docs/WEF_Forum_IncGrwth_2017.pdf.
6. Ibid.
7. Samans, R., et al. (2017) 'Rising to the challenge of inclusive growth and development', in *The Inclusive Growth and Development Report 2017*. Available at http://www3.weforum.org/docs/WEF_Forum_IncGrwth_2017.pdf.
8. Kuper, S. & Szymansk, S. (2012) *Soccernomics*. London and New York: HarperSport.
9. *The Economist* (2016) 'China has gained hugely from globalisation', 10 December.
10. *The Economist* (2016) 'Up on the farm: Inequality in China', 14 May.
11. Credit Suisse Group (2016) 'Global wealth report 2016'. Available at www.credit-suisse.com/.../research-institute/publications.html.
12. Hardoon, D. (2015) 'Wealth: Having it all and wanting more', Oxfam, 19 January. Available at http://policy-practice.oxfam.org.uk/publications/wealth-having-it-all-and-wanting-more-338125.
13. Lindert. P. H. 'Three centuries of inequality in Britain and America'. Available at http://economics.ucdavis.edu/people/fzlinder/peter-linderts-webpage/papers/three-centuries-of-inequality/Lindert%20Inequality%20chapter.pdf.
14. OECD (2016) 'Income inequality remains high in the face of weak income recovery'. Available at http://www.oecd.org/social/OECD2016-Income-Inequality-Update.pdf.
15. The World Bank. 'The role of trade in ending poverty'. Available at http://www.worldbank.org/en/topic/trade/publication/the-role-of-trade-in-ending-poverty.
16. Author's notes, October 2016, used with permission.
17. FAO, IFAD, UNICEF, WFP and WHO (2017) 'The State of Food Security and Nutrition in the World 2017. Building resilience for peace and food security'. Rome, FAO. Available at http://www.fao.org/3/a-I7695e.pdf.
18. Quoted in Harrison, T. (2017) 'The cost of a cup of tea', *Church Times*, 16 June. Available at https://www.churchtimes.co.uk/articles/2017/16-june/features/features/the-cost-of-a-cup-of-tea.
19. Email to author. 'Kibuye district, Rwanda', June 2017. Used with permission.
20. *Church Times* (2017) 'The cost of a cup of tea', 16 June.
21. *Christian Aid News*, Harvest edition (2017) Malawi team, publicity material.
22. D'souza, J. (2004) *Dalit Freedom Now and Forever: The Epic Struggle for Dalit Emancipation*. Centennial, CO: Dalit Freedom Network.
23. US Congressional Committee on International Relations (2006) Serial 109–116, p. 23. Available at http://commdocs.house.gov/committees/intlrel/index.htm.
24. Cox, O. (1948) *Caste, Class and Race*. New York: Modern Reader Paperbacks, pp. 11, 14.
25. Dirks, N. B. (2001) *Caste of Mind: Colonialism and the Making of Modern India*. Princeton, NJ: Princeton University Press.

26. Dumon, L. (1980) *Homo Hierarchicus: The Caste System and its Implications*. Chicago: University of Chicago Press.
27. Cox, O. (1948) *Caste, Class and Race*. New York: Modern Reader Paperbacks, p. 16.
28. Gidla, S. (2017) *Ants Among Elephants: An Untouchable Family and the Making of Modern India*. New York: Farrar, Strauss and Giroux.
29. *Christian Aid News*, Spring edition (2009) 'Bihar'. Available at www.christianaid.org.uk/bihar.
30. Nehru, J. (1985) *The Discovery of India*. New Delhi: Oxford University Press, p. 522.
31. Milanovic, B. (2016) *Global Inequality: A New Approach for the Age of Globalisation*. Cambridge, MA: Bellknap.

Chapter Four: Half the World: Identity Wars

1. McVeigh, K. (2006) 'Woman sues bank for £11m over "bullying mini Hitler"', *The Times*, 11 May.
2. Available at www.rnh.com/show/60/The-King-and-I.
3. Wollstonecraft, M. (1792/2010) *A Vindication of the Rights of Woman: With Strictures on Political and Moral Subjects*. London: Vintage.
4. Euronews (2017) 'BBC reveals gender pay gap'. Available at http://www.euronews.com/2017/07/19/bbc-reveals-gender-pay-gap.
5. Osbourne, S. (2017) '"No equal pay for women until men have babies", says former BBC Today presenter Sue MacGregor', *Independent*, 31 July.
6. Revesz, R. (2017) 'BBC Gender pay gap: Clare Balding says public broadcaster should not treat women as "discount items"', *Independent*, 25 July.
7. Watties, J. (2017) 'Storm at Google over engineer's anti-diversity manifesto', CNN Money. Available at www.money.cnn.com.
8. Crispin, J. (2017) *Why I Am Not a Feminist*. London: Melville House Publishing.
9. Kaplan, A. (2016) *Women Talk More Than Men … and Other Myths About Language Explained*. Cambridge: Cambridge University Press.
10. Baren-Cohen, S. (2003) *The Essential Difference*. London: Penguin.
11. Guiso, L., et al. (2008) 'Diversity: Culture, gender, and math'. *Science* 320(5880): 1164–5.
12. Eliot, L. (2012) *Pink Brain, Blue Brain: How Small Differences Grow into Troublesome Gaps – and What We Can Do About It*. London: Oneworld Publications.
13. Fine, C. (2011) *Delusions of Gender: The Real Science behind Sex Differences*. London: Icon Books.
14. Abelmoneim, J. (2017) 'No more boys and girls: Can our kids go gender free?' BBC Two, 23 August. Available at http://www.bbc.co.uk/programmes/b092pjs2.
15. Sapolsky, R. (2017) *Behave: The Biology of Humans at our Best and Worst*. London: Bodley Head.
16. Saini, A. (2017) *Inferior: How Science got Women Wrong – and the New Research that is Rewriting the Story*. London: Fourth Estate.
17. Mackie, E. (2009) *Rakes, Highwaymen and Pirates: The Making of the Modern Gentlemen in the 18th Century.* Baltimore: Johns Hopkins University Press.
18. Wollstonecraft, M. (1792/2010) *A Vindication of the Rights of Woman: With Strictures on Political and Moral Subjects*. London: Vintage.

19. James, H. (2007) *Portrait of a Lady*. London: Penguin.
20. Phillips, A. (1987) *Feminism and Equality*. Oxford: Blackwell, p. 1.
21. Eisenstein, H. (1985) *The Future of Difference*. New Brunswick, NJ: Rutgers University Press.
22. Wark, P. (2006) *The Times*, 22 February.
23. Hawley, G. (2016) *Right-Wing Critics of American Conservatism*. Kansas: University Press of Kansas.
24. Daniel (1980) and Martin & Roberts (1984) as discussed in Coyle, A. & Skinner, J. (eds.) (1988) *Women and Work*. Basingstoke: MacMillan Education, p. 3. Also Hakim, C. (1979) *Occupational Segregation*. Research Paper no 9, DoE. London: HMSO, p. 29. Landry, C., et al. (1985) *What a Way to Run a Railroad*. London: Comedia Press, p. 57. Ferguson, K. (1984) *The Feminist Case Against Bureaucracy*. Philadelphia: Temple University. Martin, P. (1990) 'Rethinking feminist organisations'. *Gender and Society* 4: 182–206. Jackall, R. (1988) *Moral Mazes: The World of Corporate Managers*. New York: Oxford University Press.
25. Equal Opportunities Commission (2007) *Sex and Power: Who Runs Britain?* London: Equal Opportunities Commission.
26. *The Economist* (2010) 'Older and wiser', Special Report on Germany, 13 March.
27. Dominelli, L. (2002) *Anti-Oppressive Social Work Theory and Practice*. Basingstoke: Palgrave Macmillan, p. 20.
28. Wolf, N. (1991) *The Beauty Myth*. London: Vintage.
29. United Nations Fourth World Conference. Available at http://www.un.org/womenwatch/daw/beijing/.
30. Kristoff, N. D. & Wu Dunn, S. (2010) *Half the Sky*. London: Virago.
31. UN (2015) 'United Nations millennium development goals'. Available at www.un.org/millenniumgoals/bkgd.shtml.
32. BBC News (2006) 'India "loses 10m female births"', 9 January. Available at http://news.bbc.co.uk/1/hi/world/south_asia/4592890.stm.
33. Hussain, Z. (2005) 'Courageous rape victim fights back', *The Times*, 15 March.
34. US State Department (2010) 'Human Rights Report: Iran'. Available at https://www.state.gov/j/drl/rls/hrrpt/2010/nea/154461.htm/.
35. *The Economist* (2010) 'The worldwide war on baby girls', 5 March.
36. *The Economist* (2010) 'Gendercide', 13 March.
37. Shoneyin, L. (2010) *The Secret Lives of Baba Segi's Wives*. London: Serpent's Tail.
38. Channel 4 (2008) *The Qu'ran*, documentary, Channel 4, UK. Examples of self-reporting by Egyptian women, 14 July.
39. Watson, H. (1992) *Women in the City of the Dead*. London: Hurst, p. 184.
40. Mernissi, F. (1985) *Beyond the Veil*. London: Al Saqi Books, pp. 18–19.
41. Ahmed, A. (1988) *Discovering Islam*. London: Routledge, p. 185.
42. Qu'ran - Sura 4: 34.
43. Hossein Nasr, S. (1975) *Ideals and Realities of Islam*. London: George Allen Unwin, p. 112.
44. Qu'ran - Sura 18: 46.
45. El Saadawi, N. (1982) *The Hidden Face of Eve: Women in the Arab World*. London: Zed Books.
46. Egyptian Center for Women's Rights (2008) 'Clouds in Egypt's sky, sexual harassment: from verbal harassment to rape'. Available at http://ecwronline.org/.

47. Hirsi Ali, A. (2006) *The Caged Virgin*. Free Press.
48. Sullivan, A. (1997) *Same-Sex Marriage: Pro and Con*. New York: Vintage.
49. Bernstein, M. (2002) 'Identities and politics: Toward a historical understanding of the lesbian and gay movement'. *Social Science History* 26(3): 531–81.
50. Bell, D. & Valentine, G. (1995) *Mapping Desire: Geographies of Sexualities*. London: Routledge.
51. Bernstein, M. (2002) 'Identities and politics: Toward a historical understanding of the lesbian and gay movement'. *Social Science History* 26(3): 531–81.

Chapter Five: War on the Skin

1. Ferguson, N. (2007) *The War of the World*. London: Penguin.
2. Rex, J. (1961) *Key Problems of Sociological Theory*. London: Routledge and Kegan Paul.
3. Onwuachi-Willig, A. (2013) *According to Our Hearts: Rhinelander v. Rhinelander and the Law of the Multiracial Family*. Princeton: Yale University Press.
4. Rex, J. (ed.) (1981) *Apartheid and Social Research*. Paris: UNESCO.
5. Dunn, A. (2017) 'The competitive advantage of racial equity', Shared Value Initiative. Available at https://sharedvalue.org/groups/new-research-competitive-advantage-racial-equity.
6. Technology Quarterly (2017) 'Targeting tumours', *The Economist*, September. Available at https://www.economist.com/technology-quarterly/2017-09-16/treating-cancer.
7. Letter to the *London Times*, 10 October 2017, following publication of the UK Race Disparity Audit that day, which can be found at https://www.gov.uk/government/publications/race-disparity-audit.
8. McGarry, A. (2017) *Romaphobia*. London: Zed Books.
9. Reid, S. (2008) 'It was the week's most shocking picture: Gipsy girls dead on a beach ignored by sunbathers …', *Daily Mail*, July 26.
10. Bungwe, R. (2002) 'Refugee', in *Credit to the Nation*. The Refugee Council.
11. Smith, M. M. (2006) *How Race Is Made: Slavery, Segregation, and the Senses*. Chapel Hill: University of North Carolina Press.
12. Jones, S. (1993) *The Language of the Genes: Biology, History and the Evolutionary Future*. London: Harper Collins.
13. Buck, P. (1937) *The Road to Reunion, 1865–1900*. New York: A. A. Knopf.
14. Al.com (2017) '"Fight or die white man": Alabama man leading the push for Southern secession'. Available at http://www.al.com/news/index.ssf/2017/08/alabama_man_leading_the_push_f.html.
15. BBC Radio 4 (2017) *The Today Programme*, 18 August. Available at www.bbc.co.uk/radio4/TheToday Programme.
16. news.com.au (2017) 'Charlottesville violence: Man charged with murder was pictured at neo-Nazi rally', 14 August. Available at http://www.news.com.au/world/charlottesville-virginia-scene-of-white-supremacist-march-amid-calls-to-seceded-from-united-states/news-story/.
17. See review by Clapp, S. (2016) 'On the Donmar Warehouse performance', *Observer*, 16 October.

18. Beckert, S. & Rockman, S. (eds.) (2017) *Slavery's Capitalism*. Philadelphia: University of Pennsylvania Press.
19. Coates, T. N. (2015) *Between The World And Me*. Melbourne: Text Publishing Company.
20. Genovese, E. (1976) *Roll, Jordan, Roll: The World the Slaves Made*. New York: Vintage.
21. Simmons, L. (2017) *The Prison School: Educational Inequality and School Discipline in the Age of Mass Incarceration*. Berkeley: University of California Press.
22. Lord McDonnell. (2017) *BBC News*. Available at www.bbc.co.uk/radio4/today programme, 10 August.
23. Ferguson, K. (2017) 'Former race tsar Trevor Phillips says it's time to admit most sex grooming gangs are Muslim amid calls for abusers to be treated as rate hate criminals and given tougher sentences', *Daily Mail*, 11 August. Available at www.dailymail.co.uk/news/article-4781426/Asian-grooming-gangs-treated-race-hate-crimes.
24. Flynn, J. R. (1980) *Race, IQ and Jensen*. London and Boston, MA: Routledge & Kegan Paul. See also Flynn's follow-up book, Flynn, J. R. (2008) *Where Have All the Liberals Gone?: Race, Class, and Ideals in America*. Cambridge and New York: Cambridge University Press.
25. McIntosh, P. (1988) *Working Paper 189. 'White Privilege and Male Privilege: A Personal Account of Coming To See Correspondences through Work in Women's Studies'*. Wellesley, MA: Wellesley College Centre for Research on Women.
26. Figes, O. (1996) *A People's Tragedy: The Russian Revolution 1891–1924*. London: Pimlico, p. 80.
27. Connelly, M. (2008) *Fatal Misconception: The Struggle to Control World Population*. Cambridge, MA: Harvard University/Belknap Press.
28. Cohen, R. & Kennedy, P. (2000) *Global Sociology*. London: MacMillan Press, p. 110.
29. Brewer, A. (1990) *Marxist Theories of Imperialism: A Critical Survey*, 2nd edn. London: Routledge.
30. Duara, P. (ed.) (2004) *Decolonisation: Perspectives from Now and Then*. London: Routledge, p. 3.
31. Gutierrez, G. (1973) *A Theology of Liberation*. London: SCM Press, p. 85.
32. Fanon, F. (1986) *Black Skin, White Masks*. London: Pluto.
33. *Hotel Rwanda*, see review in www.bbc.co.uk/films/2005/02/17/hotel_rwanda_2005_review.shtml.

Chapter Six: Intact Bodies, Wounded History

1. The Equality Trust 'Why more equality?' Available at https://www.equalitytrust.org.uk/why-more-equality.
2. Oliver, M. (1996) *Understanding Disability: From Theory to Practice*. Basingstoke: MacMillan.
3. Davis, L. (1997) *The Disability Studies Reader*. New York: Routledge.
4. Finkelstein, V. (2005) 'Reflections on the social model of disability: The South African connection'. Available at http://disability-studies.leeds.ac.uk/files/library/finkelstein-Reflections-onthe-Social-Model-of-Disability.pdf, cited in Evans, C. (2017) 'Accessible buses: Are they commercially viable?' An MPhil thesis submitted to the University of Reading, cited with kind permission by Clive Evans.

5. UPIAS (1976) 'Fundamental principles of disability'. Available at http://disability-studies.leeds.ac.uk/library/, cited in Evans, C. (2017) 'Accessible buses: Are they commercially viable?' Unpublished MSc thesis.
6. Oliver, M. (1996) *Understanding Disability: From Theory to Practice*. Basingstoke: MacMillan.
7. Tregaskis, C. (2002) 'Social model theory: The story so far'. *Disability & Society* 17(4): 457–70.
8. Kitchin, R. (2000) 'The researched opinions on research: Disabled people and disability research'. *Disability & Society* 15(1): 25–47.
9. Oliver, M. (1996) *Understanding Disability: From Theory to Practice*. London: MacMillan Press.
10. Nathanson, D. (1987) *The Many Faces of Shame*. New York: The Guilford Press.
11. Monagha, K. (2005) *The Disability Discrimination Legislation*. Oxford: Oxford University Press, p. 2.
12. Nathanson, D. (1992) *Shame and Pride: Affect, Sex and the Birth of the Self*. New York: W. W. Norton.
13. James, O. (2008) *Contented Dementia: 24 Wraparound Care for Lifelong Wellbeing*. London: Vermilion.
14. Braddock, D. L. & Parish, S. L. (2001) 'An institutional history of disability', in Albrecht, G. et al. (eds.) *Handbook of Disability Studies*. London: Sage, p. 49.
15. United Nations (1982) *World Programme of Action Concerning Disabled Persons*. New York: Author.
16. Department of Health (2001) *Valuing People: A New Strategy for Learning Disability for the 21st Century*. London: Department of Health.
17. Joint Committee on Human Rights (2008) *Seventh Report*, 22 January. London: House of Commons.
18. Lynch, K., Baker, J., & Lyons, M. (2009) *Affective Equality: Love, Care and Injustice*. Basingstoke: Palgrave MacMillan.
19. NICE (2011) 'Common mental health problems: Identification and pathways to care'. Available at http://www.nice.org.uk/guidance/cg123.
20. McManus, S., et al. (eds.) (2009) *Adult Psychiatric Morbidity in England – 2007: Results of a Household Survey*. NHS Information Centre for Health and Social Care. Available at http://www.hscic.gov.uk/pubs/psychiatricmorbidity07.
21. Patel, V., et al. (2010) 'Mental disorders: Equity and social determinants', in Blas, E. & Sivisankara Kurup, A. (eds.) *Equity, Social Determinants and Public Health Programmes*. Geneva, Switzerland: World Health Organization.
22. Das-Munshi, et al. (2008) cited in McManus, S., Bebbington, P., Jenkins, R., & Brugha, T. (eds.) (2016) *Mental Health and Wellbeing in England: Adult Psychiatric Morbidity Survey 2014*. Leeds: NHS Digital. Available at http://content.digital.nhs.uk/catalogue/PUB21748/apms-2014-full-rpt.pdf.
23. McManus, S., et al. (eds.) (2016) *Mental Health and Wellbeing in England: Adult Psychiatric Morbidity Survey 2014*. Leeds: NHS Digital. Available at http://content.digital.nhs.uk/catalogue/PUB21748/apms-2014-full-rpt.pdf.
24. Lynch, K. (2009) 'Affective equality: Who cares?' *Development* 52(3): 410–15.
25. Baker, J., et al. (2004) *Equality: From Theory to Action*. Basingstoke: Palgrave MacMillan.
26. Kimmel, M. S. (2005) *The Gender of Desire: Essays on Male Sexuality*. Albany: State University of New York Press.

Chapter Seven: Moral Outrage: Religious and Philosophical Arguments

1. From the Philippines, 3 March 2017. Women's World Day of Prayer. Available at https://www.wwdp.org.uk/news.
2. Author's parish notes – used with permission.
3. Heyman, S. (2009) 'On the criminalisation of hate speech', in Hare, I. & Weinstein, J. (eds.) *Extreme Speech and Democracy*. Oxford: Oxford University Press.
4. Amos 2 v 6–7.
5. Bible, New International Version, International Bible Society, 1 Corinthians 10 v 17.
6. Ibid.,1 Corinthians 12 v 13.
7. Ibid., Galatians 3 v 28.
8. Josephus (1926) *The Life. Against Apion*, translated by Thackeray, H. St. J. Loeb Classical Library 186. Cambridge, MA: Harvard University Press, ii.201.
9. Dunn, J. D. G. (1993) *The Epistle to the Galatians*. London: A. & C. Black, p. 207.
10. Schmidt, M. (1962) *John Wesley: A Theological Biography*, Vol. 1. London: Epworth Press, p. 110.
11. Bible, New International Version, International Bible Society, Ephesians 2 v 14–15.
12. Ibid., Galatians 3 v 28.
13. Ibid., 1 Corinthians v 12.
14. Pugliucci, M. (2017) *How to be a Stoic*. London: Rider.
15. Navia, L. E. (2005) *Diogenes the Cynic*. Amherst, NY: Humanity Books.
16. Nussbaum, M. C. (1997) *Cultivating Humanity: A Classic Defence of Reform in Liberal Education*. Cambridge, MA and London: Harvard University Press.
17. Parfit, D. (1998) 'Equality & priority', in Mason, A. (ed.) *Ideals of Equality*. Oxford: Blackwell, p. 3.
18. Baker, P. (ed.) (2008) *The Putney Debates: The Levellers*. London: Verso.
19. Rees, J. (2016) *The Leveller Revolution*. London: Verso.
20. Locke, J. (1963) *Two Treatises of Government*, edited by Laslett, P. Cambridge: Cambridge University Press.
21. Montesquieu (1973) *Persian Letters*. Harmondsworth: Penguin.
22. Herder, J. G. (1968) *Reflections on the History of Mankind*, edited by Marvel, F. Chicago: University Chicago Press.
23. Kant (1948) *Groundwork for the Metaphysics of Morals*, translated by Paton, H. J. London: Routledge, pp. 80–7.
24. Ibid., pp. 80–7.
25. Kant (1996) *The Metaphysics of Morals*. Cambridge: Cambridge University Press, p. 428.
26. Taylor, C. (1992) *Multiculturalism & Politics of Recognition*. Princeton, NJ: Princeton University Press, p. 59.
27. Rousseau, J. (1984 edition) *A Discourse on Inequality*. Harmondsworth: Penguin Books, p. 105.
28. McDonald, C. & Hoffman, S. (eds.) (2011) *Rousseau and Freedom*. Cambridge: Cambridge University Press.
29. Wolker, R. (2012) *Rousseau, the Age of Enlightenment and their Legacies*. Princeton, NJ: Princeton University Press.
30. Rousseau, J. J. (2008) *Confessions*. Oxford: Oxford University Press.

31. Billington, J. H. (1980) *Fire in the Minds of Men: Origins of the Revolutionary Faith*. London: Temple Smith, p. 71.
32. Callinicos, A. (2000) *Equality*. Cambridge: Polity Press, p. 20.
33. Schama, S. (1989) *Citizens: A Chronicle of the French Revolution*. London: Vintage.
34. Zeldin, T. (1979) *France 1848–1945: Ambition and Love*. Oxford: Oxford University Press, pp. 199–200.
35. Outlaw, L. (1995) 'Racial and ethnic complexities in American life', in Harris, D. (ed.) *Multiculturalism from the Margins*. Westport, CT: Bergin & Garvey.
36. Taylor, A. (2016) *American Revolutions: A Continental History 1750–1804*. New York: W. W. Norton.
37. White, R. (2017) *The Republic for Which it Stands: The United States during Reconstruction and the Gilded Age 1865–1896*. Oxford: Oxford University Press.
38. Stone, L. (1977) *The Family, Sex and Marriage in England, 1500–1800*, quoting Astell, M. (1706) *Reflections on Marriage*.
39. Eisenstein, Z. R. (1981) *The Radical Future of Liberal Feminism*. Boston, MA: Northeastern University Press in a discussion of Elizabeth Cady Stanton, ch. 7, pp. 145–73.
40. de Tocqueville, A. (1994) *Democracy in America*, 1st edn. London: David Campbell.
41. Ware, C. (1970) *Woman Power: The Movement for Women's Liberation*. New York: Tower Publications, p. 3.
42. Tawney, R. H. (1964) *Equality*. London: Unwin.
43. Marx, K. (1970) 'Critique of the Gotha Programme', in Marx, K. & Engels, F. (eds.) *Selected Works*, Vol. 3. Moscow: Progress Publishers, pp. 9–30, 19.
44. Marx, K. (1976–81) *Capital*, Vol. 1. Harmondsworth: Penguin, pp. 272–3, 279, 280, 382.
45. Elster, J. (1985) *Making Sense of Marx*. Cambridge: Cambridge University Press, ch. 4.
46. Phillips, A. (1987) *Feminism and Equality*. Oxford: Blackwell, p. 1.
47. Bell, L. (1993) *Rethinking Ethics in the Midst of Violence*. Lanham, MD: Rownham & Littlefield, p. 71.
48. Hooks, B. (1984) 'Feminism: A movement to end sexist oppression', in *Feminist Theory: From Margin to Center*. Boston, MA: South End Press, pp. 17–31.
49. Munro, R. (1997) *Ideas of Difference: Stability, Social Spaces & the Labour of Division*. Oxford: Blackwell, p. 18.
50. Rawls, J. (1971) *A Theory of Justice*. Cambridge, MA: Harvard University Press.
51. Rawls, J. (1993) *Political Liberalism*. Cambridge, MA: Harvard University Press.
52. Freeman, S. (2008) *Rawls*. London: Routledge.
53. Nozick, R. (1974) *Anarchy, State and Utopia*. New York: Basic Books.
54. Sandel, M. (2009) *Justice: What's the Right Thing to Do?* New York: Farrar, Straus and Giroux.
55. Sher, G. (2015) 'Why we are moral equals', in Steinhof, U. (ed.) *Do All Persons have Equal Moral Worth?* Oxford: Oxford University Press.
56. Arnesson, R. (2015) 'Basic equality: Neither acceptable no rejectable', in Steinhof, U. (ed.) *Do All Persons have Equal Moral Worth?* Oxford: Oxford University Press.
57. Steinhof, U. (2015) 'Against equal respect and concern, equal rights and egalitarian impartiality', in Steinhof, U. (ed.) *Do All Persons have Equal Moral Worth?* Oxford: Oxford University Press.

Chapter Eight: Why Inequality Matters: Economic and Practical Arguments

1. See OECD 'Inequality'. Available at http://www.oecd.org/social/inequality.htm.
2. Gornick, J. & Jantii, M. (2013) *Income Inequality: Economic Disparities and the Middle Class in Affluent Countries*. Palo Alto, CA: Stanford University Press.
3. The World Bank. 'GINI index (World Bank estimate)'. Available at http://data.worldbank.org/indicator/SI.POV.GINI.
4. OECD Income Inequality. Available at https://data.oecd.org/inequality/income-inequality.htm.
5. Harrison, G. (1988) 'Wordsworth's "The Old Cumberland Beggar": The economy of charity in late eighteenth-century Britain'. *Criticism* 30(1): 23–42.
6. OECD May 2015 'In it together: Why less inequality benefits all'. Available at http://www.oecd-ilibrary.org/employment/in-it-together-why-less-inequality-benefits-all.
7. Gornick, J. & Jantii, M. (2013) *Income Inequality: Economic Disparities and the Middle Class in Affluent Countries*. Palo Alto, CA: Stanford University Press.
8. Congressional Budget Office (2010) 'Average federal tax rates'. Available at https://www.cbo.gov/publication/42870, cited by Stiglitz, J. (2012) *The Price of Inequality*. London: Allen Lane.
9. No figures available at the time of writing for 2017 but see report on the CBO figures until 2013. Available at http://www.heritage.org/taxes/report/cbo-report-distribution-income-and-taxes-shows-taxes-matter.
10. Roberts, A. (2017) *Superfast, Prime-time, Ultimate Nation: The Restless Invention of Modern India*. London: Profile.
11. Scanlon, T. M. (2014) 'The 4 biggest reasons why inequality is bad for society', TED. Available at http://ideas.ted.com/the-4-biggest-reasons-why-inequality-is-bad-for-society/.
12. Piketty, T. (2014) *Capital in the Twenty-First Century*. Cambridge, MA: Belknap Press.
13. Ostry, J. D., Berg, A., & Tsangarides, C. G. (2014) *Redistribution, Inequality, and Growth*. Washington, DC: International Monetary Fund. Available at http://www.imf.org/external/pubs/ft/sdn/2014/sdn1402.pdf.
14. Stiglitz, J. (2012) *The Price of Inequality*. London: Allen Lane, p. 43.
15. Commenting on BBC Radio 4, World at One (8 August 2017) on Buchan, I., Kontopantelis, E., Sperrin, M., Chandola, T., & Doran, T. (2017) 'North-South disparities in English mortality1965–2015: Longitudinal population study'. *Journal of Epidemiology and Community Health* 71(9): 928–36.
16. Stiglitz, J. (2012) *The Price of Inequality*. London: Allen Lane, p. 3.
17. OECD 'Inequality'. Available at http://www.oecd.org/social/inequality.htm. OECD 'Inequality and education'. Available at http://www.oecd.org/social/inequality.htm#education.
18. OECD 'Inequality'. Available at http://www.oecd.org/social/inequality.htm. OECD 'Inequality and education'. Available at http://www.oecd.org/social/inequality.htm#education.
19. 'How closely is the distribution of skills related to countries' overall level of social inequality and economic prosperity?' Available at https://www.oecd.org/edu/skills-beyond-school/EDUNAEC1.pdf.

20. Doucouliagos, C. (2017) 'Don't listen to the rich: Inequality is bad for everyone', *The Conversation*, August 6. Available at https://theconversation.com/dont-listen-to-the-rich-inequality-is-bad-for-everyone.
21. Equality and Human Rights Commission (2017) *Being Disabled in Britain: A Journey Less Equal*. Available at https://equalityhumanrights.com/en/publication-download/being-disabled-britain-journey-less-equal.
22. See https://www.livability.org.uk/.
23. Evans, C. (2017) *Accessible Buses: Are they Commercially Viable?* An MPhil thesis submitted to the University of Reading, cited with kind permission by Clive Evans.
24. Shaw, S. J. (2005) 'Theme 4 Social Dimensions of Urban Land Management – Tackling social exclusion in transport: Principles into practice?' CABERNET 2005, Proceedings of First International Conference on Managing Urban Land, Belfast.
25. Shakespeare, T. (2013) *Disability Rights and Wrongs Revisited*. London: Routledge.
26. BBC Radio 4 (2009) *Crossing Continents*, 18 May.
27. Hewlett, S, A. (1987) *A Lesser Life*. London: Michael Joseph, p. 91.

Chapter Nine: The Argument from Intensified Social Comparison

1. Centre for Labour and Social Studies (2012) *Why Inequality Matters*. Available at http://classonline.org.uk/docs/Why_Inequality_Matters.pdf.
2. Snowdon, C. (2010) *The Spirit Level Delusion: Fact Checking the Left's New Theory of Everything*. Ripon: Democracy Institute/Little Dice.
3. Wilkinson, R. & Pickett, R. (2010) *The Spirit Level: Why Equality Is Better for Everyone*. London: Penguin, p. 13.
4. *The Divide*. Available at www.thedividedocumentary.com.
5. Marmot, M. (2005) *Social Determinants of Health*. Oxford: Oxford University Press.
6. Wilkinson, R. & Pickett, R. (2010) *The Spirit Level: Why Equality Is Better for Everyone*. London: Penguin, p. 21.
7. Ibid., p. 25.
8. Ibid., p. 28.
9. Marmot, M. (2004) *The Status Syndrome: How Social Standing Affects Our Health and Longevity*. New York: Henry Holt, p. 33.
10. Marmot, M. (2004) *The Status Syndrome: How Your Social Standing Directly Affects Your Health and Life Expectancy*. London: Bloomsbury.
11. Centre for Labour and Social Studies (2012) *Why Inequality Matters*. Available at http://classonline.org.uk/docs/Why_Inequality_Matters.pdf.
12. Stiglitz, J. (2012) *The Price of Inequality*. London: Allen Lane.
13. Wilkinson, R. & Pickett, K. (2009) *The Spirit Level: Why More Equal Societies Almost Always Do Better*. Harmondsworth: Penguin Books.
14. Ferrie, J. E. (ed.) (2004) *Work, Stress and Health: The Whitehall II Study*. London: Public and Commercial Services Union. Available at https://www.ucl.ac.uk/whitehallII/pdf/wii-booklet.
15. Frank, R. (1999) *Luxury Fever*. New York: Free Press.
16. De Neve, J.-E. & Oswald, A. (2012) 'Happiness pays: Measuring the effect of subjective well-being on later income using sibling fixed effects'. Presented at the Royal Economic Society's 2012 Annual Conference at the University of Cambridge.

17. Fliessbach, K., et al. (2007) 'Social comparison affects reward-related brain activity in the human ventral striatum'. *Science* 31: 1305–8. doi: 10.1126/science.1145876.
18. McBride, M. (2001) 'Relative-income effects on subjective well-being in the cross-section'. *Journal of Economic Behaviour & Organization* 45(3): 251–78.
19. Wilkinson, R. & Pickett, R. (2010) *The Spirit Level: Why Equality Is Better for Everyone*. London: Penguin, p. 13.
20. Husserl, E. G. (1982) *Ideas Pertaining to a Pure Phenomenology and to a Phenomenological Philosophy*, Vol. 1. Hague: Kluwer Publishers.
21. Merleau-Ponty, M. (2012) *Phenomenology of Perception*, translated by Landes, D. New York: Routledge.
22. Morris, D. (2010) 'Empirical and phenomenological studies of embodied cognition', in Gallagher S. & Schmicking D. (eds.) *Handbook of Phenomenology and Cognitive Science*. Dordrecht, New York, Heidelberg, and London: Springer, pp. 235–52.
23. James, O. (2007) *Affluenza*. London: Vermilion.
24. Weber, M. (1994) *Political Writings*, Cambridge Texts in the History of Political Thought. Edited by Lassman, P. and translated by Speirs, R. Cambridge: Cambridge University Press.
25. Festinger L. (1954) 'A theory of social comparison processes'. *Human Relations* 7(2): 117–40.
26. Deutsch, M. & Krauss, R. M. (1965) *Theories in Social Psychology*, Vol. 2. New York: Basic Books.
27. Collins, R. L. (1995) 'For better or worse: The impact of upward social comparison on self-evaluations'. *Psychological Bulletin* 119(1): 51–69.
28. Sweating, H., et al. (2009) *Social Psychiatry and Psychiatric Epidemiology* 44: 579–86.
29. Social Anxiety UK. 'What is social anxiety?' Available at http://social-anxiety.org.uk/.
30. Hobbes, T. (2005) *The Elements of Law, Natural and Politic*. Boston, MA: Adamant Media Corporation.
31. Hont, I. (2015) *Politics in Commercial Society*. Cambridge, MA: Harvard University Press.
32. Rousseau, J. J. (2016) *Discourse on the Origin and the Foundations of Inequality Among Men*. Amazon.com: CreateSpace Independent Publishing Platform.
33. Neuhouser, F. (2015) *Rousseau's Critique of Inequality*. Cambridge: Cambridge University Press.
34. Wolf, N. (1991) *The Beauty Myth*. London: Vintage, p. 73.
35. Banyard, K. (2011) *The Equality Illusion – The Truth About Men and Women Today*. London: Faber & Faber, p. 33.
36. Sales, N. J. (2016) *American Girls: Social Media and the Secret Life of Teenagers*. New York: Knopf.
37. Lee, P. (2016) *Deloittes Mobile Consumer Survey 2016*. Deloitte. Available at https://www2.deloitte.com/uk/en/pages/technology-media-and-telecommunications/articles/mobile-consumer-survey.html.
38. Twenge, J. (2017) 'Have smartphones destroyed a generation?' *The Atlantic*, September. Available at https://www.theatlantic.com/magazine/archive/2017/09/has-the-smartphone-destroyed-a-generation/534198/.
39. Twenge, J. (2000) 'The age of anxiety? Birth cohort change in anxiety and neuroticism, 1952–1993'. *Journal of Personality and Social Psychology* 79(6): 1007–21.
40. Collishaw, S., et al. (2004) 'Time trends in adolescent mental health'. *Journal of Child Psychology and Psychiatry* 45(8): 1350–62.
41. Orenstein, P. (2016) *Girls and Sex: Navigating the New Landscape*. New York: Harper.

42. Scott, L. (2015) *The Four-Dimensional Human: Ways of Being in the Digital World*. London: Heinemann.
43. World Economic Forum (2017) 'Shaping the future implications of digital media for society'. Available at https://www.weforum.org/projects/human-implications-of-digital-media.
44. Rivera, M. (2017) *Big Data: How Much Is Too Much?* World Economic Forum. Available at https://www.weforum.org/agenda/2017/02/big-data-how-much-is-too-much/.
45. Dickerson, S. & Kemeny, M. (2004) 'Acute stressors and cortisol responses: A theoretical integration and synthesis of laboratory research'. *Psychological Bulletin* 130: 355–91.
46. Scheff, T. J. (1988) 'Shame and conformity: The deference-emotion system'. *American Sociological Review* 53: 395–91.
47. Wilkinson, R. & Pickett, R. (2010) *The Spirit Level: Why Equality Is Better for Everyone*. London: Penguin, p. 13.

Chapter Ten: The Psychodynamic Argument: Marx versus Freud

1. Collins, P. H. (1986) 'Learning from the outsider within: The sociological significance of black feminist thought'. *Social Problems* 33(6): s14–s32.
2. Wilkinson, R. & Pickett, R. (2010) *The Spirit Level: Why Equality Is Better for Everyone*. London: Penguin, p. 33.
3. Author's client notes – name withheld and used with permission.
4. Reay, D. (2005) 'Beyond consciousness'. *Sociology* 39(5): 192.
5. Bott, E. (1956) *Family and Social Network*. London: Tavistock.
6. Reay, D. (2005) 'Beyond consciousness'. *Sociology* 39(5): 192.
7. Bourdieu, P. (1999) 'The order of things', in Bourdieu, P. et al (eds.) *The Weight of the World: Social Suffering in Contemporary Society*. Cambridge: Polity Press, pp. 60–76.
8. Rubin, L. (1976) *Worlds of Pain: Life in the Working-class Family*. New York: Basic Books.
9. Steedman, C. (1986) *Landscape for a Good Woman*. London: Virago.
10. Fanon, F. (1969) *Black Skins: White Masks*. Harmondsworth: Penguin.
11. Sayer, A. (2005) *The Moral Significance of Class*. Cambridge: Cambridge University Press, pp. 201–2.
12. Reay, D. (2005) 'Emotional capital, women and social class', in Skeggs, B. & Adkins, L. (eds.) *Feminists Evaluate Bourdieu*. London: Blackwell, pp. 57–74.
13. Dorling, D. (2010) *Injustice: Why Social Inequality Persists*. Bristol: Policy Press, pp. 5–11, et seq.
14. Bradshaw, J. & Finch, N. (2003) 'Overlaps in dimensions of poverty'. *Journal of Social Policy* 32(4): 513–25.
15. Offer, A. (2006) *The Challenge of Affluence: Self-control and Well-being in the United States and Britain since 1950*. Oxford: Oxford University Press, pp. 190–6.
16. Centre for Economic Performance's Mental Health Policy Group (2006) *The Depression Report: A New Deal for Depression and Anxiety Disorders*. London: CEPMHPG London School of Economic and Political Science.

17. Reeves, R. (2017) *Dream Hoarders: How the American Upper Middle Class Is Leaving Everyone Else in the Dust, Why that Is a Problem, and What to Do About It*. New York: Brookings Institution Press.
18. Marx, K. (1969) 'The German ideology', in Feuer, L. S. (ed.) *Marx and Engels: Basic Writings on Politics and Philosophy*. London: Fontana.
19. Horkheimer, M. (1993) 'The present situation of social philosophy and the Tasks of an Institute of Social Research', in Horkheimer, M. (ed.) *Between Philosophy and Social Science. Selected Early Writings*. Cambridge, MA: MIT Press, pp. 1–14.
20. Ibid.
21. Jeffries, S. (2016) *The Lives of the Frankfurt School*. London: Verso, p. 141.
22. Freud, S. (2010) *Civilization and Its Discontents Paperback*. Eastford, CT: Martino Fine Books.
23. Fromm, E. (2013) *Marx's Concept of Man: Including 'Economic and Philosophical Manuscripts'*. London: Bloomsbury, p. 26.
24. Fromm, E. (2011) *Escape from Freedom*. Open access: Ishi Press.
25. Fromm, E. (1963) *The Sane Society*. London: Routledge & Kegan Paul, pp. 18–19.
26. Marcuse, H. (1955) *Eros and Civilisation: A Philosophical Inquiry into Freud*. Boston, MA: Beacon Press.
27. Marcuse, H. (1961/2002) *One-Dimensional Man: Studies in the Ideology of Advanced Industrial Society*. London: Routledge Classics.
28. Dorling, D. (2010) *Injustice: Why Social Inequality Persists*. Bristol: Policy Press, p. 99.
29. Sontag, S. (2009) *Against Interpretation and Other Essays*. London: Penguin Classics.
30. Sartre, J.-P. (2003) *Being and Nothingness*, Part 4, Chapter 1. London: Routledge.
31. Lukács, G. (1971) *The Theory of the Novel*. Cambridge, MA: MIT Press.
32. Hegel, G. W. F. (1874) *The Logic. Encyclopaedia of the Philosophical Sciences*, 2nd edn. London: Oxford University Press, p. 9.
33. Hegel, G. W. F. (1977) Preface to *The Phenomenology of Spirit*, translated by Miller, A. V. Oxford: Clarendon Press, secs. 50, 51, pp. 29, 30.
34. Marx, K. (1970) *Capital, Afterword*, Vol. 1, Second German edn. Moscow: Progress, p. 29.
35. Parsons, T. (1954) *Revised Analytic Approach to Social Stratification – Essays in Sociological Theory*. Glencoe, IL: Free Press.
36. Goffman, I. (1974) *Frame Analysis: An Essay on the Organisation of Experience*. New York: Harper & Row.
37. Habermas. J. (1984) *The Theory of Communicative Action*. Boston, MA: Beacon Press.
38. Miller, P. (1987) *Domination and Power*. London: Routledge.
39. Habermas, J. cited in Eder, K. (2007) 'Cognitive sociology and the theory of communicative action'. *European Journal of Social Theory* 10(3): 389–498.
40. Honneth, A. (1995) *The Struggle for Recognition: The Moral Grammar of Social Conflicts*. Cambridge: Polity Press.
41. Marx, K. (1976) *Capital*, Vol. 1. Harmondsworth: Penguin, pp. 344–5.
42. Marx, K. (1973) *Grundrisse Foundations of the Critique of Political Economy*. Harmondsworth: Penguin, p. 83.
43. Gay, P. (1989) *Freud: A Life for Our Times*. Basingstoke: Papermac.
44. Foucault, M. (1977) *Discipline and Punish: The Birth of the Prison*. London: Penguin.
45. Vatikiotis, M. (2017) *Blood and Silk: Power and Conflict in Modern Southeast Asia*. London: Weidenfeld & Nicolson.

46. Freud, S. (1997) *The Interpretation of Dreams*. Ware: Wordsworth Editions.
47. Jones, E. (1964) *The Life and Work of Sigmund Freud*. Harmondsworth: Penguin Books, p. 11.
48. Freud, S. (1900) *The Interpretation of Dreams*. Ware: Wordsworth Editions, motto on the title page.
49. Jones, E. (1957) *The Life and Work of Sigmund Freud*, Vol. 2. London: Hogarth Press, pp. 439–40, 457–8.
50. Crews, F. (2017) *Freud: The Making of an Illusion*. London: Profile.
51. Gellner, E. (1993) *The Psychoanalytic Movement: The Cunning of Unreason*. London: Fontana, p. xiii.
52. See for example Damasio, A. (1999) *The Feeling of What Happens*. San Diego: Harvest (Harcourt).
53. Freud, S. (1974) *Introductory Lectures on Psychoanalysis*. Harmondsworth: Pelican Books, p. 278.
54. Fairbairn, R. (1952) *An Object Relations Theory of the Personality*. New York: Basic Books.
55. Funder, D. C. (1997) *The Personality Puzzle*. New York: W. W. Norton, p. 257.
56. Barrat, B. B. (1993) *Psycho-Analysis and the Post-Modern Impulse: Knowing and Being since Freud's Psychology*. Baltimore: John Hopkins University.
57. Prochaska, J. O. & Norcross, J. C. (1994) *Systems of Psychotherapy: A Trans-theoretical Perspective*. Pacific Grove, CA: Brooks/Cole Publishing, p. 39.
58. Horney, K. (1950) *Neurosis and Human Growth*. New York: W. W. Norton.
59. Makari, G. (2008) *Revolution in Mind: The Creation of Psycho-analysis*. London: Duckworth.
60. Turner, C. (2011) *Adventures in the Orgasmatron: Wilhelm Reich and the Invention of Sex*. London: Fourth Estate.
61. Lacan, J. (1988) *The Ego in Freud's Theory and the Techniques of Psychoanalysis*, edited by Miller, J.-A. New York: W. W. Norton.
62. Parker, I. (2010) *Lacanian Psychoanalysis: Revolutions in Subjectivity* (Advancing Theory in Therapy). London: Routledge.
63. Prochaska, J. O. & Norcross, J. C. (1994) *Systems of Psychotherapy: A Trans-theoretical Perspective*. Pacific Grove, CA: Brooks/Cole Publishing, p. 81.
64. Adler, A. (1939) *Social Interest*. New York: Putnam.

Chapter Eleven: A Theory of Social Relativity

1. Waytz, A. (2009) 'The psychology of social status', *Scientific American*, December. Available at https://www.scientificamerican.com/article/the-psychology-of-social/.
2. Mencken, H. L. cited in Frank, R. (1999) *Luxury Fever*. New York: Free Press.
3. Townsend, P. & Abel Smith, B. (1965) *The Poor and the Poorest*. London: G. Bell & Sons.
4. Townsend, P. (1979) *Poverty in the United Kingdom*. London: Penguin.
5. Stiglitz, J. (2012) *The Price of Inequality*. London: Allen Lane, p. 105.
6. Bertrand, M. & Morse, A. (2013) *Trickle-Down Consumption*. NBER Working Paper, No. 18883.
7. Clark, A. E. & Senik, C. (2011) *Will GDP Growth Increase Happiness in Developing Countries?* Paris School of Economics Working Paper, No. 2010–43.

8. Van Hoorn, A. (2007) *A Short Introduction to Subjective Well-Being: Its Measurement, Correlates and Policy Uses: Is Happiness Measurable and what do those Measures Mean for Policy?* OECD. Available at www.oecd.org/site/worldforum06/38331839.pdf.
9. Diener, E., et al. (2010) 'New measures of well-being: Flourishing and positive and negative feelings'. *Social Indicators Research* 39: 247–66.
10. Diener, E., et al. (1985) 'The satisfaction with life scale'. *Journal of Personality Assessment* 49: 71–5. See also Pavot, W. & Diener, E. (2008) 'The satisfaction with life scale and the emerging construct of life satisfaction'. *Journal of Positive Psychology* 3: 137–52.
11. Clark, A. E. & Oswald A. J. (1996) 'Satisfaction and comparison income'. *Journal of Public Economics* 61(3): 359–81.
12. Easterlin, R. A. (1995) 'Will raising the incomes of all increase the happiness of all?' *Journal of Economic Behaviour & Organization* 27(1): 35–47.
13. Einstein A. (1916) *Relativity: The Special and General Theory* (translation 1920). New York: H. Holt and Company.
14. Folsing, A. (1998) *Albert Einstein*. Harmondsworth: Penguin Books, p. 381.
15. Einstein, A. (2010) *Relativity: The Special and General Relativity*. Eastford, CT: Martino Fine Books.
16. Parducci, A. (1984) 'Value judgments: Toward a relational theory of happiness', in Eiser, J. R. (ed.) *Attitudinal Judgment*. New York: Springer, pp. 3–21.
17. Parducci, A. (1968) 'The relativism of absolute judgments'. *Scientific American* 219: 85.
18. Franks, R. (2007) *Falling Behind*. London: University of California Press, p. 89.
19. Diener, E. & Suh, E. M. (1997) 'Measuring quality of life: Economic, social & subjective indicators.' *Social Indicators Research* 40(1–2): 189–216. See also Diener, E. & Seligman, M. E. P. (2004) 'Beyond money. Toward an economy of well-being'. *Psychological Science in the Public Interest* 5(1): 1–31.
20. Thompson, W. & Hickey, J. (2005) *Society in Focus*. Boston, MA: Pearson.
21. Ehrenreich, B. (1989) *Fear of Falling: The Inner Life of the Middle Class*. New York: Harper Collins.
22. Runciman, W. G. (1966) *Attitudes to Social Inequality in Twentieth Century England*. London: Routledge, p. 14.
23. Merton, R. K. & Rossi, A. S. (1957) 'Contributions to the theory of reference group behaviour', in Merton, R. K. (ed.) *Social Theory and Social Structure*. Glencoe, IL; Free Press.
24. Stouffer, S. A., et al. (1949) *The American Soldier. 1. Adjustments During Army Life*. Princeton, NJ: Princeton University Press, pp. 250–3.
25. Sapolsky, R. M. (2004) 'Social status and health in humans and other animals'. *Annual Review of Anthropolology* 33: 393–418.
26. Cummins, D. D. (2000) 'How social environment shaped the evolution of mind'. *Synthese* 122(2000): 3–28.
27. Zink, C., et al. (2008) 'Know your place: Neural processing of social hierarchy in Humans'. *Neuron* 58(2): 273–83.
28. Wheeler, L. (1966) 'Motivation as a determinant of upward comparison'. *Journal of Experimental Social Psych*ology 2(Suppl 1): 27–31.
29. Minkel, J. R. (2006) 'Poor people living in well-to-do neighborhoods die sooner'. *Scientific American,* December. Available at https://www.scientificamerican.com/article/poor-people-living-in-wel/.
30. De Botton, A. (2005) *Status Anxiety*. London: Penguin.

31. Office of National Statistics (2013) 'Women in the labour market: 2013'. Available at https://www.ons.gov.uk/employmentandlabourmarket/peopleinwork/employmentandemployeetypes/articles/womeninthelabourmarket/2013-09-25.
32. Rawls, J. (1999) *A Theory of Justice*, revised edn. Cambridge, MA: Harvard University Press.
33. Leiter, B. (2002) *Nietzsche on Morality*. London: Routledge.
34. Martin, C. & Evans. D.-N. (2013) *Nietzsche's 'Thus Spoke Zarathustra'*, A Reader's Guide. Bloomsbury Academic.
35. Nietzsche, F. W. & Caro, A. D. (2014) *Beyond Good and Evil: On the Genealogy of Morality*. Stanford: California.

Chapter Twelve: The Politics of Positions

1. BBC Radio 4 (2012) *The Today Programme*, 24 July. Available at www.bbc.co.uk/radio4/TheToday Programme.
2. Whitton, E. (2003) *Humanistic Approach to Psychotherapy*. London: Whurr Publishers, p. 39. See also Thorne, B. (2001) *Therapeutic and Spiritual Dimensions*. London: Whurr Publishers.
3. Berne, E. (2010) *The Games People Play*. Harmondsworth: Penguin Life.
4. Husserl, E. (2012) *Ideas: General Introduction to Pure Phenomenology*. London: Routledge.
5. Berne, E. (2016) *Games People Play: The Psychology of Human Relationships*. Harmondsworth: Penguin.
6. Foucault, M. (2000) *Power*. New York: New Press.
7. Sartre, J.-P. (2007) *Existentialism and Humanism*. London: Methuen.
8. Nietzsche, F. W. (2003) *The Genealogy of Morals*. Mineola, NY: Dover Publications Inc.
9. Foucault, M. (2002) *The Order of Things: An Archaeology of the Human Sciences*. London: Routledge.
10. Davies, B. & Harré, R. (1990) 'Positioning: The discursive production of selves'. *Journal for the Theory of Social Behaviour* 20: 46.
11. Sayer, A. (2005) *The Moral Significance of Class*. Cambridge: Cambridge University Press, pp. 201–2.
12. Mead, G. H. (1934) *Mind, Self and Society*. Chicago: University of Chicago Press.
13. Alzheimer's Society. 'My name is not Dementia'. Available https://www.alzheimers.org.uk/download/downloads/id/876/my_name_is_not_dementia_people_with_dementia_discuss_quality_of_life_indicators.pdf.
14. Author's client notes – name withheld and used with permission.
15. Elliot, C. (2003) *Better than Well: American Medicine Meets the American Dream*. New York: W. W. Norton.
16. Orbach, S. (2009) *Bodies*. London: Profile Books.
17. Author's client notes – name withheld and used with permission.
18. Appignanesi, L. (2008) *Mad, Bad and Sad: A History of Women and the Mind Doctors from 1800 to the Present*. London: Virago.
19. Johnstone, L. & Dallos, R. (2013) *Formulation in Psychology and Psychotherapy*. London: Routledge.

20. Levine, M. (2008) *The Price of Privilege: How Parental Pressure and Material Advantage are Creating a Generation of Disconnected and Unhappy Kids*. New York: Harper Perennial.
21. Patton, P. (2000) *Deleuze and the Political*. New York: Routledge.
22. Levi-Strauss, C. (1974) *Structural Anthropology*. New York: Basic Books.
23. Author's client notes – name withheld and used with permission.

Chapter Thirteen: Understanding the Triggers: Indifference, Indignity and Inequality

1. Miller, A. (2000) *Death of a Salesman*. Harmondsworth: Penguin Plays.
2. Author's client notes – name withheld and used with permission.
3. Ellison, R. (1952) *Invisible Man*. New York: Random House.
4. BBC (2012) *The World Tonight*, 9 May. Available at www.bbc.co.uk/WorldTonight.
5. Unite For Sight. 'Module 2: Why bottom up instead of top down?' Available at http://www.uniteforsight.org/community-development/course1/module2.
6. Author's client notes – name withheld and used with permission.
7. Swann, W. Jr. (1999) *Resilient Identities: Self, Relationships, and the Construction of Social Reality*. Basic Books: New York.
8. Philipps, A. (2010) *On Balance*. London: Hamish Hamilton.
9. 'Sarah's Bubble'. Available at www.timetochange.org.uk.
10. Smith, M. M. (2006) *How Race Is Made: Slavery, Segregation, and the Senses*. Chapel Hill: University of North Carolina Press.
11. Winnicott, D. (1953) 'Transitional objects and transitional phenomena'. *International Journal of Psychoanalysis* 34: 89–97.
12. Cooley, C. H. (1902) *Human Nature and the Social Order*. New York: Scribner.
13. Feyneyhough, C. (2008) *The Baby in the Mirror: A Child's World from Birth to Three*. London: Granta Books.
14. Reddy, V. (2008) *How Infants Know Minds*. Cambridge, MA: Harvard University Press.
15. Trinh, M. (1992) *The Framer Framed*. London: Routledge.
16. Sartre, J.-P. (2003) *Being and Nothingness: An Essay on Phenomenological Ontology*. London: Routledge.
17. Author's client notes – name withheld and used with permission. See also Spence, J. (1988) *Putting Myself in the Picture*. London: Real Comet Press.
18. Author's client notes – name withheld and used with permission.
19. Ibid.
20. Sartre, J. P. (1958) *Being and Nothingness*. London: Methuen, p. 231.
21. Derrida, J. (2008) *Psyche: Inventions of the Other*. Stanford: Stanford University Press.
22. Author's client notes – used with permission.
23. Sartre, J. P. (1958) *Being and Nothingness*. London: Methuen, p. 47.
24. Ibid., p. 221.
25. Honneth, A. (1995) *The Struggle for Recognition: The Moral Grammar of Social Conflicts*. Cambridge: Polity Press.
26. Honneth, A. (2003) *Redistribution or Recognition?: A Political-Philosophical Exchange*, co-authored with Fraser, N. London: Verso.

27. Honneth, A. (2007) *Reification: A Recognition-Theoretical View*. Oxford: Oxford University Press.
28. Taylor, C. (1992) *Multiculturalism and the Politics of Recognition*. Princeton, NJ: Princeton University Press.
29. Williams, R. R. (2000) *Hegel's Ethics of Recognition*. Berkeley: University of California Press.
30. Taylor, C. (1992) *Multiculturalism and the Politics of Recognition*. Princeton, NJ: Princeton University Press, pp. 24 and 50.
31. Ibid., p. 38.
32. Arendt, H. (1958) *The Human Condition*. Chicago: University of Chicago Press, p. 184.
33. Markell, P. (2003) *Bound by Recognition*. Princeton, NJ: Princeton University Press.
34. BBC Two (2012) *The Indian Ocean*, documentary, 22 April.
35. Vaughan, A. T. (1995) 'The origins debate: Slavery and racism in seventeenth century Virginia', in Vaughan, A. T. (ed.) *Roots of American Racism: Essays on the Colonial Experience*. New York: Oxford University Press, p. 171.
36. Gaita, R. (2000) *A Common Humanity: Thinking about Love, Truth and Justice*. London: Routledge, p. xxi.
37. Sartre, J. P. (1958) *Being and Nothingness*. London: Methuen, p. 231.
38. Tallis, R. (2009) *The Kingdom of Infinite Space: A Fantastical Journey Round your Head*. New Haven, CT: Yale University Press.
39. ITV (2010) *Piers Morgan Lives*, documentary, 7 November.
40. Author's client notes – name withheld and used with permission.
41. Lynch, K., Baker, J., & Lyons, M. (2009) *Affective Equality: Love, Care and Injustice*. Basingstoke: Palgrave MacMillan.
42. Honneth, A. (1992) 'Integrity and disrespect: Principles of a conception of morality based on the theory of recognition'. *Political Theory* 20(2): 187–201.
43. Remnick, D. (2010) *The Bridge: The Life and Rise of Barack Obama*. New York: Knopf.
44. Larsen, N. (2000) 'Imperialism, Colonialism, Postcolonialism', in Schwarz, H. & Ray A. (eds.) *A Companion to Post-Colonial Studies*. Oxford: Blackwell, p. 41.
45. Rose, D. (2006) 'Don't be rude to old patients, doctors told', *The Times*, 4 October, quoting Cayton, H.'s article in the *Journal of the Royal Society of Medicine*.
46. American Psychiatric Association (1980) *Diagnostic and Statistical Manual of Mental Disorders: DSM-III*. Washington, DC: American Psychiatric Association.
47. Leader, D. (2011) *What Is Madness?* London: Hamish Hamilton.
48. Vollman, W. (2009) *Imperial*. New York: Viking.
49. Lindsay, B. (ed.) (1983) *Comparative Perspectives of Third World Women: The Impact of Race, Sex and Class*. New York: Praeger, p. 298.
50. Cutrufelli, M. R. (1983) *Women of Africa: Roots of Oppression*. London: Zed Press.
51. Nussbaum, M. (1992) 'Human functioning and social justice'. *Political Theory* 20(2): 207.
52. Hearn, J. (1998) *The Violences of Men*. London: Sage, p. 212. See also Bly, R. (1990) *Iron John: Men and Masculinity*. London: Rider Books.
53. Martin, D. (2007) 'Split religion: How much modern politics and revolutionary violence owe to enlightenment excesses, malformed theology, and the disorders of faith', *Times Literary Supplement*, 10 August.

54. Rosen, M. (2012) *Dignity: Its History and Meaning*. Cambridge, MA: Harvard University Press.
55. Kateb, G. (2011) *Human Dignity*. Cambridge, MA: Harvard University Press.

Chapter Fourteen: Inequality's Inner Thread: Towards a New Social Category

1. Ahmed, S. (2017) *Living a Feminist Life*. Durham, NC: Duke University Press Books.
2. Crenshaw, K. (1989) 'Demarginalizing the intersection of race and sex: A black feminist critique of antidiscrimination doctrine, feminist theory and antiracist politics'. *University of Chicago Legal Forum* 140: 139–67.
3. Author's client notes – name withheld and used with permission.
4. Travis, A. (2010) 'John Denham's subtler approach to race and class carries new risk'. *Guardian*, 14 January. Available at https://www.theguardian.com/society/2010/jan/14/john-denham-communities-equality-race. Reporting a speech by Labour Communities Secretary John Denham.
5. *The Economist* (2017) 'Blurring the rainbow', 20 May.
6. Friere, P. & Shor, I. (1987) *A Pedagogy of Liberation*. London: Macmillan.
7. Ibid., p. 112.
8. International Boulevard (2012). Available at http://www.internationalboulevard.com/the-light-of-your-ferocity-garcia-marquez-on-the-future-hugo-chavez/.
9. *Shorter Oxford English Dictionary*, 3rd edn. (2008) Oxford: Oxford University Press.
10. Bottomore, T. B. (1991) *A Dictionary of Marxist Thought*. Cambridge, MA: Wiley-Blackwell.
11. Silver, H. (1994) 'Social exclusion and social solidarity'. *International Labour Review* 133(5–6): 531–78.
12. Sen, A. (1985) *Commodities and Capabilities*. Amsterdam and New York: Elsevier Science. Also, Nussbaum, M. (2011) *Creating Capabilities the Human Development Approach*. Cambridge, MA: Belknap Press, pp. 30–1.
13. Wolff, J. & De-Shalit, A. (2008) *Disadvantage*. Oxford: Oxford University Press.
14. Author's client notes – name withheld and used with permission.
15. Data for 2009 from the Department of Children, Schools and Families.
16. Campbell, D. (2010) 'More than 40% of domestic violence victims are male, report reveals', *Guardian*, 15 January.
17. Available at www.manzapper.newgrounds.com/.
18. Motz, A. (2008) *The Psychology of Female Violence*. London: Routledge.
19. Available at www.mankind.org.
20. Bourke, J. (2007) *Rape: A History from 1860 to the Present*. London: Virago.
21. Sweeting, H., et al. (2009) 'Social psychiatry and psychiatric'. *Epidemiology* 44: 579–86.
22. Gaita, R. (2000) *A Common Humanity: Thinking About Love, Truth and Justice*. London: Routledge, p. xxi.
23. Joseph, G. & Lewis. J. (1981) *Common Differences: Conflict in Black and White Feminist Perspectives*. Boston, MA: Beacon Press.
24. Said, E. (1978) *Orientalism*. Harmondsworth: Penguin.
25. Marchand, S. L. (2009) *German Orientalism in the Age of Empire: Religion, Race and Scholarship*. Cambridge: Cambridge University Press.

26. McLintock, A. (1991) *Imperial Leather: Race, Gender and Sexuality in the Imperial Context.* London: Routledge; or Mills, S. (1991) *Discourses of Difference, Women's Travel Writing and Colonialism.* London: Routledge.
27. Rich. A. (2003) Notes towards a politics of location, in Rich, A. (1984) *Blood, Bread and Poetry: Selected Prose 1979–1985.* London: Little Brown & Co.
28. Norman, B. (2007) '"We" in redux: The Combahee River collective's black feminist statement'. *Differences* 18(2): 104.
29. Gilroy, P. (2000) *Between Camps: Race, Identity and Nationalism at the End of the Colour Line.* London: Allen Lane–Penguin.
30. Rex, J. (1986) *Race and Ethnicity.* Milton Keynes: Open University Press.
31. Kanneh, K. (1998) 'Black feminisms', in Jackson, S. & Jones, J. (eds.) *Contemporary Feminist Theories.* New York: New York University Press, p. 88.
32. Jewish Virtual Library (2011) 'Jews in Islamic countries: The treatment of Jews'. Available at https://www.jewishvirtuallibrary.org/the-treatment-of-jews-in-arab-islamic-countries-2.
33. *Ottowa Citizen* (2014) 'Pierre Trudeau was right about Quebec'. Available at http://ottawacitizen.com/news/national/column-pierre-trudeau-was-right-about-quebec.
34. *BBC News* (2017) 'Catalonia's bid for independence from Spain explained'. Available at www.bbc.co.uk/news/world-europe-29478415.
35. Appleton, J. (2017) 'Self, society and alienation', a talk at The Academy on 15 and 16 July. Available at https://notesonfreedom.com/2017/05/31/gender-neutral-identity-and-the-pronoun-obsession/.
36. Ibid.
37. Dolezal, R. (2017) *Full Color: Finding My Place in a Black and White World.* New York: BenBella Books.
38. Hynes, C. (2017) 'Rachel Dolezal's pick-your-race policy works brilliantly – as long as you're white', *Guardian*, 27 March.
39. Dolezal, D. (2016) 'Who is the "You" of you?' TED. Available at https://blog.ted.com/rachel-dolezals-tedx-talk/.
40. Fogg Davis, H. (2017) *Beyond Trans.* New York: NYU Press.
41. Foner, P. S. (ed.) (1970) *W. E. B. DuBois Speaks: Speeches and Addresses, 1920–1963.* New York: Pathfinder Press.
42. Levi-Strauss, C. (1963) *Structural Anthropology.* New York: Basic Books, Ch. 7.
43. Derrida, J. (1981) *Positions*, translated by Bass, A. Chicago: University of Chicago Press, p. 41.
44. Saito, Y. (2008) *Everyday Aesthetics.* Oxford: Oxford University Press.
45. Jerram, L. (2011) *Streetlife: The Untold Story of Europe's Twentieth Century.* Oxford: Oxford University Press.
46. Rutherford, J. (ed.) (1990) *Identity: Community, Culture, Difference.* London: Lawrence & Wishart, pp. 21–2.
47. Foucault, M. (1970) *The Order of Things: An Archaeology of the Human Sciences.* London: Tavistock, p. 340.
48. Robbins, B. (2000) 'Towards a new humanistic paradigm', in Schwarz, H. & Ray A. (eds.) *A Companion to Post-Colonial Studies.* Oxford: Blackwell, p. 567.
49. BBC Radio 4 *News at Six.* 16 June, 2009.
50. Mohanty, C. T. (1989) 'Under Western eyes: Feminist scholarship and colonial discourse'. Quoted in Ang, I. 'I'm a feminist but ... "other" women and post-national

feminism', in Lewis, R. & Mills, S. (eds.) *Feminist Post-Colonial Theory: A Reader*. Edinburgh: Edinburgh University Press, p. 193.
51. Martineau, H. (2012) *How to Observe Morals and Manners*. Los Angeles, CA: Hardpress Publishing.
52. Walters, M. (1976) *The Right and Wrongs of Women*. Harmondsworth: Penguin, p. 339.

Chapter Fifteen: The Effect of Inequality: Demoralisation, Resignation and the Protest

1. As quoted in the Talmudic tractate Berakhot (55b).
2. Eagleton, T. (1990) *The Ideology of the Aesthetic*. Oxford: Blackwell, p. 230.
3. Wascher, C. A. F. & Bugnyar, T. (2013) 'Behavioral responses to inequity in reward distribution and working effort in crows and ravens'. *PLoS ONE*. doi:10.1371/journal.pone.0056885.
4. Essler, J. L. (2017) 'Domestication does not explain the presence of inequity aversion in dogs'. *Current Biology* 27(12): 1861–5.
5. Hollis, M. (2011) *Now All Roads Lead to France: The Last Years of Edward Thomas*. London: Faber.
6. Hartscok, N. (1990) 'Foucault on power: A theory for women', in Nicholson, L. J. (ed.) *Feminism/Postmodernism*. New York: Routledge, pp. 157–75.
7. Deleuze, G. (1993) *The Deleuze Reader*, edited by Bounds C. V. New York: Columbia University.
8. Jones, M. (2002) *The Social Psychology of Prejudice*. Upper Saddle River, NJ: Prentice Hall.
9. Gladwell, M. (2008) *Outliers: The Story of Success*. London: Allen Lane.
10. Parsons, T. (1951) *The Social System*. New York: Free Press.
11. Biko, S. (1986) *I Write What I Like*. San Francisco: Harper & Row.
12. Oquendo, M. A., et al. (2004) 'Instability of symptoms in recurrent major depression: A prospective study'. *American Journal of Psychiatry* 161(2): 255–61.
13. Reay, B. (2004) *Rural Englands*. Basingstoke: Palgrave Macmillan, p. 145.
14. Fischer, L. (1997) *The Life of Mahatma Gandhi*. London: Harper Collins, p. 163.
15. Reddie, R. (2012) *Martin Luther King Jnr: History Maker.* Oxford: Lion Hudson.
16. Tutu, D. (1977) 'Black theology/African theology: Soul mates or antagonists', in Appiah-Kubi, K. & Sergio Torres, S. (eds.) *African Theology En Route: Papers from the Pan African Conference of Third World Theologians*, December 17–23.
17. Burney, F. (2012) *The Court Journals and Letters of Frances Burney*, Vol. 1. Sabor, P. (ed.); Vol. 2. Cooke, S. (ed.) Oxford: Clarendon Press.
18. Boo, K. (2012) *Behind the Beautiful Forever: Life, Death and Hope in a Muslim Slum*. London: Portobello Books.
19. Meeropol, R. (2009) *An Execution in the Family: One Son's Journey*. New York: St Martin's Griffin.
20. Tavris, C. (1989) *Anger: The Misunderstood Emotion*. New York: Simon & Schuster.

Chapter Sixteen: The Politics of Equal Worth

1. Dalrymple, W. (2009) *Nine Lives*. London: Bloomsbury, p. 40.
2. Girard, R. (2016) *Things Hidden Since the Foundation of the World*. London: Bloomsbury Revelations.

3. Lewis, B. (2008) *Hammer and Tickle: A History of Communism Told through Communist Jokes*. London: Weidenfeld & Nicolson.
4. Applebaum, A. (2012) *Iron Curtain: The Crushing of Eastern Europe, 1944–56*. London: Allen Lane.
5. Hoffman, A. (2009) *My Happiness Bears No Relation to Happiness: A Poet's Life in the Palestinian Century*. London: Yale University Press.
6. Schama, S. (2008) *The American Future: A History*. Oxford: Bodley Head.
7. Hooks, B. (1990) *Yearning: Race, Gender and Cultural Politics*. Boston, MA: South End Press, p. 75.
8. Greene, G. (1991) *Our Man in Havana*. Harmondsworth: Penguin Twentieth Century Classics.
9. Perez, L. A. (2008) *Cuba in the American Imagination: Metaphor and the Imperial Ethos*. Chapel Hill: University of North Carolina Press.
10. Horowitz, I. (2008) *The Long Night of Dark Intent: A Half Century of Cuban Communism*. Piscataway, NJ: Transaction.
11. Che Guevara, E. (1960) 'On revolutionary medicine', speech to the Cuban Militia. Available at https://www.marxists.org/archive/guevara/1960/08/19.htm.
12. Carroll, R. (2008) 'Guevara's children speak out against commercialisation of iconic image', *Guardian*, 6 June.
13. Searle, J. R. (2010) *Making the Social World: The Structure of Human Civilisation*. Oxford: Oxford University Press.
14. Austin, J. L. (1975) *How to do Things with Words*, 2nd edn. Oxford: Oxford University Press.
15. See *Made in Dagenham*, film (2010).
16. Sharp, G. (2011) *Sharp's Dictionary of Power and Struggle: Language of Civil Resistance in Conflict*. Oxford: Oxford University Press.
17. Quoted in Thompson, E. P. (1980) *The Making of the English Working Class*. Harmondsworth: Penguin, p. 108.
18. Tolstoy, L. (2012) *Hadji-Murad*. London: Vintage Classics.
19. Figes, O. (1996) *A People's Tragedy: The Russian Revolution 1891–1924*. London: Pimlico, p. 368.
20. Quoted in Thompson, E. P. (1980) *The Making of the English Working Class*. Harmondsworth: Penguin, p. 108.
21. Pelling, H. (1963) *A History of British Trade Unionism*. Harmondsworth: Penguin.
22. Blair, T. (1998) Speech to Labour Party Conference, quoted in Callincross, A. (2000) *Equality*. Cambridge: Polity Press.
23. Author's client notes – name withheld and used with permission.
24. Smith, Z. (2001) *White Teeth*. London: Vintage International.
25. Du Bois, W. E. (1965) 'Address to the All-African People's Conference', in Du Bois, W. E. (ed.) *The World and Africa*. New York: International Publishers, p. 310.
26. Hall, J. (1927) *The Revolt of Asia*. New York and London: Upton Hall, p. 4.
27. Barraclough, G. (1973) *Introduction to Contemporary History*. Harmondsworth: Penguin, Ch 6.
28. Fischer, L. (1997) *The Life of Mahatma Gandhi*. London: Harper Collins, p. 345.
29. Biko, S. (1986) *I Write What I Like*. San Francisco: Harper & Row.
30. Gay, P. (2006) *Freud: A Life for Our Time*. New York: W. W. Norton.
31. Bowcott, O. & Luscombe, R. (2010) 'British family "demanded white staff at Florida hotel",' *Guardian*, 24 April.

32. Litvinoff, E. (2008) *Journey Through a Small Planet*. Harmondsworth: Penguin Modern Classic.
33. Eva Clarke. Holocaust survivor testimony, a talk presented by the Holocaust Education Trust. Available at www.het.org.uk/survivors-eva-clarke.
34. Thomas, C. (2002) 'Disability theory: Key ideas and thinkers', in Barnes, C. et al. (eds.) *Disability Studies Today*. Cambridge: Polity Press, p. 39.
35. Walker, M. (ed.) (1995) *Peta: A Feminist's Problem with Men*. Buckingham: Open University, p. 15.
36. Eisenstein, Z. (1981) *The Radical Future of Liberal Feminism*. Boston, MA: Northeastern University Press, in a discussion of Elizabeth Cady Stanton, pp. 145–73.
37. Wegner, J. R. (1988) *Chattel or Person: The Status of Women in the Mishnah*. New York and Oxford: Oxford University Press, p. 3.
38. Stevenson, B. & Wolfers, J. (2009) *The Paradox of Declining Female Unhappiness*. Cambridge, MA: National Bureau of Economic Research.
39. Morris, J. (1996) *Encounters with Strangers*. London: The Women's Press, p. 15.
40. Nagata, J. (1984) *The Reflowering of Malaysian Islam*. Vancouver: University of British Columbia Press.
41. Ong, A. (1995) '"State versus Islam": Malay families, women's bodies and the body politic in Malaysia', in Ong, A. & Peletz, M. G. (eds.) *Bewitching Women, Pious Men: Gender and Body Politics in Southeast Asia*. Berkeley: University of California Press, pp. 160–94.
42. Nasr, V. (2010) *Meccanomics: The March of the New Muslim Middle Class*. Oxford: Oneworld.
43. Tripp, C. (2006) *Islam and the Moral Economy: The Challenge of Capitalism*. Cambridge: Cambridge University Press.
44. Afzal Khan, F. (ed.) (2006) *Shattering the Stereotypes: Muslim Women Speak Out*. Northampton, MA: Love Branch Press.
45. Coleman, I. (2010) *Paradise Beneath Her Feet: How Women are Transforming the Middle East*. London: Random House.
46. Hakim, C. (1997) *Between Equalisation and Marginalisation: Women Working Part-time*. New York: Oxford University Press.
47. Murray, A. (1998) 'Debt-bondage and trafficking: Don't believe the hype', in Kempadoo, K. & Doexema, J. (eds.) *Global Sex Workers: Rights, Resistance and Re-definition*. New York: Taylor & Francis, pp. 51–64.
48. Hewlett, S, A. (1987) *A Lesser Life*. London: Michael Joseph, p. xiii.
49. Hakim, C. (2004) *Female Heterogeneity and the Polarisation of Women's Employment*. London: Athlone Press.
50. Foucault, M. (1978) *History of Sexuality Volume One*. New York: Random House.
51. Angelou, M. (1998) *I Know Why The Caged Bird Sings*. London: Longman.

Index

www.ingramcontent.com/pod-product-compliance
Ingram Content Group UK Ltd.
Pitfield, Milton Keynes, MK11 3LW, UK
UKHW021238300926
15471UKWH00013B/557

9 780755 601813